TRUTH AND RELEVANCE

Truth and Relevance

Catholic Theology in French Quebec since the Quiet Revolution

GREGORY BAUM

McGill-Queen's University Press
Montreal & Kingston • London • Ithaca

ISBN 978-0-7735-4325-6 (cloth)
ISBN 978-0-7735-4326-3 (paper)
ISBN 978-0-7735-9027-4 (ePDF)
ISBN 978-0-7735-9028-1 (ePUB)

Legal deposit second quarter 2014
Bibliothèque nationale du Québec

Printed in Canada on acid-free paper that is 100% ancient forest free (100% post-consumer recycled), processed chlorine free

McGill-Queen's University Press acknowledges the support of the Canada Council for the Arts for our publishing program. We also acknowledge the financial support of the Government of Canada through the Canada Book Fund for our publishing activities.

Library and Archives Canada Cataloguing in Publication

Baum, Gregory, 1923–, author
Truth and relevance: Catholic theology in French Quebec since the Quiet Revolution/Gregory Baum.

Includes bibliographical references and index.
Issued in print and electronic formats.
ISBN 978-0-7735-4325-6 (bound). – ISBN 978-0-7735-4326-3 (pbk.). – ISBN 978-0-7735-9027-4 (ePDF). – ISBN 978-0-7735-9028-1 (ePUB)

1. Church and social problems – Québec (Province) – Catholic Church. 2. Religion and civil society – Québec (Province). 3. Church and state – Québec (Province) – Catholic Church. 4. Catholic Church – Doctrines – History. 5. Catholic Church – Québec (Province) – History. I. Title.

BX1422.Q8B38 2014   282'.7140904   C2013-907829-0
C2013-907830-4

This book was typeset by Interscript in 10.5/13 Sabon.

Contents

Preface

The wall between French and English Canadian theological traditions has been lamented for so long that we can rejoice at this admirable panorama by Gregory Baum. The former professor at the University of Toronto (1959–86) and McGill University (1986–95) presents a long-awaited and stimulating overview of what has been said and written on the subject in Quebec since the 1960s. The reader will find in this book diverse thinkers (notably Fernand Dumont and Jacques Grand'Maison) who have contributed by varying degrees to the evolution of Catholic thought in Quebec. The reader will also be persuaded that the differences between the dominant English Canadian and French Québécois theologies, though considerable, should not prevent a fruitful exchange between the two communities, but rather encourage dialogue. Gregory Baum is among those who know that we are enriched by our differences – the other is always the mirror of oneself. This book should thus be received as an invitation to dialogue by the man who was the energetic editor of *The Ecumenist* from 1962 to 2004.

Indeed, Gregory Baum has described how his contact with Québécois political culture has modified his theological trajectory.[1] As a professor in a renowned Montreal university, an associate of le Centre justice et foi (where he now has his office), a member of Québec Solidaire, and an engaged citizen of Quebec society, he has come to view some of the problems of modern society from a typically Québécois point of view. Compared to the rest of Canada, Quebec (which is 81.2 percent francophone) distinguishes itself by a stronger feminism, a nationalism fuelled by the majority/minority relationship, active trade unionism, resilient social democracy, anticlericalism verging on antireligious sentiment, an increasing removal of Catholicism from the national culture, and vigorous francophile intellectual thought. These collective features have influenced Quebec's conception of commitment, faith, and hierarchy in the Catholic tradition. Through his years living in Quebec, Baum has come to "see Canada in another light."[2] Yet the new perspective has not reduced Baum's critical sense nor the finesse of his observations; on the contrary, it helps his readers to see through common misinterpretations that all too often produce misunderstandings and confine us to our regrettable solitudes.

Québécois (hereinafter "francophone") theology of the past decades is misapprehended if one is unaware of its divorce from the Thomist tradition that dominated theological studies before 1960. Since the nineteenth century, Thomism has been recognized as the official doctrine of the Church, a recognition punctuated by frequent admonitions. Among these were the papal encyclical *Aeterni Patris* (1879), the twenty-four theses (1914), and the *Motu Proprio* of Pius X (29 June 1914), as well as the late but unequivocal encyclical, *Humani Generis* (1950). This directive of the Vatican guided the development of higher education in Quebec (the founding of the Faculty of Theology at Laval University in Montreal in 1878), resulting in the unrivalled dominion of Thomism in the theological and philosophical studies of this province, more so than anywhere else. On the eve of the Second Vatican Council in 1962, a survey of francophone members of the Philosophical Association of Canada revealed that 82 percent identified themselves as Thomists, 9 percent as Christian existentialists, 5 percent as Aristotelians, 2 percent Augustinians, and 2 percent heterodox.[3] The problem was that the Aquinas that was being taught in the colleges and universities had a neo-scholastic bent, replacing the free use of critical reflection with an exclusivist, dogmatic teaching. Even Jacques Maritain, though committed to the renewal of Thomism, was suspected by the Quebec clergy of having dubious ideas.

The Quiet Revolution (1960–66) and the Second Vatican Council (1962–65) blew open the Thomistic catechism. The effort to overcome this theological inheritance, increasingly associated with *la grande noirceur*,[4] brought about a radical rejection of the scholastic tradition, deemed abstract and authoritarian. Catholic thinkers now argued that Quebecers had been introduced to an abstract, disembodied religious discourse that severed the connection to their historical reality. "We forget that institutions are sustained by the experience of the people. When institutions remove themselves from this source, when they become preoccupied with their regulations, ideologies and facades, they become disconnected and lose their meaning – like trees neglecting their roots, fixated on their branches. That is what happened to our Church."[5] This explains why a good deal of new theology has been developed outside faculties of theology. Readers surprised by the theological influence of Fernand Dumont, a professor in a department of sociology, should remember that in his youth he had intended to study philosophy, but was soon turned off by the scholastic monopoly barring all new and free thinking. He was not the only one to hope for a renewal of metaphysical thought through reflections from the margin. The Quebec of the last fifty years has been a rich haven of "Sunday theologians."[6]

To free themselves from dry and oppressive neo-Thomism, Quebec theologians worked hard developing a cutting critique of all thought that was disembodied, stagnant, routine, and in fact reified. I was struck by the title chosen by Baum for his book, *Truth and Relevance*, echoing the well-known distinction proposed by Fernand Dumont. The truth, Dumont argued, is in itself something cold and abstract, the simple fruit of a reasoning mind, the more or less trustworthy result of axiomatic operations. Are libraries not full of propositions which in no way affect the daily lives of people who visit them? Truths cannot elevate or transform those who encounter them without an inner movement of the heart, without subjective acceptance. Truth becomes relevance, for instance, when it responds to people's anxieties and urgent questions, allowing them to resolve their problems and transform their lives There is a big difference between proven facts that do not engage the people who accept them, and those that affect people at their deepest levels; there is the greatest difference between the truths we know and those that we truly, totally, and passionately believe. In other words, there is a great difference between truth and relevance.

Seen in this light, Dumont argued, the work of professors, authors, and theologians is very similar: it offers meaning to what would otherwise be flat and empty. The professor must by his passion embody his teaching, which, being lived by the teacher standing before the class, takes on a new dimension. The author has a similar task of dramatizing the human condition. Finally, the theologian witnesses to something which infinitely surpasses him. Each of these professions is an endeavour in meaning. Those who practice them try to make the world speak – a world that, if left to its own devices, would never say anything to anyone.

Baum is quite right in stating that Québécois theologians want to write God into the fabric of history. As he demonstrates, a pervasive panentheism marks their understanding of the workings of the world. Not only is God immanent in events (which forces us to rethink divine providence), but God also dwells within each human being (which implies that God's invitation is always and already written into people's hearts). For Québécois theologians, faith is not learned, but experienced. The Bible is not a book; it is Word. Priests are not only pastors; they must also be witnesses. Faith is a heritage that is not received, but that wins us over. The Church is not a bishopric, but rather "the Church is you," as Rémi Parent maintains in his book.[7] Christ is first of all Jesus, the man from Nazareth. Faith is not isolation; it is an encounter. In short, everywhere and always, theologians seek to develop an evangelical message for people in their historical contexts, attentive to the signs of the times and to their anxieties and hopes. This theological approach has produced what Baum identifies as typically Québécois: our theologians may have doubts about God, but never about Jesus; they adopt the preferential option for the poor; they rarely speak of sin; they are socially engaged and eager to incarnate the Gospel in their lives.

These reflections lead to the intersection of faith and culture. Quebec theologians of the second half of the twentieth century have tried to recover genuine solidarity with men and women of faith so that the Catholic Church becomes something other than a structure imported from a foreign place. They could not be satisfied with an anonymous institution, an institution from nowhere; rather, they hoped for a Church that would engage the hopes and doubts of all the faithful and thus become authentically Québécois. Hadn't that been the case, they suggested, in the first Christian communities in Jerusalem, Antioch, Corinth, and Alexandria? Hadn't the universal Word of God been heard in different accents since the beginning? Then why should Quebecers be forced to hear the Good News in a language that did not belong to them? We know that historically the Catholic clergy adopted the axiom "our language is the guardian of the faith," and that influential members of the Church, such as Canon Lionel Groulx (1878–1967), championed the nationalist movement. From the 1960s on, Quebec theologians continued to associate themselves with the quest for the affirmation of Quebec society. Distancing themselves from traditionalist ideologies of the past, they embraced the neo-nationalist turn of the Quiet Revolution, with many beginning to promote the independence of Quebec. These theologians have tried to find a connection between nationalism and Catholicism, not just culturally but also politically.

This posture may startle many English Canadian theologians who were accustomed to the moralizing and conservative thought of Quebec theology before the 1960s. Gregory Baum himself has admitted his initial discomfort with the nationalist tone of Catholic theology in Quebec. He had to learn to respect his Québécois colleagues who refused to separate their faith from their nationalistic aspirations. Some called themselves socialists or sovereignists *because* they were Christians, finding within the Gospel the motive for their engagement. Quebec theologians in fact distinguish themselves by an integral stance (*intégralisme*), unwilling to see their faith as an add-on or a piecemeal application of Catholicism; instead they search in various ways to come to terms with the modern world. Rather than restricting faith to the intimate sphere of the heart or directing it to abstract expressions of the ultimate, they hold a faith that seeks – not without difficulty – historical forms of incarnation.

These features alone are original enough to justify an overview of the type chosen by Gregory Baum in this book. Yet beyond the subject of the book, what gives value to *Truth and Relevance* is the author himself. If this book is valuable, it is because it is written with flair and vigour. Gregory Baum is above all a man of openness: openness to the transcendent, whether divine or earthly, moving to a beyond that asks humanity not to close in upon itself; openness to others, and particularly to those who are furthest away – the humble, forgotten, abandoned, and downtrodden – so as to bring them back into our circle of concern and fellowship; openness to all cultures so that we can build our faith as much on our common convictions as on the sharing of our differences. Quebec has been able to benefit from this openness for a long time. I like to think of Baum as a priceless window through which we can view the horizon – in his writings, his speeches, and his encounters.

Jean-Philippe Warren
Professor of sociology, Concordia University, Montreal

TRUTH AND RELEVANCE

A Brief Introduction

After teaching theology and religious studies at St Michael's College in the University of Toronto for twenty-six years, I moved to Montreal in 1986 to become a professor at the faculty of religious studies of McGill University, a great anglophone academic institution. Because of my association with the international Catholic review *Concilium,* articles of mine were known in Quebec's francophone theological milieu. I was invited by the Jesuit-sponsored Centre justice et foi to join the editorial committee of its monthly review *Relations*. I regarded this as a great privilege, for it allowed me to follow and participate in the public debates in Quebec society. The orientation of the Centre, I should explain, had been affected by a decision of the Jesuit Order in 1975 to commit itself to the promotion of faith and the justice demanded by faith.[1] Later, when I joined la Société canadienne de théologie, I found myself surrounded by theologians who did excellent work and argued passionately about the meaning of the Gospel for the contemporary world. My adoption by the French-speaking community led me to an intellectual adventure: the recognition of Quebec as a distinct society and the discovery of the diminished Quebec Church as a place of innovative pastoral and theological projects.

Language, a means of communication, is also a barrier stopping conversation across cultural boundaries. This is the reason why the theological and pastoral thinking developed in Quebec, though innovative and often controversial, is almost unknown in the English-speaking theological milieu. Hardly anything has been written about it in English. My book *The Church in Quebec* (1991) contains a few articles on theology.[2] David Seljak completed his doctoral dissertation at McGill University in 1995 on the reaction of the Catholic Church to the Quiet Revolution. In 2000 he published the article "The Catholic Church and Public Politics in Quebec."[3] In the collection of articles *Intersecting Voices* (2007), Carolyn Sharp published "Critical Theologies in Quebec" and Monique Dumais "Critical Feminist Theologies in Quebec."[4] This is about all that has been published in English about Catholic theology in Quebec. In June 2011, increasingly troubled by this lack of communication, I asked the department of theological studies of Montreal's Concordia University to allow me to teach a course on Catholic theology in French Quebec. The department graciously invited me to teach a summer course on this topic in May/June 2012. Instead of preparing my lectures, I decided to write a book to share my acquaintance with Catholic theology in Quebec with a wider audience.

Because Quebec, at one time a Catholic society, has the benefit of several theological faculties distributed over the province, the theological literature produced by their professors is impressive. It is not my intention to produce a complete report, nor a synthesis of this literature. I simply wish to offer a thoughtful look at this theology, influenced undoubtedly by my membership in la Société canadienne de théologie and my association with le Centre justice et foi. La Société canadienne de théologie has over the years published its proceedings in book form, producing a long list of volumes, the series *Héritage et projet*, offering a valuable entry to Quebec's theological literature. Through le Centre justice et foi I came to participate in the network of Catholic groups and individuals committed to social justice and reflecting critically on church and society.[5] As a member of this network I have a particular interest in theological and exegetical studies that speak to contemporary society, reveal its negative potential, and promote equality and social justice. The important issue for these scholars is not the truth of the Church's teaching, but its relevance: that is, its power to redeem the human heart and change the course of history. The Christian Gospel is truly proclaimed only when it is relevant, when it speaks to a given situation, sheds light on its sinful structures, and promises rescue and transformation. I have entitled this book *Truth and Relevance* because most of the theologians and exegetes mentioned in it want to announce the Gospel as a message relevant to contemporary Quebec society. The subtitle, *Catholic Theology in French Quebec since the Quiet Revolution*, indicates that this book is an introduction to Quebec's recent theological literature.

I pay, in fact, special attention to the theological currents that acknowledge the close link between faith and justice. I apologize to colleagues of mine whose work I have not mentioned, even though it deserves respect and attention.

Protestants constitute a small minority in French Quebec: they have as yet no major francophone institution that teaches theology. The main concern of their ministers is with preaching and pastoral care. Over the years, the Catholic faculties have become ecumenical in outlook: they invite Protestants to join them as professors and students. In the subtitle of the book I refer to "French Quebec" because it does not deal with the theological literature produced in Quebec's anglophone community. I say nothing of the theological ideas implicit in Charles Taylor's philosophical work, though they are a source of wisdom so far unexplored by theologians. Nor do I deal with the theological achievement of Douglas Hall, a former colleague of mine at McGill and a personal friend. Anglophone theologians in Montreal are in an intense dialogue with their colleagues in English Canada and the United States, yet rarely cross the linguistic boundary. The philosopher Charles Taylor is a special case: he is perfectly at home in French Quebec.

Vatican Council II hoped that theologians in dialogue with their culture would be able to announce and explain the Christian Gospel in a language that people are able to understand. I shall present the bold recommendations of the Council at some length. With the Council, Quebec theologians hold that the dialogue between faith and culture is an essential task of theology. Their theology is therefore unashamedly contextual: it reflects in one way or another the historical experience of the Quiet Revolution.

Because my own cultural background is quite different, I do not always see things the same way as Quebec theologians. I shall mention this difference at several points and discuss it at greater length in the book's final chapter. Because some ideas of Quebec theologians are quite radical, I occasionally cite the well-known German theologian Joseph Ratzinger, who in his youth entertained similar ideas. Let me add that at present Quebec theologians pay little attention to the conservative current in Roman Catholicism, encouraged by the Vatican and approved by Benedict XVI. This current is not based on original theological thought, nor does it stimulate creative interaction; it has an impact on the Church's life through administrative measures, putting pressure on seminaries and theological faculties and appointing clerics uninterested in theology to positions of ecclesiastical authority. The Church of Quebec, I am inclined to think, is still an open community, in dialogue with the world, struggling to find a way of practicing and announcing the Gospel so that it can be heard. It is remarkable that in the present conservative climate, Benedict XVI has occasionally still made bold theological proposals: yet they have not travelled very far, halted by a rigid clinging to the Catholicism of yesterday. In his encyclical *Spe Salvi* (2008), Benedict XVI made a statement on the task of theology that describes very well what Quebec theologians are trying to do.

> A self-critique of modernity is needed in dialogue with Christianity and its concept of hope. In this dialogue Christians too, in the context of their knowledge and experience, must learn anew in what their hope truly consists, what they have to offer to the world and what they cannot offer. Flowing into this self-critique of the modern age there also has to be a self-critique of modern Christianity, which must constantly renew its self-understanding setting out from its roots.[6]

I wish to express my thanks to Jean-Philippe Warren for his generous and thoughtful preface; to Guy Côté, a theologian and friend, who has read the manuscript and given me good counsel; to Kyla Madden, editor at McGill-Queen's University Press, for her encouragement; and to Julie Cool, who helped me make free translations of the French citations into English. I also wish to express my gratitude to le Centre justice et foi – its director Élisabeth Garant and the entire team – which has been my guide in looking at Quebec in the light of the Gospel.

A final remark of considerable importance: I wrote this book prior to the 13 March 2013 election of Pope Francis, whose vision of the Church reawakens the Catholic community to the light of the Second Vatican Council and whose ideas have a remarkable affinity with the thought of Quebec's progressive Catholic theologians.

I

The Quiet Revolution and the Catholic Church

Beginning in the 1960s, Catholic theology in Quebec participated in the efforts of the emerging Quebec nation to invent a new discourse through which to express its collective aspirations, until then largely buried.[1] Theologians asked themselves what the Gospel has to say to the people of Quebec as they exercise their power, redefine their identity, and discover their cultural creativity. In this first chapter I shall discuss what happened to the Church during and after the Quiet Revolution. The Church was challenged by this cultural upheaval; and to respond to these challenges, the Quebec bishops set up a study commission to produce pastoral recommendations that would allow the Church to participate in the making of the new society. I shall present a summary of these recommendations, for they had a strong influence on the work of theologians. Yet despite the Church's effort to renew itself at Vatican Council II and in Quebec, the province eventually became a secular society, turning its back on the religion that had accompanied it over the centuries. Beginning in the late 1970s, the social-democratic values of the Quiet Revolution were challenged by the neo-liberal culture dominant in North America, yet the theologians, as we shall see, remained faithful to the new humanism and denounced the emerging culture marked by individualism, consumerism, and competitiveness.

THE QUIET REVOLUTION[2]

The province of Quebec moved rather late into cultural and political modernity.[3] The provincial government, prior to 1960, protected traditional, pre-modern cultural ideals, restricted religious and political pluralism, and refused to regard the State as responsible for the social development of the population. The government had no ministry of education, no ministry of health, and no ministry of social welfare. Maurice Duplessis, the premier of Quebec during most of the years between 1936 and 1959, defended this policy in unbending fashion. He wanted private societies to organize education, health services, and social assistance. The Catholic Church was pleased to fulfill this role for the francophone population: it assumed responsibility for the organization of schools and colleges, hospitals and health care centres, and assistance to people in need. As a result, the Church's organizational presence became ubiquitous. English-speaking Quebecers, about twenty percent of the population, were not dissatisfied with this government policy, for it allowed them to organize their own institutions without government interference.

In this situation the cultural power of the Church in French Quebec was excessive. It defined Quebec's cultural identity in opposition to the Protestant and secular culture of North America. It demanded unanimity within its own ranks and supported the government in its opposition to pluralism. The Church was sustained in its activities by the faith of the vast majority of the people. Their ardent piety produced a culture of solidarity and mutual aid. An intense faith inspired vast numbers of young people to become priests, sisters, and brothers dedicated to serve in their own society and in the missions overseas. This profound loyalty to the Church may seem like an anomaly in the middle of the twentieth century. Yet whenever a Catholic people conquered by an empire of another religion struggles for its collective survival, the Church becomes a symbol of identity and resistance. This happened in Poland, Ireland, and Quebec.

There were signs in the 1940s and 1950s that the unanimity in the Catholic Church was being challenged. Joseph Charbonneau, the archbishop of Montreal, broke ranks with the other bishops in his support for non-confessional institutions and his interventions in favour of labour strikes.[4] The review *Cité libre,* published by intellectuals relying on liberal Catholic thought coming from France, criticized what it called the clerico-nationalist, corrupt, and undemocratic regime of Duplessis.[5] Two priests, Gerard Dion and Louis O'Neill, produced a book in 1956 that criticized Duplessis's reactionary policies and advocated democratic and egalitarian ideas.[6] Examining activities and events in these two decades, historians have come to recognize the social currents within Catholicism that prepared the

Quiet Revolution.[7] Still, despite these moments of anticipation, when a Liberal government was elected on 22 June 1960, a cultural explosion took place that truly deserves the name of "Quiet Revolution."

Quebecers thought of themselves as a gifted and autonomous people with energy, ideas, and the will to construct their own society. If we follow Émile Durkheim's vocabulary designating as "effervescence"[8] the collective experience of peoples at dramatic turning-points in their history, we may say that for Quebecers the Quiet Revolution was a time of effervescence. People wanted to catch up with modern society, be open to pluralism, participate in democratic decision-making, express themselves in art and literature free of censorship, and create a modern educational system qualifying students to advance in the fields of science and technology. The agents of this cultural upheaval also wanted to free themselves from the economic domination of the English-Canadian elites and assume full political responsibility for their society.

At the same time, the promoters of the Quiet Revolution wanted Quebec to remain faithful to its distinctive cultural tradition and not be assimilated into the other North American societies. They wanted Quebec to resist the individualistic culture of these societies and preserve its own heritage of solidarity and co-operation. Many of them called their vision "socialism" in a wide sense ranging from co-operatism and social democracy to Marxist-inspired social reconstruction. Like other nations caught in a pre-modern culture, Quebecers wanted to catch up with modernity and yet remain a distinctive society.

As a consequence of the Quiet Revolution, Quebecers gradually ceased to think of themselves in ethnic terms, a part of the French-Canadian nation from sea to sea. They began to think of Quebec as their own nation, defined in terms of citizenship, rather than ethnicity. While this altered self-perception disappointed the French-Canadian minorities in other Canadian provinces, it gradually opened Quebec society to ethnic and cultural pluralism, *le Québec au pluriel*.

The Quiet Revolution also initiated the process of secularization. The promoters of secularism, at first a small minority, accused the Catholic Church of having supported the reactionary regime of Maurice Duplessis, now called *la grande noirceur* (the great darkness), and of having impeded the entry of Quebec into North American modernity. The secularists now looked upon Catholicism as part of *la grande noirceur*. Their intention was to secularize

Quebec's self-perception and replace the religious story that had defined Quebec's identity in the past with the secular self-definition of a people eager to discover its power, talent, and originality. When the Liberal government created ministries of education, health, and social assistance, and secularized the ecclesiastical institutions that had been serving these purposes, the Catholic Church lost a great deal of its power and influence in society. Only in the school system did the bishops retain a certain hold, even if it was no longer under their direct control.[9]

A significant number of Catholics welcomed the declericalization of their society. At this time, the Second Vatican Council (1962–65) advocated a new openness to modernity, emphasized the responsibility of the laity, supported the autonomy of secular institutions, and expressed respect for religious pluralism. Some Catholics wanted a quiet revolution in the Church itself. The review *Maintenant* published by the Dominicans became an ardent supporter of ecclesiastical reform.[10] The institutional changes and the lively debates among Catholics made the Church uncertain about its future. It had lost its cultural power and institutional presence, yet the majority of its members still remained ardent believers. Yet by the end of the 1960s a growing number of Catholics became indifferent to their religious tradition and disassociated themselves from their parishes. The society itself was becoming increasingly secular.

THE DUMONT COMMISSION

The social transformation initiated by the Quiet Revolution affected Catholics in the practice of their faith. The cultural effervescence released a spirit of freedom in the Church and inspired Catholics to engage in new pastoral experiments, such as setting up base communities.[11] Some Catholic Action groups became involved in radical politics. To foster the internal cohesion of the Church and institute common pastoral policies, the bishops appointed a Commission in 1968 to consult the Catholics of the province, listen to their problems and spiritual aspirations, and recommend a set of pastoral policies that would allow the Church to respond creatively to the new Quebec. As chair of the Commission the bishops appointed Fernand Dumont, a learned sociologist, whom we shall meet in a subsequent chapter. The eleven members of the Commission included one bishop, Jacques Grand'Maison, a theologian whose thought we shall study further on; a number of other priests; and several laymen and women drawn mainly from the Catholic Action movement. Among the laymen was also a labour union representative, Jean-Paul Hétu.

With many Quebec Catholics, the bishops believed that the teaching of Vatican Council II on the responsibility of the particular Church entitled them to consult the Catholic people, listen to their theologians, and work toward the inculturation of the Gospel in their national community. The bishops wished to promote a Catholicism that responded affirmatively as well as critically to the new Quebec. Because the conciliar texts on the particular Church are important for understanding the effort of Quebec theologians, we shall look at them in the next chapter. At this point I will mention only two relevant sentences.

> Within the Church particular Churches hold a rightful place; these Churches retain their own traditions, without in any way opposing the primacy of the Chair of Peter, which presides over the whole assembly of charity and protects legitimate differences, while at the same time assuring that such differences do not hinder unity but rather contribute toward it.[12]

> The bishops should present Christian doctrine in a manner adapted to the needs of the times, that is to say, in a manner that will respond to the difficulties and questions by which people are especially burdened and troubled.[13]

The Dumont Commission held hearings in the towns and regions of Quebec and received briefs from individuals and groups. The Commission wanted to hear how Quebecers of faith, committed to the Catholic tradition, envisaged the future of the Church in their new society.[14]

It deserves to be mentioned that this extensive inquiry dealt with francophone Quebecers, that is to say the great majority, all of whom had been deeply affected by the Quiet Revolution. For anglophone and allophone Quebecers, less than twenty percent of the population, the Quiet Revolution presented a different kind of challenge: they had to get used to French as the language of work in commerce and industry. While the francophone majority experienced the Quiet Revolution as a liberation from colonial linguistic subjugation, the non-francophone minorities often found these changes frustrating.

The Catholics among them, a minority within a minority, did not share in the effervescence experienced by the francophone Church. To this day, the Catholicism of English-speaking Quebecers is different from the Catholicism of French Quebec.

To understand the conclusions of the Dumont Report, it is necessary to look at the methodology adopted by the Commission.[15] Having received a vast number of personal testimonies and briefs submitted by individuals and institutions, the commissioners had to decide how to move from the empirical data to principled theological reflections. They arrived at the historical judgment that the Quiet Revolution was an irreversible process, that Quebec had become a secular, pluralistic society, and that the Catholic Church no longer spoke for the whole of Quebec, but only for one sector, the community of believers. This judgment allowed the Commission to disregard the submissions of Catholics who longed for the return of the Catholicism of yesterday.

A second principle used by the Commission was the recognition that Quebec society and the Quebec Church were struggling to redefine their collective identity and hence were in favour of both change and continuity. Most Quebecers wanted to preserve the social solidarity they had inherited and, at the same time, escape from the authoritarianism of the Duplessis regime. Most Catholics felt the same way about the Church: they wanted to keep the faith they had inherited and, at the same time, escape from the authoritarian style of the old Church. Reflecting on the Church's new identity, the commissioners were not neutral agents reading the testimonies and briefs submitted to them; they were in fact ardent Catholic believers wrestling with the question of how to define the Church's identity in the new Quebec. They became convinced that a crisis of self-understanding must be resolved by both a creative response to the new and an effort to preserve the continuity with the past. Needed are both rupture and fidelity. Or conversely, the Church is both an inheritance from the past and a project for the future. This principle guided the commissioners in their work: it allowed them to disregard both the proposals of reactionary Catholics opposed to anything new and the proposals of radical Catholics who wanted the Church to become fully egalitarian, abandoning the distinction between clergy and laity, and defining its mission in purely humanitarian terms.

The Dumont Report, entitled *L'Église du Québec: un héritage, un projet*,[16] was published in 1971. New and startling was its emphasis on the Church as "communion": this implied, according to the Report, participation, pluralism, and the toleration of dissent. The Report mentioned three factors that were producing an internal pluralism in the Church: (1) Catholics react differently to the proposals of Vatican II; (2) they interpret differently the commitment to social justice; and (3) they choose, as they always did, a spirituality that corresponds to their religious experience. Because of this internal pluralism, dialogue within the Church is becoming increasingly necessary. Because the Church is a communion, the Report argues, it may not be thought of as "an immutable pyramid throughout the ages, nor as an inaccessible obelisk."[17] A highly centralized bureaucracy hides the Church's true nature as the communion of the faithful. Communion implies participation. As the Quebec people, mobilized by the Quiet Revolution, have acquired a strong sense of their social responsibility, the Catholics among them now feel that they are also responsible subjects in their religious community. The Report observes that "the democratization of secular life has not failed to influence the expectations of the faithful, whether they be lay people, religious or priests."[18]

This call for democratization, the Report insists, does not question the episcopal-papal structure of the Church, which Catholics regard as an institution *jure divino*. "The introduction of democratic ways can go a long way without compromising the Church's hierarchical structure."[19] What Catholics are asking for is simply wider consultation and co-responsibility. The faithful and their priests want to be in conversation with the bishops and participate in some way in the decision-making process that affects the Church's teaching and its pastoral policies. The Report makes provisional proposals for the setting up of ecclesiastical forums that would facilitate dialogue between the believing community and their appointed leaders.[20] Looking upon the Church as a people on pilgrimage, the Report regards the Church as forever unfinished and designates its internal organizations as *des chantiers* or building sites.[21]

At the same time, the Quebec Church remains faithful to its inheritance. The Report mentions in particular three activities characteristic of the Church throughout its history: (1) the commitment to serve the French-Canadian people; (2) the communal life marked by solidarity and shared values; and (3) the outstanding engagement of priests, brothers, and sisters in foreign missions. These activities, the Report insists, retain their vitality, even if in modified forms. The Church's commitment to the Quebec nation continues: as a minority in a pluralistic society, the Church now joins the democratic debate over issues of the common good and exercises a socio-critical function – a prophetic role – defending the weaker members of society and calling for social justice. The Church's missionary engagement finds expression today in the service Catholics offer to the world, co-operating with others in the pursuit of justice and giving witness to God in the secular society. The Church's communal life also assumes a new form: it is now open to pluralism and tolerates dissent. The Report actually "denounces the tendency of long standing, also among lay people, to reduce the response to a complex set of problems to a single official definition, especially coming from Rome."[22] In the Church there is room for responsible dissent and respectful opposition. "There exists in the Church a Christian ethics of dissent, criteria derived from gospel authenticity permitting protest, in fact a pluralism characteristic of the Catholic tradition, marked as it is by internal tensions. It is important to remind those who cling to the 'letter' – to their 'letter' – of the transcendent claim of the Spirit."[23]

The Dumont Report insisted on rupture and fidelity. The Quebec bishops were unable to implement all of its recommendations. For one, the message coming from Rome had changed. Having encouraged intra-ecclesial dialogue in his encyclical *Ecclesiam Suam* of 1964, Pope Paul VI restored the monarchical understanding of the papacy in 1968 when he published the encyclical *Humanae Vitae* condemning the use of the contraceptive pill, without having consulted the bishops and against the recommendation of the study commission appointed by him. While the Quebec bishops lacked the canonical power to democratize their Church, they responded positively to the spirit of the Dumont Report: they became tolerant, welcomed pastoral experiments, supported faith-and-justice movements, and respected the pluralism within the Church. Though the bishops now represented only a minority of Quebecers, they continued to address the people of Quebec on issues affecting the common good – not in the tone of authority, but with humility, joining the public debate in a democratic society. The Dumont Report had a great affect on theologians: it legitimized their freedom to find fault with the Catholicism of yesterday and come up with proposals that would make the Gospel relevant for the Quebec that was in the making.

Despite its openness to the democratic spirit, the Dumont Report did not raise the issue of the inferior status assigned to women in the

Church, even though among the eleven commissioners were four women. Nor did the Report please Jean-Paul Hétu, the labour union representative on the Commission. He actually refused to sign the final draft because he regarded the Report's preoccupation with Quebec's identity and the Church's well-being as middle-class concerns, indifferent to the exploitation of labour and the unjust distribution of wealth in society. We shall examine this issue at length in chapter 5.

THE CHURCH'S RAPID DECLINE

In 1968 when the Dumont Commission was holding its hearings throughout the province, Catholics participated in great numbers, eager to give testimony of their faith and express their vision of the Church. It was a time of religious enthusiasm. Yet in 1971, when the Report was finally published, the enthusiasm had largely disappeared: the Catholic population was no longer interested in religious issues. This at least was the impression of Fernand Dumont.[24]

Vast numbers of Catholics distanced themselves from the Church in the years that followed. They still called themselves Catholics when filling out forms or responding to the census, yet they increasingly looked upon the Church's religious discourse as a foreign language.[25] In a period of ten years the Catholic Church lost more than half of its active members – or even two thirds, as some social scientists claim. Lively movements continued to flourish in the Catholic Church, in particular the charismatic renewal[26] and a faith-and-justice current, also called the Catholic Left, but these represented small minorities. Quebec, a Catholic society, underwent a rapid secularization that was altogether unique. There exists no historical parallel for this on the European continent.

The cause of this unusual development is undoubtedly complex: it was produced by the interaction of several historical factors. An article on this issue, published in 2006 by the Quebec sociologist Nicole Laurin, begins with this paragraph: "The decline of the Church of Quebec during the 1960s has attracted the attention of historians and sociologists. They have tried to explain this phenomenon in various ways and evaluate its consequences. Nonetheless, the breakdown of the Church remains an enigma."[27]

The article discusses the various theories proposed by Quebec social scientists to account for this puzzling development. Some of them argue that the modernization of society has secularized all Western societies and that this process was so rapid in Quebec because the social transformation initiated by the Quiet Revolution was so rapid. Other sociologists blame the Catholic Church for what has happened. The rejection of the Church, they argue, was a revolt against the Church's excessive power, its support of the political establishment, its alliance with the Duplessis regime in the 1950s, its pervasive clericalism, and its imposition of cultural conformity. Fernand Dumont, in a book published in 1964,[28] denounces the faults of Quebec Catholicism: its omnipresent clericalism, its authoritarianism prohibiting free expression, its uncritical subservience to the Vatican, its nostalgia for the regime of Christendom, and its attachment to the power it exercised in the history of Quebec. He recalls that English-speaking Canadians used to refer to Quebec as "the priest-ridden province."

Other prominent Catholics also denounced the excessive power of the Quebec clergy. When Jacques Maritain returned to France after a lecture tour in Quebec in 1934, he reported his experiences in a letter to Emmanuel Mounier. This is how Mounier remembered this letter in his diary.

> Back in Canada, Maritain told me "This time, I touched obscurantism with my fingers. The clergy take all the places, especially in education. There is a huge, although mute anti-clerical revolt among Catholic youth: it sometimes takes impudent forms – claiming positions – which is excusable." Maritain suggested that there will be an enormous religious crisis in Quebec within a decade.[29]

A similar observation was made by the French Dominican priest Alain-Marie Couturier, exiled in New York during World War II. He was a frequent visitor to Quebec, where he supported the quest of the young artists for free expression. He wrote to his friends in France, "The place the clergy has held and still holds in French-Canadian life will eventually produce a revolt."[30]

Today many Quebecers, including the theologians we shall study in this book, regard Quebec's Catholicism of yesterday as the principal cause for the rapid secularization of society. Their opinion reminds me of an eloquent passage written by Abraham Heschel, the famous rabbi of prophetic Judaism.

> Religion declined not because it was refuted, but because it became irrelevant, dull, oppressive, insipid. When faith is completely replaced by creed, worship by discipline, love by habit; when the crisis of today is ignored because of the splendor of the past; when faith becomes an heirloom rather than a living fountain; when religion speaks only in the name of authority rather than with the voice of compassion – its message becomes meaningless.[31]

In my own writings on Quebec's rapid secularization I have offered sociological reflections that take into account the multiplicity of historical factors.[32] As I mentioned above, in Catholic societies colonized by an empire of a different religion, the Church becomes a symbol of resistance and identity, fostering a passionate and often excessive piety. This happened in Poland colonized by the Orthodox Czarist Empire, and in Ireland and Quebec colonized by the Protestant British Empire. In these societies the Church became an integral part of the national myth that defined the collective spirit of the people.

In the Quiet Revolution, Quebec redefined its collective identity. In the past, the province of Quebec had seen itself as the cradle and core of the Canada-wide French-Canadian nation, a nation united by its ethnic origin, its religion, its culture, and its common language. With the Quiet Revolution, Quebecers began to affirm their province as the Quebec nation, defined not in ethnic or religious terms, but as a modern society based on citizenship and hence open to ethnic, cultural, and religious pluralism. The emerging myth defining the identity of Quebec no longer included its inherited Catholicism. Some sociologists attribute great cultural power to the symbols of a nation: the American scholar Robert Bellah even argues that these symbols constitute a "civil religion" affecting public life as well as personal consciousness.[33] One reason why the USA has remained such a religious society, he argues, is that its national myth includes reference to God, America being "God's own country." As Quebec was becoming a modern society, assuming political self-responsibility within Canada or possibly adjacent to it, a new national myth emerged that was wholly secular, affected the life of society, and secularized people's personal self-understanding.

With many sociologists I am convinced that public institutions have an effect on people's consciousness. It deserves to be remembered that prior to the Quiet Revolution, the government of Quebec had no ministry of education, no ministry of public health, and no ministry of public welfare: to the francophone population, all these services were delivered by ecclesiastical institutions, ubiquitous organisms that gave the Church a strong presence in the daily lives of the people. When, in the Quiet Revolution, education, health, and welfare were taken over by public institutions, the Church ceased to play a major role in people's daily lives, thus losing the hold on their consciousness. The rapid secularization of Quebec society, I wish to argue, is not simply the result of an angry reaction against a powerful ecclesiastical establishment; it is also, and perhaps even more so, the result of the significant institutional changes introduced during the Quiet Revolution.

The British sociologist David Martin has pointed to the significant difference between the process of secularization in Protestant and Catholic societies.[34] Protestant societies are accustomed to a plurality of Churches, some of which even accommodate liberal Christians unable to embrace the orthodox creed. Thanks to this experience of pluralism, secularization in Protestant countries is a gradual process that does not produce a cultural upheaval. By contrast, Catholic societies recognize a single Church that defines the whole of life, personal and social, and leaves no room for dissent. Here people who become non-believers disrupt the public order, and the secularization of society produces a cultural upheaval. Since dissidents reject the inherited totality, they tend to elevate their secular philosophy into a new total truth, thus producing a cultural schism between conservative believers and liberal secularists. This happened in France and other Catholic European nations.

When, in an article written twenty-five years ago, I inquired whether this theory sheds light on the secularizing process in Quebec, I argued that in Quebec a series of compromises between Catholics and secular citizens prevented the emergence of a cultural schism.[35] I referred, for example, to the willingness of the government-appointed Parent Commission on education[36] to talk to the bishops and respect some of their wishes. I also mentioned the efforts of committed Catholic believers to reduce the power of the clergy in the field of culture and education. Yet rereading my article twenty-five years later, I am no longer convinced by my own arguments: I think that a cultural schism has taken place in Quebec. The Catholic Church survives as a minority, but it has become almost invisible in the secular society. Catholic voices are not received in the debates about the social and political future of Quebec. A resentment against the Catholic Church has become part of the dominant culture. The Catholic religion continues to be associated with *la grande noirceur* of the Duplessis regime. Public opinion in Quebec is unwilling to acknowledge the progressive movements in today's Church, nor appreciate the social teaching of the Quebec bishops expressing solidarity with workers and all people left in the margin. Since many Quebecers feel that religion is a phenomenon belonging to the past, they are annoyed by immigrant groups that manifest their faith in public by the clothes they wear. Religious liberty guaranteed by law assures the private practice of religion, but some Quebecers feel that religion should have no place in the public sphere. A passionate debate is currently taking place about *la laïcité de l'État*, the separation of religion and State.[37] Ardent secularizers want the State to be neutral in regard to religion and forbid men and women working for the State to wear visible religious symbols. Most political leaders and the Catholic bishops recommend instead *la laïcité ouverte*: they want the State to be neutral in regard to religion, yet to appreciate the contributions made by the religious to society and to be generous in respecting religious signs in the public sphere. I mention this debate in the present context because it illustrates the resentment against religion that pervades Quebec society. Without attention to this cultural phenomenon, it is impossible to understand the preoccupations of Quebec theologians.

THE DECLINE OF SOCIAL DEMOCRACY

The social values and the institutions generated by the Quiet Revolution were supported by the majority of Quebecers, including the Church. They promoted social democracy, fostered personal freedom and social solidarity, and assigned to the government the responsibility for serving the common good, steering the economy, distributing the public wealth, and supporting the cultural creativity of society. Yet Quebec's social democracy was increasingly challenged by the neo-liberal policies adopted in North America and the world in the late 1970s, following the political philosophy of Margaret Thatcher, the British prime minister, and Ronald Reagan, the American president. In Canada, neo-liberal economics was recommended by the MacDonald Commission of 1985.[38] The loss of the Quebec referendum on sovereignty-association in 1980 revealed that the culture of Quebec had become more liberal, reluctant to support a collective project. As the years passed, Quebec society came to resemble more and more the other North American societies: competitive, individualistic, subject to the market, oriented toward consumption, indifferent to the common good, and unaware of the growing distance between rich and poor. In the preface to his book *Raisons communes*, published in 1995, Fernand Dumont offers a brief analysis of what Quebec society has become and concludes that what is urgently needed is another Quiet Revolution.

> Whenever the sky is grey, when the future takes on a monotone hue and politics wallows in powerlessness, we begin to dream of sudden bursts which put history back on the road. In Quebec, we think with nostalgia about the years of the Quiet Revolution, the liberation of spirits, the rejuvenation of the state, educational reforms, large-scale social programs ... In today's reality, an increasing number of problems call for mobilization and planning. Although distinctions between the social classes have diminished, our society is not becoming more egalitarian. In early 1994, Quebec had 750 000 recipients of social assistance, 400 000 unemployed; 130 000 minimum-wage workers; one person in four is functionally illiterate, 40 000 youth drop out of school without a high school diploma every year. An increasing number are left behind by the social progress ... At the same time, we are witnessing a growing disengagement from large institutions such as churches, unions and political parties. An increasing gap exists between the official discourse and the new problems that arise. The cynicism among citizens toward those in power is constantly growing.[39]

In her article on critical theology in Quebec, Carolyn Sharp[40] has shown that in each decade following the Quiet Revolution, theologians have become more critical of the social order, denouncing the growing social inequalities and at the end advocating resistance to the present orientation of society. This is a valid approach to the study of theology in Quebec. The reason why I have not followed this approach is that the theologians studied in this book have not changed their theological method as society began to abandon its social democratic values. While they became increasingly critical, theologians continued to follow the method recommended by

Vatican Council II: (1) listening to the culture to which they belong, (2) denouncing its destructive potential in the light of the Gospel, (3) discerning in the present culture the humanizing values and practices, and (4) integrating the latter into the proclamation of the Good News. The difference between theologians, as we shall see, was between reformers and radicals, the former supporting progressive political action and the latter calling for resistance to society's present orientation.

THEOLOGICAL STUDIES IN QUEBEC

The Quiet Revolution and Vatican Council II had a strong impact on the teaching of theology in Quebec. The Quiet Revolution put great emphasis on education. The Parent Report restructured the entire school system, making it an instrument for the democratization of culture, accessible to the children of all social classes.[41] The government financed the extension of Laval University and the University of Montreal, and founded the new University of Quebec, with campuses in Montreal, Chicoutimi, Rimouski, Trois-Rivières, and Gatineau. Vast numbers of students now wanted to study, think for themselves, be trained in a discipline, and graduate from a university. The evolving culture released energy and enthusiasm for the intellectual life. Thanks to the freedom initiated by Vatican Council II, Catholics now also turned to the study of theology in great numbers. Several of the above-mentioned universities had a faculty or a department of theology.

In Quebec, lay people were studying theology. They were able to find employment in the Catholic school system (abolished in 2005) where the teaching of religion was offered in every grade. Some young men studied theology to prepare themselves for the priesthood. Already prior to the Vatican Council, some bishops had moved the seminary to the university campus, a move that was almost universally adopted after Vatican II. Since the critical dialogue of theology with the national culture was now recommended, the bishops were ready to integrate seminary education into the faculty or the department of theology. While the bishops were no longer in control of these faculties and departments, they entertained a trusting relationship to them.

In some universities the situation became more complex. The University of Montreal and Laval University had been founded as

Catholic universities and their faculties of theology had been recognized canonically by Rome. Yet in the wake of the Quiet Revolution, these universities severed their institutional link to the Catholic Church and became secular, a process that made the theological faculties lose their canonical status. In Montreal this led to a public conflict in 1967. When a priest professor of theology decided to leave the priesthood, the archbishop of Montreal, Paul Grégoire, insisted that he be dismissed, yet since he had academic tenure, the University of Montreal was unable and unwilling to do so. In response the archbishop decided to withdraw the seminarians from the university and restart the seminary under his control.

The University of Sherbrooke, founded as a Catholic university with a canonically approved faculty of theology, has not sought to change its status. Yet after 1970 the university made little use of its Catholic name; only the faculty of theology continued to live up to its canonical status. It is in fact the only Catholic faculty in Quebec that has canonical recognition. St Paul University in Ottawa, Ontario, a bilingual institution, is also canonically approved by Rome.

Located in secular universities, the faculties of theology now engage in dialogue with the social sciences to gain a better understanding of their society and of the Church's mission within it. As the society became increasingly pluralistic, the faculties of theology adopted an ecumenical policy: they hired Protestant and Anglican professors and admitted students belonging to their Churches. More than that, the faculties of theology expanded their field of teaching and research to include religious studies, that is to say critical scholarly attention to non-Christian religions, especially those practiced in Quebec society. When, in the year 2005, the Ministry of Education secularized the entire school system and introduced an obligatory course on ethics and religious culture, the faculties of theology and the departments of religious studies began to prepare teachers for the new course.

The evolution of the theological faculties of Quebec has been studied and described in several articles by Gilles Routhier,[42] prominent theologian and historian, currently the dean of Laval University's faculty of theology. Several of his publications deal with the reception of Vatican Council II in various parts of the Church and the place of ecclesiastical authority in the development of Catholic theology. In his articles on the theological faculties in Quebec, Routhier replies to critics who complain that the location of these faculties within secular universities leads to the estrangement of theologians from the Church and to the neglect of the pastoral function of theology. Routhier argues persuasively that a team of theologians located in a secular university renders an indispensable service to the Church, which is itself situated in a secular society. According to Vatican Council II, the proclamation of the Gospel is not a doctrine introducing society to new ideas, but a message that illumines the social reality of the present, denouncing its destructive implications and supporting its humanistic aspirations. Since the Gospel is meant to redeem and transform the human milieu, theologians must be in dialogue with the culture of their society, respect its pluralism, bring to light its potential for evil, and honour its concern for justice and peace. Theologians must present the paschal mystery as a source of hope, helping believers to lead redemptive lives. Teaching theology in a sealed-off seminary, Gilles Routhier argues, is unlikely to offer adequate preparation for the exercise of pastoral ministry in a pluralistic society.

Routhier is aware that various models for the teaching of theology exist in the Catholic Church. In the USA, theology is taught in departments of Catholic universities; in France, theology is taught in Catholic Institutes that have no right to call themselves universities (except in Alsace); in Germany, a concordat assures the presence of canonical theological faculties within secular universities; and in Ontario, Catholic theology is taught in Catholic faculties federated with Protestant and Anglican faculties, as, for instance, in the Toronto School of Theology. Routhier argues that none of these models fit into the evolution of university education in Quebec. While the relations of the Quebec faculties to Rome are complex and sometimes difficult, their relations to the bishops and the Catholic community have been very good. Routhier writes, "While it is true that the transfer of theology from the seminary to the university and the diversification of the student body have changed [the relationship to the Church], they have not broken this relationship, but transformed it."[43]

Since the days of Vatican Council II, Quebec theologians have produced a considerable body of literature. There are four francophone theological reviews: *Laval théologique et philosophique*, founded at Laval University in 1945; *Théologique*, founded in 1993 at the University of Montreal; *Eglise et théologie*, recently renamed *Théoforum,* published at St Paul University since 1970; and *Science et Esprit*, published by le Collège universitaire dominicain in Ottawa since 1998. La Société canadienne de théologie, founded in 1964, meets once a year. Until 2009, the proceedings of these meetings were published in book form almost every year; they constitute the substantial collection *Héritage et projet* brought out by the publisher Fides in Montreal. The volumes of research and reflection published by Quebec theologians are addressed to a variety of publics, some to their academic colleagues, some to pastors and pastoral agents, and some to the wider society. I wish to mention in particular the network "Culture et foi," founded in 1995, which provides a website fostering the innovative ideas and practices in the Catholic Church. It makes available to the reader articles of critical theologians, decrees of the papal and episcopal authorities, and declarations on controversial theological issues made by Catholic groups and institutions. The website provides an accessible archive for contemporary theological developments.

Theology is not confined to the university. Bishops rely on the co-operation of theologians in writing their pastoral letters and public statements. The Dumont Report, mentioned above, offered theological proposals for the renewal of the Church, based on the testimonies of the Catholic people and elaborated by a commission that included lay people and theologians. The Dumont Report recognized that Catholic men and women reflecting on the meaning the Gospel has for their lives and their society are in fact generating Catholic theology. In the 1970s the network "Les politisés chrétiens"[44] produced theological texts; and later, beginning in 1985, "Le groupe de théologie contextuelle québécoise,"[45] a circle of lay people including a few academic theologians, held meetings at regular intervals and produced theological statements addressed to society. This circle is in solidarity with the social movements at the base of society and tries to articulate what the Gospel means for people pushed to the bottom of society. The decline of the values promoted by the Quiet Revolution and the growing inequalities produced by neo-liberal economic policies did not stop the theological reflections of engaged Catholics; they did not abandon their trust in the messianic promises of Jesus.

There is no denying that the secularization of Quebec society threatens the flourishing of the academic study of theology. Because there are fewer students, a number of departments of theology have been closed and the surviving faculties and departments now include the study of the world religions. While the guild of professional theologians has become smaller, it still displays an extraordinary vitality.

2

Vatican Council II on Faith and Culture

During Vatican Council II, André Naud, a greatly respected theologian, was the theological adviser of Cardinal Léger, the archbishop of Montreal. Since I worked at the Council as a "peritus" at the Secretariat for Christian Unity, I often met Naud, and we occasionally worked together. A few years later, in the article "La théologie au Québec,"[1] he argued persuasively that theology, faithful to the Gospel and the Church's tradition, must shed light on the historical framework of the believing community and, for this reason, needs to be rethought in every age. Naud lamented that Quebec's theological heritage was poor, reflecting the cultural dependency of French Canada's colonial existence. We had no great authors, he wrote, nor an original school of thought. In the late nineteenth century our seminaries had introduced the neo-scholastic theology that Pope Leo XIII had made normative for Catholic theological education. This Roman theology, a weak echo of the thought of Saint Thomas, presented itself as universal, as valid in all parts of the Church, be it in Europe or the Americas. In Quebec, Naud wrote, we inherited "a theology of Christendom without problems, without challenges, without anguish, a theology that possessed the truth securely, an abstract theology unrelated to people's lives." This is now changing, Naud continued. Theologians have begun to wrestle with the meaning of God's revelation in the historical conditions created by the Quiet Revolution.

In his article Naud acknowledges that the Roman theology was in fact contextual: it was the Church's answer to religious ideas proposed by in the nineteenth century by philosophers and religious thinkers. On one side were "the fideists" who held that faith was a matter of experience at odds with rational thinking, and on the other side were "the rationalists," mainly German idealists, who held that philosophy could demonstrate the truth of divine revelation. The innovative idea of the Roman theology was to distinguish between credibility and faith. That divine revelation was a credible truth, not an illusion or a fairy tale, could be demonstrated rationally. This was the reply to the fideists. Yet since divine revelation transcends human intelligence, it cannot be demonstrated by reason; it can only be received as divine gift. This was the answer to the rationalists.

At the present time, Naud argued, the Church is challenged by different philosophies. In particular, the Church's message is accused of being otherworldly, lifting believers out of their historical context and relating them to heaven and eternity. Today theology must show that the Gospel summons believers to assume responsibility for their lives and their society. Naud concludes that theologians in Quebec must produce their own theological reflections.

THE PROPOSALS OF VATICAN COUNCIL II

The need for a new theology was recognized by Vatican Council II (1962–65). Here the Catholic Church redefined its relationship to the modern world: it now recognized human rights, religious freedom, and the co-responsibility of citizens for their society, and it respected religious pluralism and fostered co-operation of Catholics with non-believers in the service of the common good. The values of the Quiet Revolution – freedom, solidarity, democracy, and collective responsibility – were in keeping with the new Catholic teaching.

Of great importance for the evolution of theology in Quebec were three innovative recommendations made by Vatican Council II.

The Creativity of the Particular Church

The Council retrieved the forgotten ecclesiology of the ancient Christian authors, the so-called Church Fathers, that recognized the relative autonomy of the particular Church. The Council acknowledged that the Catholic Church, i.e. the Church Universal under the authority of the pope, is in fact an immense community of Churches, all in communion with one another and all respecting the papal primacy. The Catholic Church is not an ecclesiastical realm in which the local Churches are ecclesiastical provinces, governed by bishops who derive their authority from the pope. According to *Christus Dominus*, the conciliar decree on bishops, "Bishops exercise their episcopal office, received through episcopal consecration, in communion with and under the supreme authority of the supreme pontiff" (no. 3). Bishops receive their pastoral authority sacramentally. Their Churches, we are told in *Lumen Gentium*, the conciliar constitution on the Church, are embodiments of the Church of Christ. Particular Churches are portions of this one Church; they render present this one Church in their region. The conciliar documents state this quite clearly, even if they do not emphasize it, nor explore its implications. Here are three brief texts from *Lumen Gentium*.

> Within the Church particular Churches hold a rightful place; these Churches retain their own traditions, without in any way opposing the primacy of the Chair of Peter, which presides over the whole assembly of charity and protects legitimate differences, while at the same time assuring that such differences do not hinder unity but rather contribute toward it. (no. 13)

> The individual bishop is the visible principle and foundation of unity of his particular Church, fashioned after the model of the universal Church. In and from such individual Churches there comes into being the one and only Catholic Church. (no. 23)

> This Church of Christ is truly present in all legitimate local congregations of the faithful which, united with their pastors, are themselves called Churches in the New Testament. For in their locality these are the new People called by God, in the Holy Spirit and in much fullness. (no. 26)

In his commentary on Vatican Council II, the young Joseph Ratzinger assigned great importance to the recognition of the local or regional Church:

> Catholic theology recognizes ... the multiplicity of Churches existing within the framework of the one, visible Church of God, each of which represents the totality of the Church. In close communion with one another they help build up, within a framework of a unity born of a vigorous multiplicity, the one Church of God ... This plurality of Churches has in fact increasingly

> receded in favour of a centralized system; in this process the local Church of Rome has, so to speak, absorbed all the other local Churches. This state of affairs ... the Council has attempted to correct.[2]

The Quebec theologian and historian Gilles Routhier writes:

> The move from an ultramontane Church to a "national" Church – one that does not look Roman – did not happen unexpectedly. With its theology of the local Church, its attention to culture, its re-evaluation of the ministry of bishops, its doctrine of episcopal collegiality, and its recognition of the jurisdiction of episcopal conferences, Vatican Council II was the culmination of a process that had begun at the end of the nineteenth century and which gained momentum in the first half of the twentieth century.[3]

That the Council had recognized the theological status of the local or regional Church, and its creativity and relative autonomy, persuaded the bishops of Quebec to enlarge the mandate of the Dumont Commission, asking it to consult the faithful and propose pastoral recommendations for a Roman Catholicism appropriate for Quebec.

Faith in Dialogue with Culture

The conciliar document on bishops, *Christus Dominus*, made the innovative proposal that the bishop of the Church should "adapt" the Christian message to make it relevant to the issues that preoccupy the local congregation. This is an allusion to the pastoral approach that has subsequently been referred as the "inculturation" of the Christian message.

> The bishops should present Christian doctrine in a manner adapted to the needs of the times, that is to say, in a manner that will respond to the difficulties and questions by which people are especially burdened and troubled. They should also guard that doctrine, teaching the faithful to defend and propagate it. In propounding this doctrine they should manifest the maternal solicitude of the Church toward all men whether they be believers or not. With a special affection they should attend upon the poor and the lower classes to whom the Lord sent them to preach the Gospel.[4]

The expression "adapt" or "adapted preaching" needs clarification. As it stands it could be falsely interpreted as a surrender to the dominant culture. The need to rethink and reformulate the Gospel in response to the cultural conditions of a particular Church is expressed more clearly in the conciliar document *Gaudium et Spes*.

> From the beginning of her history the Church has learned to express the message of Christ with the help of the ideas and terminology of various philosophers, and has tried to clarify it with their wisdom. Her purpose has been to adapt the Gospel to the grasp of all as well as to the needs of the learned ... Indeed this accommodated preaching of the revealed Word ought to remain the law of all evangelization. For thus the ability to express Christ's message in its own way is developed in each nation.
>
> At the same time there is fostered a living exchange between the Church and the diverse cultures of people. To promote such an exchange, especially in our days, the Church requires the special help of those who live in the world, are versed in different institutions and specialties, and grasp their innermost significance in the eyes of both believers and unbelievers. With the help of the Holy Spirit, it is the task of the entire People of God, especially pastors and theologians, to hear, distinguish and interpret the many voices of our age, and to judge them in the light of the divine Word, so that revealed truth can become more deeply penetrated, better understood and set forth to greater advantage.[5]
>
> Recent studies and findings of science, history and philosophy raise new questions which affect human lives and demand new theological investigations. Within the requirements and methods proper to theology, theologians are invited to seek continually for more suitable ways of communicating doctrine to the men and women of their times; for the deposit or the truths of faith are one thing and the manner in which they are enunciated, in the same meaning and understanding, is another. In pastoral care, sufficient use must be made not only of theological principles, but also of the findings of the secular sciences, especially of psychology and sociology, so that the faithful may be brought to a more adequate and mature life of faith.
>
> May the faithful live in close union with the other people of their time and may they strive to understand perfectly their way of thinking and judging, as expressed in their culture. Let them

> blend new sciences and theories and the understanding of the most recent discoveries with Christian morality and the teaching of Christian doctrine, so that their religious culture and morality may keep pace with scientific knowledge and with the constantly progressing technology. Thus they will be able to interpret and evaluate all things in a truly Christian spirit.[6]
>
> It is to be hoped that many of the laity will receive a sufficient formation in the sacred sciences and that some will dedicate themselves professionally to these studies, developing and deepening them by their own labors. In order that they may fulfill their function, let it be recognized that all the faithful, whether clerics or laity, possess a lawful freedom of inquiry, freedom of thought and of expressing their mind with humility and fortitude in those matters on which they enjoy competence.[7]

These are remarkable paragraphs. They ask Catholic theologians to be in dialogue with their culture, learn from the sciences and the wisdom of their age, evaluate the many voices in the light of God's Word, and detect in this culture insights that help them express the Catholic faith. We are told that "accommodated preaching of the revealed Word ought to remain the law of all evangelization." Catholic truth is one, but its presentation is multiple. Each nation, we are told, must proclaim the one truth in a manner that allows its people to grasp and practice it.

This accommodated preaching involves bishops, theologians, and the people. Bishops are searching for a more effective pastoral ministry; theologians reread the Scriptures and study the wisdom of the age; and the people have religious experiences that guide their lives in the society to which they belong. To make the Christian message relevant to the local or regional congregation, dialogue within the Church becomes a pastoral necessity. Thanks to this dialogue, (1) the Gospel is able to critically illuminate the culture of the society and (2) the humanistic values of this culture can be lifted up to become part of Catholicism in that place.

Vatican Council II itself was a special event of creative dialogue. One result of this dialogue has been the Church's positive response to the secular values of human rights and freedoms. In the ambiguity of modern culture, the Council discerned people's democratic aspirations as values in keeping with the Christian message; and relying on new theological insights, the Council integrated these values into the contemporary form of Catholicism.

In subsequent papal teaching, this pastoral process has been called 'inculturation.' In the encyclical *Redemptoris Missio* (1990), John Paul II defined inculturation as "the incarnation of the gospel in native cultures and also the introduction of these cultures into the life of the Church."[8] Another version of this definition in the same encyclical is "the intimate transformation of authentic cultural values through their integration in Christianity and the insertion of Christianity in the various human cultures." To allow this process to take place in the local or regional Churches, the conciliar decree on the Church's missionary activities, *Ad Gentes*, recommends that seminarians, in their study of theology, be in dialogue with the wisdom inscribed into their own culture:

> Let the minds of the students be kept open and attuned to an acquaintance and an appreciation of their own nation's culture. In their philosophical and theological studies, let them consider the points of contact which mediate between the traditions and religion of their homeland on the one hand and the Christian religion on the other. (no. 20)
>
> Likewise, priestly training should have an eye to the pastoral needs of that region; and the students should learn the history, aim, and method of the Church's missionary activity, and the special social, economic, and cultural conditions of their own people. Let them be educated in the ecumenical spirit, and duly prepared for fraternal dialogue with non-Christians. (no. 21)
>
> All this demands that studies for the priesthood be undertaken, so far as possible, in association and living together with their own people. (no. 22)

That preaching the Gospel called for a dialogue between faith and culture was a topic dear to John Paul II. On his trip to Canada in 1984, he relied on the Gospel to denounce currents in Canadian culture, and at the same time detected in the same culture elements in keeping with the Gospel that deserved integration into theology and gave relevance to Christian preaching.[9] While people in the communist world were oppressed politically, he said, and people in the Third World were oppressed economically, Canadians, he continued, were culturally oppressed: their consciousness was invaded by individualism, competitiveness, and the addiction to consumerism, mediated by the dominant culture of their society. At the same time, the cultural current that made Canadians work for social justice and resist economic and political imperialism was in keeping with the Gospel and deserved the support of Christian preaching. To show his approval of the liberation theology produced by the Canadian bishops at that time, the pope cited and slightly extended a sentence from their 1983 statement "Ethical Reflections on the Economic Crisis."

> The needs of the poor must take priority over the desires of the rich, the rights of workers over the maximization of profits, and the preservation of the environment over uncontrolled industrial expansion, and production to meet social needs over production for military purposes.[10]

The Bible, the Soul of Theology

Of utmost importance for Catholic theologians was the emphasis Vatican Council II put on the reading of the Bible. We are told that theology must begin with the study of the Scriptures and continue again and again to refer back to them.

> Sacred theology rests on the written word of God, together with sacred tradition, as its primary and perpetual foundation. By scrutinizing in the light of faith all truth stored up in the mystery of Christ, theology is most powerfully strengthened and constantly rejuvenated by that word. For the Sacred Scriptures contain the word of God and since they are inspired, really are the word of God; and so the study of the Bible is, as it were, the soul of sacred theology.[11]

On his visit to Canada in 1984, John Paul II showed that this turn to the Scriptures brings out the redemptive character of Christian doctrine: this doctrine is not an abstract truth, but transforms human consciousness and eventually society itself. This is how I presented the pope's message in my article on that visit.

> The Pope grounded his call for justice in his Christology. Every sermon of his contained a social message. He never spoke of God and Jesus Christ without drawing attention to the impact of

dogma on society. In line with his first encyclical, *Redemptor hominis*, John Paul II presented a "transformist" Christology. The self-revelation of God in Jesus Christ is for the Pope a disclosure of the divine mystery and at the same time an illumination of our ambiguous human reality as well as a thrust towards its transformation. Divine revelation illuminates and transforms the world.[12]

THEOLOGY IN QUEBEC: CONTEXTUAL AND TRANSFORMATIVE

Vatican Council II had a profound influence upon the Church of Quebec. We saw in chapter 1 that the bishops appointed the Dumont Commission to consult the faithful and their theologians in order to propose pastoral policies to make the Church relevant for the people of Quebec. Theologians, following the guidelines of Vatican II, paid attention to the cultural, political, and economic challenges of their society. They gave priority to the Scriptures, looked upon theology as transformative, denounced the unjust or oppressive features of their society, and supported in the name of their faith the humanizing values of the Quiet Revolution. Their theology was contextual. They wanted to proclaim the universal truth of the Gospel in a form that was relevant to the historical situation of their society.

Jacques Racine, a prominent theological and pastoral thinker, has described in one sentence the effort of theologians to respond to and participate in the Quiet Revolution:

"Dedicated Christians and theologians in particular have tried to contribute to the construction of a modern Quebec identity, attentive to what the Church and religious experience could offer to motivate, critique and support this endeavour."[13]

Catholic theology in English-speaking Canada moves in various directions. Most of the time, the theological literature is addressed to a Catholic readership distributed over the English-speaking world. Its main purpose is to communicate theological ideas that are appropriate and relevant in the industrialized societies of the West. English-speaking theologians rarely refer their ideas to issues related specifically to Canadian society. The great Canadian philosopher-theologian Bernard Lonergan, whose important work addresses not only theologians but also scientists and moral philosophers, had worldwide influence, stimulating thinkers to do new research and develop their own ideas. Yet Lonergan has never analysed nor addressed specifically

Canadian concerns: he did not regard this as part of his task as a theologian. Moreover, Canadian theologians want their books to be read outside of Canada and hence prefer to publish them in New York or London, leaving aside specifically Canadian concerns. Political theology does exist in Canada,[14] yet relating the Christian message to the struggle to transform Canadian society is done only by a minority of theologians. Women theologians are more likely to relate the Gospel to conditions of inequality imposed upon their society.

Theologians in Quebec, like other intellectuals in the province, tend to relate their scholarly work to the problems of their society. Most of the time their reflections are contextual. One reason for this is that Quebecers see themselves as a nation with an unfinished political identity. The federalists among them look forward to a new Canadian constitution that recognizes Quebec as a nation within Canada, and the independentists aspire to a sovereign republic of Quebec closely allied to Canada. Intellectuals in Quebec are also worried that the cultural power of English in North America will undermine their mother tongue, which is currently the public language of their society. Today globalized, neo-liberal capitalism speaks English the world over. Quebecers also realize that a large percentage of immigrants settling in Montreal prefer to integrate into the English-speaking minority, keeping the door open to the rest of the North American continent. There are thus political reasons why intellectual activity in Quebec is never unrelated to the concerns of the social order.

Theologians in Quebec relate their work to society for another reason. In the past, the Catholic bishops, speaking in the name of the entire nation, exerted pressure upon the government and used their authority to tell people what politicians to support. Anglo-Canadians often referred to Quebec as "the priest-ridden province." When, after the Quiet Revolution, church-going Catholics became a minority in Quebec, bishops, theologians, and lay leaders continued to address the public on social and political issues – now, however, no longer in defence of the establishment, but as critics, applying Catholic social teaching to their society. The Catholic leadership in Quebec now exercises a prophetic role.

It is possible to summarize the preceding remarks by saying that theologians in Quebec practice a contemporary form of fundamental theology. In the nineteenth century, fundamental theology, also known as apologetics, tried to offer a rational demonstration of the credibility of divine revelation. This included philosophical arguments proving God's existence, historical arguments proving that Jesus was a reliable witness, and biblical arguments proving that the Catholic Church was the true Church founded by Jesus. Apologetics was not theology in the proper sense; it did not begin with faith in divine revelation; it addressed itself to outsiders, persuading them that the Catholic faith was not a surrender to an irrational myth, but the acceptance of a message that was rationally credible.

Apologetics of this kind is no longer practiced. Today fundamental theology tries to present the Christian faith as shedding light on contemporary culture by responding to its questions and anxieties and by confirming and enhancing its insights and virtues. Fundamental theology is addressed to believers and secular people alike, revealing the relevance of the Gospel for contemporary society. Doctrine here becomes Good News for the present. Karl Rahner has been credited as the first theologian to rethink fundamental theology in this way,[15] an approach that was followed in the first part of the conciliar document *Gaudium et Spes*.

I remember the debate among the bishops at the Council about how to address the world community in the document that was to become *Gaudium et Spes*. Should the Church speak to the world in terms of reason and natural law (as did the encyclicals on Catholic social teaching prior to Pope John XXIII)? Or should the Church simply proclaim the biblical message to humanity? The bishops decided upon an innovative approach: they wanted the conciliar document to describe the complexity of modern society, reveal its destructive dimension and its potential for good, and then present the Christian message and mystery as God's gracious reply to these contemporary conditions. This approach, the bishops thought, would reveal the relevance of the Gospel to the believing community and at the same time make outsiders understand why believers experience the Gospel as enlightenment and as a power that changes their lives. I explained this new approach in the commentary on *Gaudium et Spes* which I published in 1967,[16] yet I did not realize at the time that this was an echo of Karl Rahner's fundamental theology.

Since God's revelation is "for us and for our salvation," Christian doctrine is redemptive; it is not a conceptual truth making us learned about God, but a saving truth that changes our self-perception and our perception of the world. All reflection on doctrine can become fundamental theology. In Quebec, as I mentioned above, theology is both contextual and transformative. Because Quebec is still a society in the making, theologians see the relevance of the Gospel in its support for the creation of a more just, more humane, and more open society. What is relevant for them is the practice mediated by Christian doctrine.

In his long article "Théologie" in the encyclopedia *Catholicisme*, Christian Duquoc writes that theologians in Quebec are engaged in dialogue with the social sciences and foster pastoral practices that are relevant to the problems of society. This is more important for them, he adds, than dialogue with philosophy and the examination of the unresolved questions posed by their culture.[17] This last observation, as we shall see, does not apply to the original theology of Fernand Dumont.

THEOLOGY FOR A CHURCH IN A SECULAR SOCIETY

While the Church is trying to make the Gospel relevant to society, the majority of Quebecers have turned their backs on the Church. Engaged Catholics ask themselves the anguishing question of how Quebec, at one time a passionately Catholic society, could have become so quickly secular and harbour resentment against the Church that had accompanied the people throughout their history. Still, the great majority of the bishops refuse to be angry with the people. They do not accuse Quebecers collectively of materialism, selfishness, or treason; instead, they make an effort to understand the reasons why people resent the Catholicism they have inherited. Since one reason for this rejection has been the excessive power of the hierarchical Church over Quebec's public culture, especially during the Duplessis regime, the bishops did not object to the declericalization of society initiated by the Quiet Revolution and welcomed the new humanistic values – such as freedom of speech, respect for pluralism, democratic participation, and the promotion of social and economic justice.

It is instructive to contrast the sympathetic approach to Quebec society taken by the Catholic Bishops Conference of Quebec with the aggressive tone adopted by Cardinal Marc Ouellet, archbishop of Quebec City from 2002 to 2010. He represented the conservative current encouraged by the Vatican, yet was unable to influence his brother bishops. In October 2007, both the cardinal and the Catholic Bishops Conference submitted briefs to the Bouchard-Taylor Commission set up by the Quebec government to recommend rulings for settling conflicts over religious symbols in the public sphere.

Cardinal Ouellet writes:

> The real problem in Quebec is the spiritual vacuum created by the religious and cultural rupture, a substantial loss of memory resulting in crises in the family and in education, leaving citizens disoriented, unmotivated, subjected to instability and wed to ephemeral and superficial values. This spiritual and symbolic void erodes Quebec's culture from within, disperses its vitality and generates insecurity, uprooted from continuity with the Gospel and the sacramental values which sustained it from the beginning. A people whose identity was so strongly forged for centuries by the Catholic faith cannot empty itself of its substance overnight without all sorts of serious consequences. This explains the disorientation of young people, the dramatic decline in marriages, the low birth rate and the alarming numbers of abortions and suicides.[18]

The Catholic Bishops Conference writes:

> In an ever moving, pluralist society such as ours, it is necessary for all to enter "the mode of dialogue." Dialogue among citizens and groups; dialogue between religious people and those who have no religious affiliation; and dialogue between the religions. The democratic ethos in which we find ourselves demands that we be open [with] one another. Being in "the mode of dialogue" requires, first of all, recognizing and accepting one's own identity, including one's religious identity wherever this applies. This holds true for all, including the members of the francophone majority. This is not the rejection of the differences among us; on the contrary, it is the attitude required for a fruitful dialogue founded on mutual respect. We must not be afraid to remember the religious Catholic background of the majority of our fellow citizens, for it marks our common history, our culture and our landscape.[19]

The Bishops Conference's readiness to engage in dialogue is shared by the theologians of Quebec.

Quebec historians and social scientists are currently debating whether and to what extent the Quiet Revolution deserves to be called a revolution.[20] Some historians recall that the industrialization of Quebec had already occurred at the end of the nineteenth century; that Liberal governments, especially between 1939 and 1944 under Adélard Godbout, had favoured democratic rights; and that Quebec's subsequent social evolution in the 1960s was similar to developments in many other Western countries. Quebec historians and social scientists are now engaged in a hermeneutical debate over how to read historical events and historical documents. Theologians are familiar with hermeneutics: they realise that interpreting an event or a text always involves a conscious or unconscious commitment to a particular perspective. The Quiet Revolution was experienced differently by different people, and its present interpretation is guided by the ideas to which the commentators attach special importance. For believing Catholics, the Quiet Revolution was truly a revolution: accompanied by Vatican Council II, it dramatically changed Catholic life in Quebec and, a few years later, caused the rapid secularization of society. For believing Catholics, the Quiet Revolution brought about a cultural transformation and a clearly defined difference between "before" and "after." According to the Dumont Report this passage involved both "rupture" and "fidelity."

To understand the work of theologians in Quebec, it is important to realise that for them something radical has taken place: the inherited Catholicism has been left behind and a new kind of Catholicism is taking shape, to which they wish to contribute. This was, in fact, the position taken by the Dumont Commission. Theologians in Quebec see themselves as servants of the future. In reliance on the Gospel, they face the dark side of contemporary society, offer a critique of the Catholic tradition, and propose the reform of Church and society – a project, they believe, that can only be done in the Holy Spirit. Their effort is encouraged by the above-quoted observation of Benedict XVI in his encyclical *Spe Salvi* of 2008: "Flowing into the self-critique of the modern age there also has to be a self-critique of modern Christianity, which must constantly renew its self-understanding setting out from its roots."[21]

GOD'S PRESENCE IN HISTORY

A characteristic of modern culture is the recognition that human beings are responsible for the world in which they live. No one thinks anymore that God created the world as it is at the beginning of time; we have become conscious that a complex evolution has produced the world to which we belong. Men and women, we now feel, have a certain responsibility for what kind of people they become and what kind of society they construct. While historically people accepted the hierarchical structure of society as the work of divine providence, in the modern age people are aware that society is man-made, that it can be reconstructed, and that they bear a responsibility for what it will be like in the future. Human beings are called – called by God – to create themselves and their world. We read in *Gaudium et Spes*, "We are witnesses of the birth of a new humanism, one in which man is defined first of all by his responsibility towards his brother and toward history"[22] – a phrase that must be adjusted to reflect the equality of men and women. A superficial reading of this conciliar quotation suggests that it refers to a humanism without reference to God – a Promethean effort of self-creation and self-redemption. Yet a careful reading of this sentence, taking into account the theology proposed by *Gaudium et Spes*, recognizes that the reference is to a humanism to which God is present as summons, grace, and horizon.

If the human vocation is to exercise historical responsibility, the message of God in heaven and the salvation of souls seem to lose their relevance and to distract people from their essential task as "artisans and authors of the culture of their community" fostering "the spiritual and moral maturity of the human race" – expressions used in *Gaudium et Spes*. Faith in dialogue with culture, as we have seen, says both a resolute No to certain of its aspects and a creative Yes to others. In the present context, faith says No to a humanism that becomes a Pelagian project of self-redemption or an ideology of inevitable progress; yet it says Yes to the struggle for peace and justice and the creation of a humane society. Christian believers hold that God's self-revelation in Jesus Christ intends to rescue humanity from self-destruction and appoint it to strive for a civilization of love. The Gospel does not intend to save souls; it wants men and women to be faithful to their human vocation, a fidelity that prepares them for the age to come. The God of the Bible is here not seen as a supreme being above history, ruling the world from His heavenly throne, but as a personal presence in history, summoning and empowering men and women to realize their human vocation and become engaged in the creation of a just and compassionate society.

The French philosopher Maurice Blondel, writing at the end of the nineteenth century, was the first Catholic thinker who rejected the idea, promoted by neo-scholasticism, that the created world was a finished reality, ruled by the wise providence of God in heaven. Blondel called this idea "supernaturalism" or "extrinsicism." He discarded the idea that the world was a finished entity to which the Gospel was added as a heavenly message, as it were, from the outside. He argued that people in modern culture are unable to accept a proposal as true that does not correspond in some way to the questions they have asked themselves and to the issues that preoccupy them. A truth uttered from the outside, unrelated to their experience, cannot be assimilated; if it is accepted nonetheless, it remains a foreign body in human consciousness and prevents people from thinking clearly. Blondel wrote that if an angel entered his office with a message from another world, he would have to say, "I am sorry, this does not concern me: my human vocation (*le métier de l'homme*) is to be concerned with the present world." We ourselves and the world to which we belong, he insisted, are not finished entities; they are still in the making, being constituted by our ongoing thoughts and actions.

After rejecting God as the great Outsider, Blondel produced a phenomenology of the human quest of self-realization, a quest that, if sustained faithfully, will carry humans toward an encounter with Transcendence. The God in whom Blondel believed was the great Insider, the mystery immanent in human life, the gracious dimension of man's making of man. Here the Gospel is not a message from another world, added to human life from without, but the proclamation of the transcendent mystery immanent in history, summoning and enabling people to fulfill their human destiny. Christian revelation, Blondel believed, confirmed and illuminated the creative and redemptive dynamics operative in the lives of people everywhere.

Though Blondel was criticized by neo-scholastic theologians, his thought influenced several Thomistic philosophers, the so-called Transcendental Thomists,[23] among whom Karl Rahner and Bernard Lonergan are the best known. In Protestantism it was the German theologian Paul Tillich who moved beyond classical theism, affirming God beyond God, God as *Lebensgrund*, grounding human life and rescuing it from its self-destructive potential.

When I read Blondel in the late 1960s – I was a professor of theology at St Michael's College in Toronto at the time – I was profoundly impressed by his method of immanence. I had the idea at the time, which I developed in my book *Man Becoming*,[24] that a theological shift was taking place in the Christian Churches from the widely held theism, in the Catholic tradition articulated in neo-scholasticism, to "panentheism," the belief in God's redemptive immanence in human history and the cosmos.

In Quebec, as we shall see in the next chapter, Fernand Dumont was greatly impressed by Maurice Blondel and with him recognized that humans in quest of their full humanity are brought in touch with Transcendence. Jean Richard, the translator and interpreter of Paul Tillich, introduced Quebec theologians to Tillich's panentheism that recognized divine Transcendence in people's ultimate concern. It is my impression that the Quebec theologians discussed in the present book think of God as present in human history, as Word and Spirit, calling and empowering men and women to practice love, justice, and peace and to move toward the full realization of their humanity.

The contemporary turn to panentheism is, as we have seen, the result of the dialogue of faith with modern culture, in particular with the new sense of personal and collective responsibility for who we are and who we will be. This theological turn also sheds the light of the Gospel on several other issues that have assumed importance in the present age.

(1) Panentheism generates an open attitude towards other religious and cultural traditions, assuring us that God is at work in them in a hidden way, generating, despite all obstacles, the desire for love, justice, and peace. That God addresses people redemptively, whatever their particular tradition, is recognized by Vatican Council II in a short paragraph of *Gaudium et Spes,* stating that the Spirit offers to every human being, in a manner known only to God, the possibility of sharing in divine redemption.[25] It follows that the significant division in today's world is not between believers and non-believers, as is sometimes suggested by ecclesiastical documents,[26] but between the people committed to love and truth and the people committed to conquest and the lies necessarily associated with it.

(2) In traditional theism God was thought to be the omnipotent ruler of the universe, obliging theologians to admit that while God did not will evil, God allowed it, for otherwise it could not take place. Today many believers protest against the idea that God has allowed the Holocaust, the atomic bombing of Hiroshima, and the horror of the recent genocides. According to panentheism, God exercises power in human history, not as a ruler from above, but as Word addressing people's minds and as Spirit strengthening their will. The evil in

history, whose origin is enigmatic, is neither willed nor allowed by God. The cause of evil is us. There is no room in God's providence for genocides and mass killings; we engage in them against the divine will. God's providence here refers to the paschal mystery and other redemptive events in human history, rescuing us from self-destruction.

(3) The emphasis on divine immanence also gives new meaning to the transpersonal titles given to God in the Scriptures. Calling God Light, Life, Love, and Truth discloses the manner in which God is present in human life and sustains people in their faith. The transpersonal titles of God now lead believers to contemplative prayer: God is not simply a "thou" facing us, but also the Light, Life, Love, and Truth in which we have our dwelling.

(4) Feminist theologians have made the Church aware that traditional theism, seeing God as heavenly king, produced masculine images of the Divine that legitimated patriarchal cultures and the lower status of women in society. By contrast, in panentheism God is a gracious presence in human history, the matrix of human becoming, no longer imaged in patriarchal terms.

This dialogue of faith and culture is not peculiar to Quebec; it is occurring in all Western and non-Western societies. Because Quebecers have reacted so negatively to the Church and have stopped reflecting on their faith, theologians in Quebec are particularly eager to find an alternative discourse about God and the order of redemption.

3

Introducing Fernand Dumont

Fernand Dumont (1927–1997) was a sociologist turned philosopher who became an original theorist and an influential public intellectual. He obtained his doctorate from the Sorbonne in Paris, was in personal conversation with the philosophers of France, became professor of the social sciences at Laval University, and was greatly admired as an independent and innovative scholar. His special interests, pursued in several volumes, were the cultural and epistemological presuppositions of the social sciences and, more generally, the dialectical interaction of culture and human consciousness. As one of the few Quebec intellectuals who remained a believing Catholic, Dumont reflected on his faith, participated in church life, and published long theological essays. His autobiography *Récit d'une emigration* (1997) reports that in the 1960s and 1970s, he had been associated with the Dominican review *Maintenant* and written many articles on theological topics. After his passing in 1997, his major writings were republished as *Œuvres complètes* in five large volumes.

I discovered the work of Fernand Dumont only after I had decided to write the present book. I knew, of course, that he had been appointed by the Quebec bishops in 1968 to chair the commission, subsequently called the Dumont Commission, on the future of the Quebec Church. Now, looking at my bookshelves, I found his *Une foi partagée* (1996), which I had bought years ago, but had never read. Reading it now instantly convinced me that Dumont was an original theological thinker. I should have known this, for when in 1987, late in his life, he acquired a doctorate in theology from Laval University, I was a member of the committee that evaluated his thesis. Yet lacking sympathy for his approach to theology, I did not recognize the greatness of his work. Now I reread his thesis, published as *L'institution de la théologie* (1987), a learned, profound, and imaginative book, the originality of which has not yet been recognized in the theological literature.

As I continued reading his work, I recognized the prominence of this Quebec thinker. I am surrounded by professors of theology and believe that we do good work and contribute to a better understanding of the Gospel and the Catholic tradition. Fernand Dumont, I am convinced, is a thinker on a higher level: he is original and systematic, well acquainted with the intellectual traditions of the West, enjoying uncommon powers of analysis and synthesis, and remaining situated in the concrete conditions of his own society. The Acadian historian Julien Massicotte writes,

> Reading Dumont's work is like an odyssey through the worlds of sociology and philosophy, literature, economics and political philosophy, psychology and psychoanalysis, history and epistemology, among others. For the work is not only learned; Dumont was also a poet and a man of action.[1]

I see here a certain parallel to the theological milieu in English Canada: many professors do very good work and make important contributions, while one thinker is outstanding, located on a higher level: Bernard Lonergan, Catholic theologian and philosopher of the sciences, whose work has achieved prominence in the English-speaking world and whose collected works in many volumes are being published by the University of Toronto Press. There is no obvious affinity between Lonergan and Dumont. Lonergan, as a Kantian of sorts, holds that fidelity to the cognitive operations is the way to the truth, while Dumont, closer to Dilthey and Troeltsch, holds that prior to knowledge is a belief or a perspective, mediated by culture or an alternative horizon.

FIRST AND SECOND CULTURE

I have tried to understand Fernand Dumont's thought by taking into account his experiences as a child and a young man. He was born in a modest milieu, the Quebec proletariat – he uses this term to refer to the labourers who worked in broken English in the factories owned and managed by members of the English-speaking elite. Dumont's parents, like so many Quebecers at the time, were generous, loyal, and courageous, sustained in their hard life by their Catholic faith and the parish to which they belonged. As a child Dumont still experienced the low place assigned to French Canadians in Canadian society: with the exception of a relatively small middle class, they were poor farmers and workers with minimal access to education or social progress. The money they earned, the stamps they used, and the packaged groceries they bought were all in English. They often felt they lived in a foreign country. Because the young Dumont was gifted, loved reading, and understood the books he read, he was helped by the teaching brothers to go to good schools and to university. As an educated person he entered the culture of the learned, began to dialogue with intellectuals in Quebec and beyond, and adopted the political ideals of democracy, freedom of speech, and shared social responsibility, values not appreciated by the Duplessis regime. Changed became also Dumont's Catholicism. Because he left the culture of his origin, he called his autobiography *Récit d'une émigration* (The Story of an Emigration).[2] Rupture and distance were important words for him: they suggested not only opening the door to creativity but also, sadly, losing access to the sources of life.

The disruptive and enlightening experience of leaving one's original milieu, shared by many French Canadians, persuaded Fernand Dumont to distinguish between the *first culture* in which people are born and which shapes their perception of the world, and the *second culture* into which they move through education, work, and social involvement, altering their perspective on human life. Dumont was convinced that people's first culture nourished them throughout their lives. As a member of the educated class and a public personality, Dumont remained faithful to his origins: he respected the religion and the language of his parents; he looked upon their culture of faith, generosity, and hard work as the source of his own intellectual creativity. He experienced in his own life the rupture with his first culture as well as the continued rootedness in it.

The relation between the first and the second culture preoccupied Dumont in his entire intellectual work. He used this distinction to compare the milieu to which people belonged and the tasks they undertook or the horizon toward which they aspired. People are shaped by their past, yet stay free to transcend it; yet their freedom will be creative only if they remain rooted in their inherited culture. Dumont coined phrases to express this relationship, such as rupture and fidelity or, inversely, *héritage et projet*. We saw in chapter 1 that the Dumont Commission published its Report under the title *Un héritage, un projet*. Dumont himself became a critic of the Catholic Church and an advocate of the Quiet Revolution, yet his bold proposals for the future remained attached to Quebec's Catholic history. Reflecting on the relation between first and second culture led Dumont, as we shall see, to formulate his theological understanding of human existence.

This chapter is an introduction to Dumont's theological thought.[3] I shall mainly examine his *Une foi partagée* and only make a few references to his earlier theological writings. His major study *L'institution de la théologie* is a masterpiece that deserves to be presented and analyzed in a monograph. Applying his sociology of knowledge to the thought and imagination of Christian theologians throughout the centuries allows Dumont to offer an original interpretation of the Catholic tradition, embracing Newman's attention to the development of doctrine and Blondel's concern with immanence and faith as action. The book, a learned, innovative contribution to the Church's theological self-understanding, has not as yet been received by the theological community outside of Quebec. So far no English or German translation has been made.

Une foi partagée begins with these sentences. "This book will appear strange in the intellectual landscape of the present. It deals with a faith that is still alive, which makes some people smile, leaves others totally indifferent, and leads not a few to the threshold of embracing it."[4] And in his autobiography, Dumont writes, "In editing *Une foi partagée* I wanted to address myself to Christians and those who are not."[5] Yet his intention was not to invite Quebecers who have become secular to return the Catholic faith. What he wanted was a conversation with them. He tried to understand their point of view, but he also wished to be understood by them and, together with them, agree on how to promote a culture that would make Quebec a just and flourishing society.

FAITH IN GOD

Dumont's first point in *Une foi partagée* is that faith and reason are not opposed, but related positively to one another, interacting in all human beings, be they religious or secular. For Dumont, faith and reason are anthropological constants. As proof he offers the following reflections.

He distinguishes three functions of human reason. First, reason active "on the ground floor" enables us to do our daily work, co-operate with people around us, and act responsibly in society. Second, reason active 'on the first floor' produces the sciences: it measures, aims at clarity and precision, and accepts as true only what can be empirically verified. Third, reason 'in the basement' is engaged in restless questioning, asking why we are doing what we are doing, whether there is any meaning in it, and whether we are doing the right thing. Reason in the basement disturbs us by asking questions for which there may be no certain answer, such as "who am I?" or "who are we?" or "what is our destiny?" Because reason in the basement continues to ask questions, we are not locked into the culture in which we are born, nor totally determined by social and ideological structures. Because this reason continues to ask questions, we can never be completely certain of the answers we have found.

That we are without definitive answers does not paralyze us. We are able to act and think and live because as children we receive a life orientation by the culture in which we are born; or because later, as adults, making a wager, we opt for a set of values and look at the world from our chosen perspective. Dumont calls this "believing" or "having faith," for this orientation whether inherited or chosen is not demonstrable. Believing is not necessarily something religious. In this philosophical work, Dumont shows that a certain believing precedes and guides the social sciences. Without believing, people would be unable to think, act, or orient their lives. Faith is an anthropological constant. For Dumont, faith precedes the development of culture, the use of reason, and the constitution of the sciences.

Having faith does not mean that the questioning of "reason in the basement" stops. Because the questioning continues, there is never a last word. Dumont argues that the reasoning in the basement moves people to pose ever deeper questions. They will eventually acknowledge that there are questions for which human reason has no answer and that reality transcends their comprehension. Dumont calls this mysterious reality that people seeking self-understanding are led to acknowledge "Transcendence without a name." Because human reason is ever restless, this Transcendence will again and again engage them.

As actors, people also cannot help but relate themselves to a good that exceeds their powers and constitutes a transcendent horizon. Dumont argues that the internal dynamics operative in thinking and acting carries human beings to the threshold of the Absolute and relates them to an unknowable Transcendence. For some persons, the nameless Transcendence has a religious meaning, while for others it does not.

> Existence starts with questions, not certitudes: what is the meaning of this world? Why is there evil and suffering? Before it can be a series of affirmations, belief is preceded by being open to the big questions at the core of the human condition. Questions of this magnitude force us to turn to a horizon that can sustain them. In other words, there is no awareness without its relationship to the Transcendent.
>
> At first, Transcendence appears as the other side of ourselves, a hypothetical vis-à-vis that forces us to ask questions beyond the monotony of our work and our daily conversations. Transcendence is at first without a name, producing the anguish that is the source of our feeling of existing. It imposes upon nature its modification through language, art, and knowledge, which cast upon the world an inescapable shadow of anxiety before it becomes an affirmation of meaning.[6]

Dumont does not deal with the question "Is there a God?" or "Does God exist?" This question, he argues, presupposes that God – if God exists – is a supreme being above human history, residing in a distant beyond, about whose existence philosophers debate with rational arguments. With the Catholic philosopher Maurice Blondel, Dumont rejects this presupposition as 'extrinsicism.' He discards the idea that God is somewhere else, external to the process by which human beings constitute themselves and build their world. With Blondel, Dumont argues that humans are moved forward by a necessary internal dynamics to recognize a Transcendence operative in their lives. The horizon of people's self-making is not produced by themselves; instead this horizon makes them restless and summons them to change and realize their human potential. This argument, we note, is not a metaphysical one; it is founded instead on a phenomenology of human existence deemed verifiable by deep and thoughtful observation.

As a Christian, Dumont believes that the Gospel reveals the drama of the human struggle, that the divine message revealed in the Scriptures responds to questions humans are bound to ask, and that the God of Jesus Christ is the transcendent Light and Power that allows men and women to actualize their humanity to the full.

At the same time, Dumont recognizes the danger of credulity. Faith demands that critical reason, reason in the basement, continues to ask critical questions.

> The issue of believing may not be reduced to fabricating a strong opinion or nurturing consoling fantasies. Believing is to keep the question that sparked it at the heart of one's assent. In all of our experiences, particularly the highest and most significant, believing takes into account the doubt, a doubt that does not weaken the consent.[7]

There is another reason why Dumont is not interested in the rational demonstration of God's existence proposed by some philosophers. Such proofs, he argues, offer at best abstract truth. Yet abstract truth does not raise existential questions, nor transform human consciousness. Truth is not enough, Dumont insists; what counts is relevance, receiving an answer to urgent life-related questions. God does not appear as the conclusion of rational reflections, he argues; God comes as an answer, ever to be rethought, to the vital questions with which people wrestle in a given historical context. Truth is significant only if it changes consciousness, resituates personal life, and prompts a new practice.

The relationship between first and second culture implies for Dumont an understanding of human beings as ever restless and yet rooted – striving for what lies beyond, yet relying on a foundation laid in childhood. This dynamic anthropology, I suggest, has often been invoked in the French intellectual tradition. Pascal had already proposed that "man is always more than man," recognizing in humans a spiritual impulse to move forward, transcending themselves without ever stopping. Maurice Blondel, as we saw in the preceding chapter, also recognized in people an inner dynamics that made them restless, reaching towards their self-realization in the love of a truth that transcended them. Dumont echoes this conviction. He writes, "Man is greater than himself; he cannot come up to his measure unless he moves beyond it; the same can be said of societies and cultures."[8] I recently came across this remarkable sentence of Albert Camus:

> That man is the only creature that refuses to be what he is, means that the human dimension – his grandeur and dignity,

> including the achievements of science, the arts and human love – can only arise from his own choice, in an endless search to become ever more the creator of himself and of his world which, attuned to his quest, become more human with him.[9]

Camus thought that the dynamics implicit in human existence move people who are faithful to it towards self-transcendence – to an inner-worldly self-transcendence without reference to divinity. Camus did not believe in God. By contrast, philosophers such as Blondel and Dumont were convinced that this inner-worldly self-transcendence was summoned forth by an unreachable horizon and sustained by a power not of human origin: the presence of Another. These thinkers believed in God.

If I understand him correctly, Dumont's version of panentheism supposes that human life has a religious dimension. If faith is an anthropological constant orienting human beings towards a nameless Transcendence, then humans, stirred by their inner promptings, will relate themselves to a higher power who may be God or may be an idol. How, we may ask, does Dumont distinguish between true and idolatrous worship? It is my impression that Dumont does not want to make a clean distinction between the two. For him, every faith, including the faith of Christians, contains an idolatrous or ideological dimension and thus remains ever in need of a more radical conversion to God. Reason in the basement, Dumont argues, continues to question faith, raise doubts, and search for more valid answers, critically rethinking its relationship to the Transcendent. Because of human finitude, there will never be a last word. Dumont thinks that if this kind of questioning stops, if believers think of themselves as possessing the truth, as having the final answer, as having no need to listen to others, as being unchallenged by doubts, then their Transcendent becomes an idol. Thus even the Church or Jesus or truth can become an idol in the name of which we arrogantly despise, humiliate, and persecute other human beings. Dumont holds that we are unable to think about God without bending God's image a little in our favour. Christians will have to reexamine their faith constantly in order to correct its ideological distortions.

This position has a certain affinity with the panentheistic theology of Paul Tillich, according to which all human beings, following an internal dynamics, orient themselves towards a god, a god that will destroy them, unless it be the true God.

The French spiritual author Marcel Légaut agrees that people, stirred by an inner impulse, reach toward a nameless Transcendence. He writes, "Faith is the primary option which individuals are ineluctably bound to make as they move – with courage, clarity and vigour – to the end of the path to which they are held, when confronting the conditions of their existence."[10] Légaut goes even further: he shows how God's redemptive presence in the coming to be of the human person summons forth a new form of prayer, the contemplation of union with God, inherited from the mystical tradition.[11]

Some Quebec theologians, while influenced by Dumont, do not agree that all human beings ultimately relate themselves to a transcendent reality. There are people, they argue, who do not opt for an ultimate concern. André Charron writes, "Faith is a constitutive function of the human person. Yet this function, constitutive though it be, can be left in the margin, displaced by various superficial preoccupations."[12] Charron agrees with Dumont that believing is a presupposition of all thinking and acting, yet for Charron, believing is not necessarily faith. Believing becomes faith, he argues, when what a person believes embraces totality and summons forth surrender.

I am inclined to agree with Charron. The phenomenological argument offered by Blondel, Dumont, and Tillich – each in his own way – does not fully convince me. Conversations with friends and acquaintances living dedicated lives have persuaded me that some people have a secular consciousness unrelated to an ultimate. They parcel out their time between social engagement, happiness in the family, and research in the sciences, unable and unwilling to choose a single ultimate concern. They are faithful to a set of values that cannot be reconciled under a single principle, obliging them to seek a creative balance between competing ideals. They live their finitude and incompleteness with patience, supposing that a certain internal dividedness is part of the human condition.

While I am unconvinced by Dumont's phenomenological argument, I fully share his turn to panentheism. With him I hold that God is present in human life and history. In my book *Man Becoming* (1970) I argue that God is present in human life as Word summoning us to self-knowledge, convicting us of sin, and empowering us to leave a destructive past behind, turning to a creative future. God is present in human life as Spirit prompting us to love our neighbour, participate in a community, and extend solidarity to all people in need. Human life is the primary sacrament mediating salvation to those who have ears. When people become aware that their experiences of truth, love, and solidarity are gifts to them, transcending their nature marred by excessive self-seeking, they become believers in Transcendence without a name – or believers in a religious tradition. Since the Word and the Spirit present in history rescue us from sin and self-destruction and constitute us as believers destined to be with God and repair the unjust world, I interpret panentheism as a theology of redemption.

The redemptive aspect of the Christian message does not receive much attention in Dumont's religious thought. He does not explore the theology of sin. He laments the harmful impact of "deculturation," i.e. the undermining of the inherited religious and humanistic values by the technological society, yet he speaks confidently about cultures, paying little attention to their ambiguity. He appreciates in particular the goodness of his own first culture, despite the wounds inflicted upon it by colonial domination. We shall see in the next chapter that Jacques Grand'Maison, a friend and collaborator of Fernand Dumont, has a greater awareness of the sin that marks people's personal and social lives.

FAITH IN JESUS CHRIST

As a sociologist, Dumont is keenly aware that believing does not take place in isolation. Children receive their faith from the parents and the parish; and as they grow up, it is the contact with others that affects what they believe and how they see their lives. Trivial exchanges have no impact on our self-understanding, but listening with attention and sympathy to another person challenges our own horizon, makes us more compassionate, and prompts us to ask questions about ourselves. Dumont refers to Martin Buber, Gabriel Marcel, and Emmanuel Lévinas as thinkers who have shown the transforming power of attentive encounters. According to Lévinas in particular, the attentive encounter with another makes us discover our ethical vocation: the other is a person who has a claim on our respect, whose face says to us, "Do not hurt me, do not kill me, stand with me in my life's struggle." We constitute ourselves as human persons through the encounter with others – with other persons or with their ideas, their art, and their creative activities.

In *Une foi partagée* Dumont admits that after the horrors of the twentieth century and, on a different level, after the thinkers known as the authors of suspicion (such as Marx, Nietzsche, Freud, and Foucault), it has become difficult to believe in humanity, escape the trap of nihilism, and commit oneself to an abiding faith. Yet even in the present, what save us, what make us grow and realize our spiritual potential, are significant encounters with others. As I am writing these lines, I find in the August 2011 issue of *Relations* a paragraph by Brigitte Haentjens, a Quebec artist, that celebrates the significance of encounters.

> It seems to me that encounters are necessary and lead to changes which are sometimes profound. They can be abstract or concrete (a painting, a thought, a book, a place, a country). Sometimes, they are simply human. They often reveal to us an unknown part of ourselves. Or they shake up the established order, the well-trodden path, opening interior doors which had hitherto been sealed. Some of them heal us or symbolically give birth to us. We become aware of their impact later, when, looking back, we try to understand the paths we have walked in our lives.[13]

The life-changing encounter central in Dumont's life has been his listening to Jesus in the Scriptures and the Church's liturgy. The Quebec philosopher received his faith from his family and his parish – his first culture; but later on, as an educated person, his faith was challenged, sustained, and guided by his attentive listening to Jesus. The important message revealed by Jesus is that the nameless Transcendence actually has a name: the God of the Bible whom Jesus calls his Father and whom he makes visible for us.

> The testimonies of Jesus recorded in Scripture are more than proof of his existence or simply a recollection of his words; they actually invoke, throughout history and thanks to it, the identity of God. For the slightest glimpse of what God is for us is Jesus Christ.[14]

Dumont pays special attention to the historical Jesus announced in the synoptic gospels. Here Jesus is the prophet speaking with authority and announcing God's coming reign; at the same time, he is a man similar to us, troubled, exposed to temptations, capable of changing his mind, sometimes sad and sometimes joyful, in need of prayer and in search of friends. Jesus does not present himself as God incarnate; he is reticent about his identity; he seems to discover only gradually what his mission is. Dumont sees Jesus as an enigmatic personality not at home in any of the religious circles or parties of his day. He is powerful and vulnerable, sovereign and humble, a follower of the Law and independent of it, conservative (protecting the local culture against Rome's imperial invasion) and radical (critical of the official interpretation of his religion). Psychology is unable to solve the riddle of his personality: he appears unique, inimitable, mysterious.

This Jesus, Dumont continues, is utterly attractive, and at the same time deeply disturbing. He raises questions about our lives, demands that we change our ways, and calls us to love God and our neighbour. Jesus will not leave us alone; he continues to challenge our selfishness and encourages our efforts to follow his lead. Our conversation with him is without end. Jesus utters different messages at different occasions, depending on the challenges we encounter in our concrete situations. In his earthly life, he challenged the religious authorities and the imperial rule, even though his prophetic witness would cost him his life. Dumont is not surprised that the message of Jesus heard by Christians, including biblical scholars, is related to the profound questions that trouble them. He fully understands that oppressed people hear in the Gospel the promise of liberation. Jesus sheds light on the lives of people whatever their situation. His figure transforms their existence; his message is ever relevant. Because we trust him, Dumont continues, we are willing to believe his friends and disciples, testifying that he was raised from among the dead and is now alive.

For Dumont, Jesus is both the revealer of a message and God's self-revelation. As revealer he sheds light on human existence, discloses the name of God, and makes known the path of the beatitudes; yet he is himself revelation because in his life, death, and resurrection, God's hidden face has become visible in history. In this Dumont follows the orthodox Christology of the Church.

Dumont realizes at the same time that Jesus is read differently by various groups and persons. He acknowledges that some believers in Jesus do not see him as God incarnate, and some biblical scholars only accept the earliest witnesses to Jesus of the Aramaic-speaking community that make no reference to his divinity. Dumont is not greatly troubled by this: what counts for him is not the abstract truth about Jesus, but his power to transform the human heart and consciousness. Truth is not enough; what counts is relevance. Those who believe his message are judged, forgiven, healed, and lifted up. Even believers with an abridged understanding of Jesus can experience his transformative power. Dumont regrets that the ecclesiastical magisterium has often reduced the Gospel to a series of doctrines, forgetting the primary importance of the redeeming encounter with Jesus, which takes place in the imagination.

Here are two quotations from the young Joseph Ratzinger that express similar convictions. "Christian belief offers truth as a way, and only by becoming a way has it become man's truth. Truth as mere perception, as mere idea, remains bereft of force; it only becomes man's truth as a way that makes a claim upon him."[15] "The essence of faith demanded by a Christology [correctly] understood is ... entry into the universal openness of unconditional love. ... Has Harnack's 'all that counts is love' been swallowed up by a Christological dogmatism? ... That this can happen, and has indeed happened more than once in history, we are well aware. But that this corresponds to the intention of the concept of faith must be emphatically denied."[16]

FAITH AND THE IMAGINATION

It is not easy to give a precise definition of what Dumont means by Christian faith.[17] It is a special kind of believing, a self-perception and perception of the world in reliance on Jesus. Children of Christian families assimilate this perspective through their first culture. Yet as they grow up and join the second culture, they may have to hear the Christian message anew. Their faith now implies both rupture and fidelity, leaving behind their childhood perception and becoming faithful to a deeper dimension of Christian revelation. Faith, Dumont holds, always includes a kind of conversion, a turn from self-love to other-love. In modern society, faith remains restless. It is challenged by rational questioning, and as people's life situation changes, they search anew for a relevant faith that addresses their problems. That is why Dumont insists that doubt plays an essential part in the quest for a living faith. Challenged by new historical conditions, believers may no longer be convinced by the answers that made sense to them in the past; they now listen anew to the message and the life of Jesus, ready to be addressed by God's Word. Dumont thinks that in the modern world Christian faith cannot survive unless it is again and again sustained by attentive listening to Scripture, openness to the work of the Spirit, and the believers' own significant religious experiences.

For Dumont, Christian faith is not equivalent to holding as true a set of doctrines. Christian faith, as we saw, is the embrace of God's revelation in Jesus as a challenging perspective from which believers may see their world and act in it. Faith summons them to hope, love, and universal solidarity. This life-giving encounter with Jesus, Dumont holds, takes place in the imagination.

In the neo-scholastic tradition, the imagination is the faculty that allows us to create images of what has happened or what we wish had happened or will happen. Here the imagination cannot be trusted as a source of truth. Dumont has a totally different understanding of the imagination. In his entire philosophical work he argues that people's imagination allows culture to have an impact on their consciousness and, more importantly, enables them at certain creative moments to transcend their culture and envisage the new. This idea is well expressed in a short passage of the French philosopher Gaston Bachelard, for whom Dumont has great respect.

> Despite its etymology, the imagination is not the ability to form images of reality; it is rather the ability to form images that surpass reality, that sing reality ... The imagination does more than create things and stories; it creates new life, it creates a new spirit; it opens the eyes to new ways of seeing.[18]

In his studies of the presuppositions of the social sciences, Dumont shows that the rational investigations of researchers are in fact guided by the imagination that pictures the world for them. The culture to which we belong exercises its influence through the imagination. Religion makes people see reality in a certain way and guides their daily lives through the figures and symbols alive in their imagination. As an example Dumont mentions the impact of Abraham on the self-understanding of people in Judaism, Christianity, and Islam. The Abraham story has exerted great power throughout history, even if archaeologists should find proof that he never existed. It is not the truth of Abraham's adventures that counts, but their relevance, their power to affect people's self-understanding. In a similar way other biblical happenings have a life-orienting impact on people's minds, such as the Exodus in the Old Testament and Christ's life, death, and resurrection in the New Testament.

I have been introduced to the power of the imagination by the sociology of knowledge of German social philosophers, Max Scheler and Karl Mannheim in particular, whom Fernand Dumont does not cite. According to these authors, the social movements for social justice in the West, whether reformist or radical, have been sustained by the messianic imagination revealed in the Old and New Testaments. The promise of God's coming reign continues to affect the imagination of people, even if they are non-believers, summoning forth the energy to become involved in struggles for social justice.

The power of the imagination is a central theme of Riccardo Petrella's recent book, *Désir d'humanité: Le droit de rêver*,[19] which shows that both the turn to neo-liberal capitalism and the maximization of profit and the turn to movements of social justice and ecological responsibility are, at their origin, the product of people's dreams: on the one hand the bad dream of limitless personal profit and on the other the good dream of a just and humane society. Petrella uses this analysis to assure the people involved in the social movements, today a small minority, that their struggle, far from being useless, is the embodiment of their dreams and hence has the power to effect the transformation of capitalist society.

Fernand Dumont reminds the reader that Jesus himself taught in images, parables, symbolic gestures, and dramatic events. Our author regrets that the ecclesiastical magisterium has moved away from this mode of teaching, putting the primary emphasis on concepts. As we shall see further on, Dumont recognizes the importance of doctrines or normative statements of belief; yet he thinks that if they become the primary medium of handing on the faith, they foster routine, conformity, and the decline of commitment.

Reading what Dumont says of the role of the imagination in communicating the Christian message makes me think of the Canadian catechism, *Viens vers le Père* or *Come to the Father,* produced in Quebec in the 1960s. This catechism appealed to the imagination of children: it proposed short biblical passages and provided colourful images, expecting the teacher to ask the children what these quotations and images meant to them. Teaching catechism was here not intended to communicate to children abstract religious concepts, but rather to stimulate their imagination, making them hear in the biblical words and images authoritative messages about how to understand themselves and act in relations to others. I remember the pedagogy of Sister Margaret Ordway, who taught the catechism *Come to the Father* in Toronto in the 1970s. She would ask the children, "What do you hear when you read this biblical passage?" or

"What message does this picture suggest to you?" This catechism was designed to summon forth the children's imaginative powers, allowing them to discover the redemptive and transformative meaning of the Christian Gospel.[20] I now recognize that the authors of this catechism entertained an idea of the imagination derived from the French philosophical tradition for which Dumont had great sympathy and which he developed in his own way. Since *Come to the Father* did not put enough emphasis on abstract doctrinal formulations, the Canadian bishops eventually demanded that it be replaced by a more traditional catechism.

GIVING WITNESS

Dumont held that faith in Jesus urges believers to give witness to him in their lives. Giving witness was more important than teaching dogma. Doctrines are objective and universal; they speak to the intellect, have a clearly defined meaning, and can even be taught by persons who do not believe in them. By contrast, testifying to one's faith in a word or gesture is a concrete act in a particular situation. Giving testimony reveals the deep conviction of the witness in a manner that speaks to the imagination and has not one, but many meanings. Receiving the testimony, Dumont adds, challenges the recipient and calls him or her to a self-questioning:

> The affirmation made by giving testimony reveals the witness and affects the totality of the person to whom it is addressed. True, there are false testimonies that do not correspond to reality or to concrete experiences. Verification is not excluded. Yet as what is said does not offer proof in itself, the witness offers his life as a testimony of his credibility or he reveals the vital importance of what he transmits. It is the same for the one who receives the testimony: he is unable to discuss the witness's message at a distance from himself, without his personal assent or rejection.[21]

In a secular society such as Quebec, where the Church's teaching finds no hearing, it is Christian witness that gives visibility to faith and projects it in the public imagination. Witnessing is more important than professing the faith in so many words. One chapter of Dumont's *Une foi partagée* offers short biographies of men and women who, in our own day, have given witness to their faith and affected their community. The witnesses chosen include personalities whose dedication is known in Quebec and intellectuals such as Emmanuel Mounier and Simone Weil whose reputations are worldwide. Dumont himself tried to be a witness of Christian faith as a thinker, a teacher, a public intellectual, and a family man.

Dumont's emphasis on giving witness makes me remember a remark made in the 1970s by the Jewish philosopher Emil Fackenheim, suggesting that if Pius XII in World War II had condemned Hitler's genocide of the Jews and been imprisoned upon Hitler's orders, no God-is-dead movement would have occurred after the war. Dumont's analysis of the power of gestures and images also reveals the great harm done to the Catholic Church's public credibility by the crimes committed by a long list of pedophile priests and their pervasive presence in the mass media.

Deserving attention is that Dumont had no intention whatever of converting to the Catholic faith his Quebec colleagues and acquaintances who had dropped out of the Church and become secular. He had respect for non-believers who were committed to truth and justice in their own way. He wanted to understand them, and in turn be understood by them. We shall see further on that Dumont was a humble believer. He did not think that Catholics were better than the followers of other traditions, nor did he want the Church to pretend it held the whole truth and had no need of the truths of other communities. Christian faith, Dumont argues, affects human beings on two levels: it offers them new meaning and initiates them to an alternative practice. For him, Jesus is both sage and prophet. Dumont does not confine the impact of faith to the promised rescue from contempt, poverty, and oppression. He has the impression that Latin American liberation theology has neglected the wisdom dimension of the Gospel and thus failed to enter into dialogue with the world of thought.[22] He does not want to reduce truth to the cognitive dimension of liberative practice. Since Latin American liberation theology is constituted by a variety of currents, Dumont's criticism calls for careful qualifications.

Dumont recognizes in his own way the political dimensions of the Gospel. Christian faith is concrete and contextual and hence contains a message addressed to society. This is how he describes this message:

> Christians share with others the work and responsibility for society. Like all others, they are attentive to the concerns of this world: they face the important decisions for the future of a group or a society. Loyalty requires that they not impose their social and political opinions in the name of religion; nonetheless, faith concerns the future of the world, the coming of a justice that we may not await passively. Witnessing and engagement go together.[23]

While Christian faith calls for social engagement, Christians will have different ideas about what this engagement involves. As we shall see, the theologians of Quebec wrestle with this question. In most situations, there is not a single answer. Dumont appreciates the plurality of options. What he objects to is a perception of faith that is so spiritual or so otherworldly that it makes believers indifferent to social injustice and the people who are its victims.

THE CHURCH

The Church as the community of believers is a topic of great concern for Dumont. Since he does not say much about it in *Une foi partagée*, I shall present some of the ideas contained in his earlier books, *Pour la conversion de la pensée chrétienne* (1964) and *L'institution de la théologie* (1987).

We saw in chapter 1 that the sociologists who have studied the rapid secularization of Quebec society have not arrived at the same conclusions. Some argue that the process of modernization, fostering personal freedom and increasing reliance on science and verifiable truths, has produced the secularization of culture not only in Quebec, but at various speeds in other Western societies. Other sociologists argue that the rejection of the Church on the part of Quebecers was a protest against the omnipresent clericalism and the Church's domination of Quebec culture. Dumont, himself a sociologist, takes both of these factors into account.

In his *Pour la conversion de la pensée chrétienne*, published in 1964, Dumont is critical of the social scientific theory that modernization leads inevitably to the loss of faith. The Quiet Revolution, he argues, was carried by the ethical ideals of solidarity and co-responsibility, values in keeping with the Christian message. In this book, he puts all the blame for the crisis of the Church upon the authoritarian character of Roman Catholicism. It was not just the pervasive clericalism against which people increasingly protested; it was also the Church's governmental apparatus, inherited from the feudal age and increasingly centralized in the nineteenth century, which appeared to them as a foreign body in modern society and to which they now objected. The ecclesiastical organization is a symbol of social values that are no longer acceptable.

In this book of 1964, Dumont offers an altogether devastating critique of the Church. Catholic theologians occasionally do this sort of thing. Here is a passage written by the young Joseph Ratzinger in 1969.

> This is the Church, the questionable creation of history, which claims to be the abiding site of [God's] revelation. We know today only too well how little, even in it, concealment of the divine presence is abolished. Precisely, when the Church believed, in all the glory of the Renaissance princedom, that it could strip away this concealment and be directly "the gate of heaven" and "the house of God," it has once again, and almost more than before, become God's disguise, with God scarcely to be found in it.[24]

In his *Une foi partagée*, written toward the end of his life, Dumont adopts a very different tone. He now greatly appreciates the renewal of the Church initiated by Vatican Council II, addressing his critical remarks principally to Quebec society, accusing it of losing the humanistic values upheld by the Quiet Revolution and turning instead to the individualism and utilitarianism promoted by unregulated capitalism. He recognizes that the culture of neo-liberalism chips away at religious values and dissolves the social solidarity needed for a social-democratic political project.

To demonstrate the cultural impoverishment produced by the technological discourse of contemporary society, Dumont introduces a distinction between the "denotation" and the "connotation" of words. The denotation of a word refers to a concrete object: thus "father" denotes this particular man, and "table" denotes this piece of furniture. By contrast, the connotation of words also communicates the associations and feelings attached to the object. Here, "father" suggests origin, protection, guidance, and care; and "table" brings to mind enjoying a common meal. Dumont argues that contemporary society, affected by science, technology, and the market, no longer hears the connotation of words; it has lost its capacity to understand the language of religion and secular wisdom traditions. The dominant matter-of-factness makes people unable to read poetry or grasp the meaning of great literature. Dumont calls this phenomenon "deculturation." At the same time, he does not accuse the whole of society of having lost its soul; he continues his dialogue with people and their movements committed to values and a social vision, be they secular or religious.

In this modern Quebec, subject to deculturizing currents, the Church is commissioned to give witness to the Gospel. In this new context, Dumont argues, the Church must (1) rethink its message so that it can be understood by the people of today and (2) reform its institutional presence so that it corresponds to the contemporary ethic of governance.

Regarding Dumont's first point: Vatican Council II refers to the rethinking of the message as "accommodated preaching of the revealed Word … the law of all evangelization."[25] Dumont shows that such processes of reinterpretation have taken place in the past. To give a well-known example, he looks at the change of meaning assigned over the centuries to the doctrine *extra ecclesiam nulla salus* (no salvation outside the Church), right up to the proposal of Vatican II that revealed in Jesus Christ, the new Adam, is God's offer of salvation to every human being. The development of doctrine, Dumont observes, implies both rupture and fidelity, i.e. breaking with the traditional teaching and uncovering the deeper meaning of the revealed message. This spiritual evolution, Dumont shows, depends on three factors: (1) the religious experience of believers, (2) the reflection of theologians, and (3) the discernment of the magisterium. The dialogue among these three groups, occasionally interrupted by conflict, allows the magisterium to formulate the norms of belief in a given context.

Dumont argues that if the magisterium in a new cultural context refuses to engage in dialogue and simply teaches Christian truth in the words appropriate for a previous period, the official teaching will no longer correspond to the religious experience of the believing community. Catholics may accept the official doctrine by an act of obedience, but they will no longer be spiritually nourished by it. Doctrine is an essential aspect of the Church's proclamation, yet if it no longer expresses how believers experience Christ's presence in their lives, doctrine becomes oppressive and undermines the Church's mission. Dumont thinks that one of the reasons why the Church of Quebec has declined so rapidly is the fact that people had accepted the official teaching simply out of obedience, not because it shed light on their religious experiences. When they discovered their freedom of speech in the Quiet Revolution, they quickly let go of the Church's teaching.

Regarding his second point: Dumont argues that the institutions of the Church are in need of reform because they provide no space for dialogue within the believing community. In democratic cultures people understand themselves as critical subjects co-responsible for the institutions to which they belong and, for this reason, regard themselves as entitled to speak their word and be heard. Because the Catholic Church does not offer its members occasions for dialogue, it is experienced as an authoritarian organization, offensive to people's contemporary self-understanding. In the absence of institutions of dialogue, permitting lay people, theologians, and bishops to listen to one another and search for answers, the Church remains unable to formulate its redemptive message in a manner comprehensible to the people of its day. I recall that the Dumont Report of 1971, discussed in chapter 1, made concrete proposals for setting up institutions of participation that would provide occasions at regular intervals for dialogue between the faithful and their pastors.

The Church must be open to the Spirit speaking in the people and attentive to the ideas of theologians in dialogue with science and the culture of their society. In today's pluralistic society, moreover, the Church must understand its mission as a service promoting the common good of the entire human family. In the light of the Gospel, the Church must denounce the sinister cultural and political currents in society, try to detect the divine presence in people's lives and in their traditions, and extend its solidarity to people in cultural and social movements promoting social justice, international peace, and ecological responsibility.

While doctrinal norms are important, Dumont argues, they do not have priority over the teaching by images, symbols, and figures, the mode in which Jesus himself announced the Good News. Dumont repeatedly mentions Cardinal Newman's observation that the bishops of the ancient Church regretted that, in response to heretical ideas, they were obliged to multiply doctrinal definitions. The quarrels at the time of the Reformation, Dumont remarks, were mainly about doctrine. Catholics and Protestants agreed on the essentials of the Christian way of life: they all wanted to trust Jesus, worship God, love their neighbour, and practice compassion. Their differences had to with doctrines that hardly touched the essence of the

Christian life. Catholics and Protestants believed that Jesus was present in the celebration of the Last Supper, yet they quarrelled passionately over the mode of this presence. The endless doctrinal definitions of faith and morals, produced in subsequent centuries, Dumont holds, were counterproductive. Catholics were no longer convinced by them. This was dramatically revealed in 1968 when Paul VI's encyclical *Humanae Vitae* on birth control failed to be received by the majority of Catholics in the Western world.

Dumont observes that Christians increasingly decide for themselves what is the right and moral thing to do. He mentions that in traditional societies, people became believers because they were embedded in a Christian community. In today's pluralistic society, he continues, people stand alone: if they resist the influence of secular culture and become believers, they do so because they trust their own judgment. In the modern context, believing is a personal decision, experienced as a divine gift. Because people rely on their own judgment in becoming believers, they also make up their own mind on what is right and wrong and what the Gospel demands that they do. Dumont calls this "the moral autonomy" of the contemporary Christian.

In discussing the Church and the Gospel, Dumont occasionally writes "No monopoly, please!" He does not challenge the universal mediation of Jesus Christ nor the claim of the Church to be God's chosen people. When he insists that the Church has no monopoly on truth and holiness, he simply wants to repudiate the ideas that Catholics are wiser and holier than others, that they are enlightened while others are blind, and that they have nothing to learn from the wisdom and virtues of the world religions and the secular humanistic traditions. Dumont holds that religious discourse must be modest. Thus he wants to reserve the word "infallibility" to God alone and prefers to speak of the guidance granted to the Church as "indefectibility."

Dumont loved this humble Church, the community of the faithful, proclaiming the Gospel, worshipping God in the liturgy, addressing society with a prophetic voice, pointing to God's presence in human life, and announcing Christ's eschatological promises.

Many of the theological ideas of Dumont are found in the writings of other Quebec theologians, not because they were directly influenced by him, but rather because as a brilliant phenomenologist, he had a sense of the ideas that were emerging in Quebec's Catholic community in his day.

4

Introducing Jacques Grand'Maison

Jacques Grand'Maison is a prolific Catholic theologian highly esteemed in the Quebec Church: he is a priest schooled in theology and political science, a pastor attentive to people's problems and aspirations, a university professor engaged in theological education, a political thinker concerned with the common good, and a social scientist doing empirical research to gain a better understanding of the Church. Grand'Maison is also a poet. He has addressed his Church and his society, decade after decade, on the social, cultural, and religious issues that affect the destiny of his people before God.[1]

Let me begin this chapter by comparing Jacques Grand'Maison and Fernand Dumont. They were friends, they appreciated one another's theological writings, and they were both members of the Dumont Commission. Yet their intellectual engagement was quite different. Dumont belonged to the academy; he was a major theorist and made substantive contributions to several disciplines. Theology was not Dumont's principal concern. His books were written for his colleagues at the university: to understand them, it was often necessary to read them twice. By contrast, Grand'Maison addressed himself most of the time to Catholics engaged in pastoral ministry or social action, an audience that included lay men and women, sisters, brothers, and priests. Grand'Maison was a practical thinker concerned with the problems of church and society. In order to resolve these problems and propose a new course of action, he listened to the Christian message and studied the social sciences with a sensitivity created by his faith. He saw himself as a pastor, not as a philosopher. To be understood by his readers beyond the academy, Grand'Maison wrote a lively prose, often adopting an imaginative style, sometimes becoming a poet and sometimes a pamphleteer. Like a painter, he did not hesitate to exaggerate to make an important point. His books were sometimes reviewed critically. He was accused of writing too quickly, citing too many authors, losing the thread of his argument, and not arriving at a final conclusion. The critical reviewers failed to see that Jacques Grand'Maison was a charismatic personality in the Catholic Church who inspired Catholics by the passages in his books that shed light on their situation and expanded their spiritual horizon.

Like Dumont, Grand'Maison is rooted in the old Quebec and has come to embrace the new. He writes:

> I am from the first and stubborn stock in the rocky land of the Laurentians.
> I am from an uncertain – if not impossible – country, but it is mine.
> I am from an anachronistic village, from an annexed city owned by speculators, from a bastard society, from a people that is now reaching a fork in the road that might be decisive.
> I am from a culture long held within its closed borders, which, against all expectations, has just crossed the border to take off on an incredible adventure.

He writes of God's presence:

> I am from a horizon of mystery which I cannot name, a mystery present in the material tasks of my daily work and my sharing with others, just as much as in the spiritual tasks of my unutterable soul, of which I must speak without ever being able to say it.[2]

The poet Grand'Maison reveals himself in such utterances over three pages. He also tells us on what occasion he woke up and became a non-conformist. In his autobiographical reflections, *Au mitan de la vie*, he writes that, as a student in Paris, he discovered in existentialism an intellectual justification of his love of freedom, his resistance to domestication, and his inclination to break out.[3] He believed that a conversion to a prophetic stance may one day revitalize the Catholic tradition. Still in Paris, he admired Richard Bach's short story *Jonathan Livingston Seagull* about the adventure of a domesticated seagull. Unhappy with the boredom of conformity and the confinement to uncritical existence, the seagull decides to escape, fly to the heights, join the wild birds, and discover liberation. Yet when the seagull returns to the domesticated flock and describes his experience of breakthrough, adventure, and freedom, no one will listen to him, and he finds himself excluded.

Despite the great difference between the intellectual and personal styles of Dumont and Grand'Maison, they share certain anthropological and theological ideas. With Dumont, Grand'Maison accepts that in order to be and to act, humans need a faith that makes them see the world in a certain way and guides their actions, a faith that, if followed without reserve, will relate them to Transcendence. The following are poetic texts, published here with their author's permission, praising the omnipresence of believing in his own and other people's lives.

There is always a faith:
At the centre of solid convictions
In the profound source of freedom
Beyond long hesitations
At the source of bold achievements,
There is always a faith.
When you get to the bottom of things
When you continue your way at night
When you live with a taste for the infinite
When you decide to make a gift of your life,
There is always a faith.
In those who see with their heart
In those who do not deceive their conscience
In those who know themselves to be a soul
In those who wager liberty against fear,
There is always a faith.
In the past and future of courageous people
In the aftermath of a just revolution
At the source of daring collective projects
At the heart of humane civilizations,
There is always a faith.
If your love is greater than your prejudice and hatred
If your spirit believes in the victory of life over death
If your hope moves beyond your disappointments
If you can be free, just, true, and strong,

There is always a faith.
Not allowing yourself to be stopped by any barrier
Going to the end of your human adventure
Building lasting solidarities
Creating new possibilities,
What is your faith?
Does it have a name, a face, a story?
Is it rooted in your land?
Can you speak of it, celebrate it, and share it?
Does it inspire your life, love and thoughts?
What is my faith?
I received it, challenged it, buried it and found it again
Always coming back to the Stranger from Galilee
He inhabits the depth and horizons of my being
A fierce passion that gives me new birth.[4]

Grand'Maison shares with Dumont the conviction that a dynamic internal to human existence moves people attentive to their inner voice to Transcendence. He writes,

> The peak of human consciousness and its vital dynamism find expression first and foremost in a wager between freedom and a deeply held personal commitment to Another, a call to transcend oneself.[5]

Grand'Maison also agrees with Dumont and, in fact, with all the members of the Dumont Commission that Quebec's inherited Catholic culture has collapsed and that Catholics, trusting in the Holy Spirit, will have to create a new presence of the Church in society.

Biblical scholars sometimes distinguish between "sages" who offer their thoughts in the light of God's Word and "prophets" who proclaim God's Word as judgment and promise to a confused or indifferent community. At a first glance one might say that Dumont was a sage and Grand'Maison a prophet. Becoming a prophet is taking a considerable risk. I will not resist the temptation to quote what Rabbi Michael Lerner, the founder and editor of *Tikkun Magazine*, had to say about this risk.

> When as a teenager I became immersed in the writings of the Prophets, I was most excited by the Prophet Jeremiah. My

> parents, who thought I was making a big mistake to have decided to become a rabbi, told me that I ... sounded like a prophet, and that one could not combine a deep prophetic vision with being a congregational rabbi, because the congregation would fire anyone who would challenge their comfortable life-style. Moreover, they warned me that people would always be offended by the "truth-telling" and "confrontational attitude" of the prophets in general and Jeremiah in particular. But their biggest challenge was this: "What's the use of being a prophet when the prophets were all such failures? They were scorned in their life-times, and their message was not really heard by those to whom it was spoken or written."[6]

Lerner and Grand'Maison took this risk. Yet we shall see that Grand'Maison is not only a prophet; he is also a sage. He develops a spirituality appropriate for the present time, laments the loss of interiority of many Quebecers who dropped out of the Church, and shows that the cultivation of an interior life is important even for secular people.

To further introduce the reader to the theology of Grand'Maison I shall select a number of theological and socio-political ideas that have preoccupied him, all of them relevant to Quebecers in the historical context created by the Quiet Revolution.

CRISE DE PROPHÉTISME[7]

In 1965 Grand'Maison published *Crise de prophétisme*, a book I regard as a significant theological breakthrough. In his preface, Roland Potvin introduces the book as an original reply to the questions raised in Fernand Dumont's *Pour la conversion de la pensée chrétienne* of 1964. Grand'Maison makes the proclamation of Christian truth relevant to people living in the modern world, in particular to Quebecers in their new society. He demonstrates on biblical grounds that the Gospel of Jesus addresses not only individuals, and not only the Christian community, but also and especially the society to which they belong. Already in the Old Testament the Hebrew prophets uttered God's Word as judgment and promise – as judgment on social injustice and religious infidelity, and as promise of God's coming reign. Judgment and promise were preached in the New Testament by John the Baptist and Jesus himself. Implied in this recognition is that the Gospel contains a political message, a message addressed to society summoning forth its conversion to greater justice. Believing in Jesus and following his path turns Christians into witnesses, testifying their commitment to justice and solidarity in the public realm. In fidelity to Scripture, the Church itself must exercise a prophetic role in the world, speaking the truth to those in power and giving hope to the people wrestling to make their society more just and more humane.

We take this insight for granted today, yet in 1965 it was new. The spirituality of engagement embraced in the 1930s by people associated with Catholic Action was interpreted as a special vocation, not a universal summons implicit in Christian faith. It was only in the late 1960s that the German Catholic theologian Johann Baptist Metz initiated what he called "political theology." This theology had a twofold task : (1) to correct the individualistic reading of the Gospel, thus retrieving its social message, and (2) to show that the divine promises not only refer to the fulfillment at the end of time, but also offer hope to people struggling to make their society more just and more compassionate. Metz's political theology was seconded by two Protestant theologians, Dorothee Soelle and Jürgen Moltmann. In total independence of this German current, Jacques Grand'Maison uncovered the political meaning of the Gospel for Quebec society.

Based on quite different historical experiences, the political dimension of the Gospel was recovered by Latin American theologians and affirmed in 1968 by the Latin American Bishops Conference at Medellin. In one way or another, the recognition of the political meaning of divine revelation spread through the entire Christian Church and affected the Catholic ecclesiastical magisterium.

In the past, the Church's relationship to society reflected its concern to protect the *bonum ecclesiae,* the Church's freedom, growth, and well-being. In most situations, the Church sought the support and protection of the powerful: the princes, the government, or the wealthy. For pragmatic reasons, without theological reflection, the Church blessed the existing social order and legitimated society in religious terms. In some situations, especially when the Catholic community constituted a minority, the Church remained aloof from society and intervened in public life only to protect the rights and interests of its flock. In modern society, marked by the separation of Church and State, the Church became free to relate itself to the society in theological terms, i.e. in the light of the Christian Gospel.

Someone might argue that ever since Leo XIII's encyclical *Rerum Novarum* of 1891, the Catholic Church had an official social teaching and thus related itself to society as an advocate of social justice. Yet because Catholic social teaching at this time was based on reason and natural law, not on the Christian message, this teaching was a guide for the "natural order" and had no impact on "the supernatural order" created by God's gift of faith, hope, and love. At that time, spirituality and the quest for holiness did not include longing for social justice nor giving public witness of solidarity with the poor and oppressed. Faith in Jesus Christ did not summon Catholics to become critics of their society, advocating the turn to social compassion and greater justice. The spiritual books used in convents, monasteries, and seminaries offered no critical reflection on social evil, on colonialism, oppression, exploitation, wars, unemployment, or impoverishment. Since the pope at the Vatican related himself to the secular world through a system of diplomatic representation, he used the polite language of the embassies and did not denounce the injustices and aggressions committed by governments. There were indeed Catholic leaders and thinkers in the nineteenth century who were active in movements of social justice and believed that in doing so they followed the Gospel, yet their religious experience was not yet integrated into the Church's understanding of its mission in the world.

The character of Catholic social teaching changed dramatically when in his encyclical *Pacem in Terris* (1963), John XXIII defended human rights and democratic pluralism in reliance on divine revelation in dialogue with human reason. Being greatly impressed by the Universal Declaration of Human Rights of the United Nations in 1948, he began to rethink the Catholic tradition. Rereading the Bible, he found, in the story of creation recorded in the Old Testament and the call of all men and women to become friends of Jesus recorded in the New Testament, a divine declaration of the high dignity of all human beings. This dignity, the pope now argued, is the theological foundation of human rights. This turn to divine revelation initiated a significant turn of Catholic social teaching. Based on God's Word in Scripture, this teaching now addresses people of faith, summons forth their commitment to social justice and solidarity, and becomes part of the Church's proclamation of the Good News.

Grand'Maison recognized this turn very early. After writing his *Crise de prophétisme*, he discovered that this social understanding of divine revelation was rapidly spreading through the Catholic Church.

He mentioned in particular that Johann Baptist Metz's political theology had made Karl Rahner change his mind. Moving beyond the existentialist understanding of the Gospel, Rahner now recognized that divine revelation called believers to political responsibility and that God was redemptively present in human history. Grand'Maison reports that Urs von Balthasar criticized Rahner for shifting the focus of attention from personal holiness to the transformation of society. Rahner replied to this that "divine revelation has not converted people as long as they have not reinterpreted their historical situation."[8] Grand'Maison fully shared this conviction.

It is not clear to me why Grand'Maison chose to call his book *Crise de prophétisme*. Since his insight in the prophetic meaning of the Gospel was not yet widely recognized in Quebec, the book laments the resistance to prophetism, rather than a crisis within it. In the Quiet Revolution, Grand'Maison argued, Quebecers have become aware of their social responsibility: they recognize that their society is redefining itself and they try to find their place in this process, while at the same time struggling to make a living, often in difficult circumstances. Grand'Maison argued that unless the sermon on Sunday morning helps Catholics gain a critical understanding of what goes on in their lives, they will not listen to the priest's message. Lay people, he claimed, increasingly reject a theology and a catechesis that do not come to grips with the historical conditions in which they live.

Grand'Maison laments that most sermons preached in the churches either engage in moralizing or simply teach Catholic doctrine. Moralizing picks on people's personal shortcomings, especially their sexual misdemeanours, while overlooking the structural evil in society, the human damage it produces, and the ethical questions it raises for the individual. Catholic doctrine is abstract truth of universal validity, yet in the realm of the Spirit, truth is not enough. What counts is relevance, shedding light on the troubling aspects of people's concrete existence and offering rescue and new life. "God's Word is life and way, as much as it is truth." He writes,

> God easily becomes an idea when no attention is paid to the actual historical presence of Jesus Christ. Without this dimension of the Judeo-Christian mystery, the existence or non-existence of God changes absolutely nothing in the human environment and people's personal experiences.[9]

To preach the Gospel as a relevant message is a task the Church must assume. To be able to do this, Grand'Maison argued, the Church will have to engage in dialogue with the social sciences, a proposal that was new and daring in 1965. This dialogue will help theologians to listen to what is going on in society, detect the destructive potential in it, and recognize the humanizing values and practices. The proper theological task is then to relate society's positive dimension to the teaching of Jesus and the presence of the Spirit. Grand'Maison made these proposals before the promulgation of the conciliar document *Gaudium et Spes*, in which "the accommodated preaching" that he recommended was presented as "the law of all evangelization."[10]

Prophecy, according to Grand'Maison, is not restricted to priests and bishops; it is the task of all the baptized. All Catholics are meant to be witnesses. The Catholic Action movement of Quebec in the 1930s had encouraged the prophetic vocation of its members. The young men and women involved in this movement realized that the Gospel had political implications and that their faith in Jesus called them to a lifestyle at odds with the dominant Catholic culture. Their spiritual motto "see, judge and act" gave them a certain independence, which in many cases produced tensions between them and the ecclesiastical hierarchy. Grand'Maison now insists that all believers are called to be witnesses and prophets. He complains that the dominant clericalism has condemned lay people to be silent. Because no one listened to them, they never learnt to express their religious experience; they were believers without a voice. Our author recognizes that this was changing: carried by the Quiet Revolution, Catholic men and women were finding their voice in the Church.

Implicit in the prophetic vocation of lay people, Grand'Maison writes, is a new relationship to priests, bishops, and popes. What is demanded is no longer unquestioning obedience, but mutual respect, dialogue, free obedience, and occasionally conscientious disagreement. The prophetic vocation of the baptized was fully recognized in the conciliar document *Lumen Gentium*,[11] yet their changed relationship to the ecclesiastical authorities was only alluded to in this document. It was the Dumont Report, as we saw earlier, that recognized the role of dissent in the evolution of Catholic teaching.[12]

Because prophets pronounce judgment on sin and proclaim promised redemption, they are tempted to exaggerate the ills of the present or the benefits expected in the future. Even readers who appreciate

Grand'Maison's writings admit that he sometimes overstates his case, carried away by his rhetorical gifts. In *Crise de prophétisme*, his denunciations are directed mainly at the clergy and the institutional Church, while in later years, disappointed by the orientation of Quebec society, his accusations and his anger are directed principally at politicians and government bureaucrats. He is critical in all directions, including the social movements of the left. In an essay on his political commitments I wrote this concluding paragraph.

> What *Crise de prophétisme* did, quite apart from its stated purpose, was define the religious identity of Grand'Maison himself … He saw himself as a prophet for his Quebec people, critical in all directions, evaluating the signs of the times, and urging the people to move in the direction of justice, compassion and solidarity. Grand'Maison would be prophet, even if it meant walking alone.[13]

THE SECOND EVANGELIZATION

Church-going Catholics have become a minority in Quebec. Through his pastoral work and his research on the problems of young people in the area of Saint-Jérome, Grand'Maison became convinced that Catholics are now confused, estranged from their inherited faith by the current emphasis on personal freedom, and unable to integrate the new message into their daily lives. Running away from guilt feelings, they prefer to avoid spiritual reflection. What is needed, Grand'Maison holds, is a second evangelization, a pastoral effort to give Catholics access to the spiritual resources that will enable them to live dedicated and meaningful lives. To launch such an effort he wrote a three-volume work entitled *La seconde évangélisation*.[14]

The present conflict in the Church, our author argues, is between "conservatives" complaining that the Church has deserted its tradition and "progressives" accusing the Church of not renewing itself consistently. Both parties are mistaken, Grand'Maison thinks. Conservatives fail to notice the spiritual continuity in the Church's renewal, and the progressives overlook that renewal is not simply the application of new pastoral policies, but the work of the Holy Spirit in people's lives. Grand'Maison wants to find a middle way, following the motto of the Dumont Report, *un héritage et un projet*. Instead of basing his "second evangelization" on a theory, old or new, he boldly proposes to base it on the religious experience of the Catholic people. As a pastor and researcher he listens to ordinary Catholics, pays attention to their problems, recognizes their spiritual struggles, and, in many cases, admires the manner in which they express their faith in Jesus Christ. It is in freedom, not in conformity to rules, he writes, that people become witnesses of their Christian faith. Finding such witnesses in all walks of life confirms Grand'Maison's conviction that the Spirit is at work in the believing community.

After reporting his empirical research, Grand'Maison names the various endeavours and activities in which his witnesses have experienced God's help: the search for meaning, fidelity in daily living, sacramental celebration, the interior life, the experience of poverty, life in community, political action, and exclusion at the margin.[15] He recalls in this context the religious experience of young Catholics involved in Catholic Action in the 1930s. Witnesses testifying that faith has the power to transform troubled lives are found among the young and the old, among simple people and the learned, among successful people and those who have failed, among lay people and priests. These are the experiences, Grand'Maison writes, that the second evangelization must encourage. In them the Spirit is at work, and through them Christ builds the Church.

Life precedes structure, Grand'Maison argues. First people speak, and after listening to them, scholars produce the grammar. Instead of protecting the inherited structures and hoping to renew Catholic life within them, the pastors must listen to the cloud of witnesses and on the basis of their experience restructure the Church's institutional life. The architect of the Church, Grand'Maison insists, is the Holy Spirit. This proposal reminds me of Johann Adam Möhler's controversial book *Die Einheit in der Kirche*[16] published in Tübingen in 1825, which presented the Holy Spirit as the author of the Church, generating its structure through the religious experiences of the faithful. Möhler corrected his thesis in his subsequent *Symbolik* of 1832, in which he acknowledged the traditional interpretation that Christ gave the Church its basic structure.

Grand'Maison does not claim to know what the Church of Quebec will look like in the future. He assumes that it will embrace only a minority of the population. He argues that structural changes are always prepared by provisional experiments with new institutions: such experiments affect people's consciousness, create an alternative imagination, and produce organizational ideas that may one day be applied to the entire institution.[17] Because many Catholics no longer find the support they need in their parish, they have joined smaller groups or attend services at Catholic centres and monasteries; Grand'Maison asks the bishops to be patient with this lack of cohesion and loose networking. It may well happen, he believes, that these provisional organizational forms may one day lead to the Church's structural renewal.

Basing himself on the experience of the witnesses, Grand'Maison describes the pastoral policies of the second evangelization. They must encourage people (1) to be rooted in Christ, (2) to break with the dominant culture, and (3) to pay critical attention to their historical context.

(1) To be rooted in Christ calls for meditative prayer and repeated revision of one's personal life. The moralizing preaching of the past gave the impression that Catholics were all right if they did not break the rules, a message that allowed them to remain on the surface of their faith. Since many of the rules no longer fit, Catholics have become confused. Of crucial importance is now the spiritual life, the encounter with Jesus Christ in Scripture and the liturgy, an encounter that will enable Catholics to deal with new challenges, follow their consciences, and give public witness of their faith. When Grand'Maison writes about the spiritual life, he is not only prophet; he is also sage, a spiritual guide.

Our author does not raise the question at this point whether such pastoral guidance can be offered in a parish or whether it calls for smaller communities.

(2) To break with the dominant culture is not a demand to reject the social-democratic values brought by the Quiet Revolution. What is to be resisted is the self-seeking utilitarianism promoted by the unregulated market system and the indifference to ethical values that have come to characterize political life. Fernand Dumont referred to this powerful trend as "deculturation," the promotion of life without depth, the domination of superficiality. Christians must rupture with the worldly world and adopt a lifestyle that expresses their fidelity to the Gospel. In his study of the witnesses, Grand'Maison gives many examples of Christian existence on different levels of Quebec society.

(3) To take into account the historical context demands that Christian believers, taking into account their location in society, search out what fidelity to the Gospel entails in their particular situation. Because of the Church's internal pluralism there is no single

measure for the life of faith, hope, and love. In dialogue with their national or regional culture and critically aware of the unjust features of their society, Christians must find an original manner of witnessing their faith in Jesus Christ.

The second evangelization focusing on the vitality of the local community calls for a new ecclesiology. Needed is a type of Church that is able, after the collapse of Christendom, to provide a new coherence to the scattered believers and the diverse communities, institute symbols of unity that respect diversity, see itself as a pilgrim people on the march, and become a visible sign of radical fraternity in the midst of the struggles for justice among the nations.

If I understand Grand'Maison correctly, he envisages the Church of the future, in Quebec and in the industrialized world in general, as a relatively small community, no longer identified with an entire nation, no longer a *Volkskirche* as the Germans call it, but representing a creative minority in society which, thanks to the power of the Gospel, has an impact far beyond its borders. The Church will become prophet: its communal life will address a critical message to society. The Church of the future, Grand'Maison anticipates, will be humble, admit that it does not have all the answers, welcome the creativity of the faithful, and be open to all who believe in Christ, without discrimination. The humble Church will symbolize in a more credible way the figure of Jesus, the loving yet demanding prophet in whom God's Word has become incarnate in human history. Grand'Maison's anticipation reminds me of Karl Rahner's similar prediction of the Church as minority.[18]

Grand'Maison is critical of the Vatican because of its unwillingness to acknowledge that Christendom, the inherited European-based Christian culture, has collapsed, and its reluctance to be open to ecclesial experiments based on the experience of contemporary Christian witnesses. He writes, "Postconciliar Rome has remained in control: it has returned to the Tridentine routine."[19] To defend its power, the Vatican operates on two registers: to explain the past errors of the magisterium (for instance, its approval of slavery and torture), the Vatican appeals to the Church's immersion in history; yet to defend its present infallibility, it presents the Church as standing above history.[20] Still, Grand'Maison refuses to be discouraged: he supports local ecclesial projects that nourish people's faith and help them to find their freedom in God. He holds, as we shall see further on, that the renewal of the Church and of society begins at the community level.

It is interesting that in an address to lay Catholics in Freiburg, Germany, on 24 September 2011, Pope Benedict XVI described the New Evangelization, a pastoral project initiated by him, in terms that that resemble Grand'Maison's proposals. These are the pope's words:

> Many people lack experience of God's goodness. They no longer find any point of contact with the mainstream Churches and their traditional structures. Why is this? … Addressing this question is the principal task of the Pontifical Council for the New Evangelization … People who lack the experience of God's goodness need places where they can give voice to their inner longing. Here we must seek new paths of evangelization. Small communities could be one such path, where friendships are lived and deepened in regular communal adoration before God. There people will speak of the small faith experiences at their workplace and within their circle of family and friends, and in so doing bear witness to a new closeness between Church and society. They come to see more and more clearly that everyone stands in need of this nourishment of love, this concrete friendship with others and with the Lord. Of continuing importance is the link with the vital life-source that is the Eucharist, since cut off from Christ we can do nothing (cf. Jn 15:5).

NATIONALISM

In the introduction to this book I mentioned that moving to Montreal in 1986 was for me the beginning of a cultural adventure, the entry into a new linguistic, political, and theological context. That I was now surrounded by friends who were nationalists made me uncomfortable at first. I decided to study the complex phenomenon of nationalism and find principles that allowed me to distinguish between ethically acceptable and ethically unacceptable forms of nationalism. I discovered that the struggle of colonized nations for political self-determination had in fact been approved by a series of covenants of the United Nations.[21] In my book *Nationalism, Religion and Ethics*[22] I relied on the ethical reflections of four religious authors, Martin Buber, Mahatma Gandhi, Paul Tillich, and Jacques Grand'Maison. The two-volume work *Nationalisme et religion*[23] by Grand'Maison is, in fact, a masterpiece, an original contribution to

Catholic social thought, which – as we shall see – has influenced the teaching of the Quebec bishops.

Allow me to mention that the body of Catholic social teaching has avoided the topic of nationalism. Since nationalist movements in the nineteenth century aimed at the creation of the modern State and hence favoured the separation of State and Church, and since Italian nationalists wanted to found an Italian State, suppressing the Ecclesiastical State on Italian soil, these movements were harshly condemned by the papacy of that century. In the twentieth century, nationalist movements in European societies were often politically reactionary, opposed to democracy and pluralism, and sometimes enjoyed the support of the Catholic Church. Because Catholic social teaching provided no ethical reflections on nationalism, politically engaged Catholics were left without any guidance.

In his first volume, Grand'Maison studies the early nationalist movements, their opposition to the feudal-aristocratic order, their creation of the modern State, and their ideal of equal citizenship. While the modern State promised to overcome the inequalities characteristic of the traditional societies, our author, ever sensitive to the dark side of social achievements, recognizes that the modern State soon introduced injustices of its own. In some cases, the State became an empire, suppressing other nations and engaging in colonial wars. Modern States, moreover, were constituted around the centres of political and economic power, thus dividing the country into privileged and underprivileged regions. While our author recognizes the right of a nation to political self-determination and hence approves of the anti-colonial struggles for self-determination, he acknowledges the turn to authoritarianism of many former colonies and hence warns against uncritical enthusiasm.

Grand'Maison also reflects critically on "the neo-nationalism" of nations within unitary States, such as Scotland and Wales in Britain, Catalonia and the Basque country in Spain, Corsica in France, and Quebec in Canada. If these nations are prevented by law from protecting and developing their cultural identity, they have an ethically grounded right of political self-determination – a right, our author insists, that has been acknowledged by the United Nations. He warns at the same time that this neo-nationalism, including Quebec nationalism, is ethically justified only if it is committed to democratic values, freedom, and pluralism.

In the second volume our author deals with the political implication of Christian faith. For Christians, he argues, there is no preferred tribe or nation; the God of Jesus embraces the whole of humanity in love. Political policies acceptable to Christians recognize all people, whatever their origin, as children of God. No one is excluded. Grand'Maison offers an extended critique of reactionary forms of nationalism, hostile to democracy and intolerant of minorities, that in some countries have had the support of the Catholic Church. In this context he denounces the Quebec nationalism between the two world wars, which was promoted by Lionel Groulx and other Catholic priests who wanted Quebec to remain a Catholic society capable of resisting the civil liberties and the cultural pluralism characteristic of secular-Protestant North America. In these pages Grand'Maison draws the slightly distorted image of Lionel Groulx, one that was popular in Quebec after the Quiet Revolution, overlooking the service rendered by this priest to enhance the collective self-confidence of Quebecers. The only nationalism that Christians may support, Grand'Maison argues, is one that envisages humanity as a family of nations and promotes universal solidarity in this framework.

Grand'Maison makes a detailed examination of the policies and ideals of the Parti Québécois, which at that time was still the official opposition in the National Assembly. He concludes that the Parti's nationalist project of sovereignty-association offers the people of Quebec the freedom to which they are entitled under conditions that guarantee democratic rights and respect for minorities. The referendum promised by the Parti Québécois, he believes, will be a *kairos*, a special historical moment, allowing the people to become adults, reject the tutelage of a higher government, and assume responsibility for their own society. Christian ethics, he holds, recommends voting in favour of sovereignty. Prior to the referendum of 1980, he published his ethical reflections on the option for sovereignty in *Le Devoir*, a position that was seconded by many theologians in the same newspaper.[24] After the loss of the referendum Grand'Maison expresses his anger with the Catholic bishops who, indifferent to the *kairos*, refused to support Quebec's political sovereignty.[25]

Yet the *kairos* did not last for long. Grand'Maison felt that the Parti Québécois was becoming increasingly indifferent to social and economic inequality. He reacted to this in a book denouncing "les promus de la Révolution tranquille," the people who had profited from the Quiet Revolution, who were now forgetting the plight of poor workers, the unemployed, and the little people in the countryside.[26] Profiting from the Quiet Revolution were professors, teachers, journalists, scientists, government employees, artists, labour leaders, and individuals belonging to the business class. Grand'Maison also became increasingly critical of society, lamenting the invasion of neo-liberal values, the waning of the humanistic ideals of the Quiet Revolution, and the loss of profound ethical convictions, especially among the young.

Prior to the referendum of 1980, the Quebec bishops refused to pronounce themselves in favour of sovereignty-association. Instead they produced a pastoral statement on nationalist movements, largely based on Grand'Maison's *Religion and Nationalism*, that made an original contribution to Catholic social teaching. In their statement of 1979, "The People of Quebec and its Political Future,"[27] the bishops acknowledge the right of self-determination of the Quebec people, a right they believed to be recognized by international law; yet they add immediately that it is not their task to tell Quebecers how to vote, whether to define their future within or without the Canadian confederation. But it is their task, they write, to offer ethical reflections on the political phenomenon of nationalism. They propose that a nationalist movement is ethical under four conditions: (1) if it intends to create a more just and more open society, (2) if it respects the human rights of minorities, (3) if it aspires to have peaceful relations with the neighbouring nations, and (4) if it does not regard the nation as the highest good – to do so would be idolatry.

Jean Richard, a theologian at Laval University, the translator and editor of Paul Tillich's collected works, did not agree with Grand'Maison's theological arguments in favour of Quebec's sovereignty. Richard begins his argument by summarizing Tillich's reflections on nationalism.[28] While nations have the right to protect their rootedness in a particular culture, the German theologian writes, justice is a higher value that must always qualify the quest for national identity. Richard then asks: what are the demands of justice in Quebec society? Referring to the writing of George Grant[29] and Douglas Hall,[30] Richard argues that the threat to Quebec's cultural identity is not its membership in the Canadian confederation, but the economic and cultural hegemony of the American empire. To defend its social-democratic ideal, Quebec must resist American imperial influence, which can be done more effectively if Quebec remains in the Canadian federation. That the Left in Quebec is usually in favour of political independence, Richard regards as a political mistake. To resist the invasion of American capital and American culture, this small society needs the link to the whole of Canada.

The debate about the future of Quebec continues in the theological community.

A CRITIQUE OF MODERNITY

Jacques Grand'Maison is opposed to all ideologies. He argues that ideologies produce fidelity to theoretical concepts, making the persons endorsing them unwilling to look at their effect on ordinary people. His sympathy is always with the people marginalized, excluded, and looked down upon. Our author defended the ideology of nationalism at a particular moment, yet – as we saw above – he soon recognized that the *kairos* did not last. In 1979, he wrote a set of articles for *Le Devoir*, later published as a book, *Au seuil critique d'un nouvel âge*, in which he denounced the political ideas of the Right and the Left, including the labour unions and the radical Catholic Left.[31] Some of his readers thought that Grand'Maison was about to become a candidate for the Parti Québécois. He himself was tormented by the question of whether to become a politician in the Parti Québécois or remain a prophet and priest committed to social justice, a free critic, unattached to any political group.

> I struggled with this dilemma for several weeks in profound darkness. One night, coming back from Montreal on the highway, I felt arising from my depths an inner truth which had lurked beneath the underbrush of all my incomplete arguments. "After all, you are a priest, for God's sake!" ... The Christians with whom I have woven Gospel ties have in turn shown me by their joy that I have chosen the remnant which maintains the fragile spark of an ever-present faith. In a society which has so quickly put out the flame of its history, in a milieu which is experiencing a spiritual and moral vacuum without precedence, I had to say that I will not put this Gospel treasure under a bushel. I would remain a poor man of God, faith and stubborn hope.[32]

In an article of mine on Grand'Maison's political stance, I concluded that he was a naysayer warning against ideologies and all political one-sidedness.[33] In 1989, in his concluding remarks at the symposium held in his honour, he surprised his audience by denouncing Quebec nationalism, his own and that of his friends. He had just read in American psychosocial literature, he told his audience, that some people, frightened by the chaos that surrounds them, withdraw into a cocoon of their own making, interrupting all relations to the world around them. We Quebec nationalists, he now continued, are in the process of cocooning ourselves.[34] Here the prophet exaggerates. His awareness of the sinister potential of all ideologies and institutions has made him utter accusations that even his best friends find unjust. Yet fully justified, in my opinion, is Grand'Maison's critique of political thinking on the Left and the Right that supposes effective institutions can be created capable by themselves of solving the concrete problems of society. People want good institutions, our author argues, that do not require them to change, i.e. to become good, just, and generous. Good institutions – as an example our author refers to the Canadian health care system – work well only if all individuals regard their participation as an ethical task, wrestling against selfishness and respecting the common good. Building society is a spiritual task for all involved in it.

Grand'Maison is suspicious of what happens at the top of society. I just found a quotation in a novel that expresses our author's attitude toward the world.

> It was the same images (on televisions). People who were bleeding, people who were hungry, people who were suffering. And then a procession of well-dressed men making endless speeches, without pity, all with the same smile and the same arrogance.[35]

The reason why Grand'Maison does not despair is his confidence that the God of Jesus Christ is at work among the people on the ground. There God summons and inspires men and women to overcome their discouragement, transcend their self-centredness, share the burdens of their neighbour, and work together for the benefit of all. God summons forth the transformation of society from the bottom up.

Rejecting both capitalism and socialism, our author recommends community development and the social economy as alternative models of social and economic activity.[36] In Quebec, a growing network of collective initiatives, co-operative ventures, self-help projects, and non-profit organizations render a multitude of services to society and provide work for vast numbers of people. These collective endeavours take place among people marginalized by society: the unemployed, part-time workers, underpaid workers, and other people living in poverty. Our author supports *le mouvement communautaire*. In this movement people express their creativity, find meaning in their work, act co-operatively, overcome their isolation, and become friends. Here people express their objection to the capitalist organization of labour by acting – not in words. Since their work is carried on in an ethical framework, people are challenged every day to live up to their own ideals. At the same time, the moral character of the social economy also contributes to its vulnerability, for selfish persons can easily create conflicts and endanger the collective enterprise.

Grand'Maison's solidarity with the people who are left out is expressed in his imaginative three-volume work entitled *Les tiers*.[37] The main point of this work is that conflicts between two powerful actors tend to overlook and render invisible the "the third ones," i.e. the people not identified with either side. In the conflict between capital and organized labour, the unemployed are *les tiers*, and in the conflict between English and French Canada, the Native peoples and the recent immigrants belong to *les tiers*. Our author understands "the option for the poor" recommended by liberation theology as a call to extend our solidarity to the people left in the bottom or pushed to the margin. In his *Les tiers* he gives many examples of peoples and groups excluded from respect and participation, showing that their struggle to be listened to has a transforming impact on the whole of society.

At the colloquium held in Grand'Maison's honour in 1989, Gisèle Turcot expressed her appreciation of his three-volume work on *les tiers*, the socially excluded. Being excluded is, in fact, the experience of women in traditional societies and continues to mark their situation in modern culture. The struggle between two groups of men tends to exclude from consciousness the subjugation inflicted upon women. An example of this, often cited by Native women in Canada, is the conflict between the federal government and the Native leaders that tends to ignore the oppressive conditions inflicted upon women by the men of their own nation. Solidarity with *les tiers*, Grand'Maison argues, was practiced by Jesus: remaining aloof from the conflict between the Jewish hierarchy and the Roman empire, he allied himself with the people of the land, the population despised by their own elite and exploited by the empire.

In *Les tiers* Grand'Maison offers in his own way a critique of modernity. The two great modern social projects, capitalist and socialist, presupposed that reason, or more precisely, techno-scientific reason, would carry history in the direction of progress – either by evolution, as held by capitalist theory, or by revolution, as held by socialist theory. These theories could not be demonstrated; they were ideologies; they claimed to be true and became the infallible guide of action. Relying on techno-scientific reason, society left ethical reasoning behind. Under the impact of capitalist theory, even democracy ceased to be guided by ethical values and became increasingly purely procedural. No attention was paid, Grand'Maison argues passionately, to *les tiers* – the exploited, the oppressed, the excluded, possibly the great majority. Our author is not becoming a conservative: he does not advocate the return to a Catholic Quebec, united in a common morality controlled from above, inhibiting personal freedom and assigning unqualified priority to the common good. Instead, he extends his solidarity to *les tiers*, to the movements at the base of society: the various forms of community development and the protection of the natural environment.

Listening to Grand'Maison makes me think of the terms "rupture and fidelity" and "first and second culture" introduced by Fernand Dumont. If modernity is defined as systematic use of reason to improve the conditions of people's personal and social lives, one can say that modernity is a rupture, a second culture, leaving behind traditional society, but – according to Dumont – the second culture will be creative and bear fruit only if it is faithful in a new way to the inherited values, the first culture. For Grand'Maison this fidelity is the solidarity with the people at the community level and the concern for protecting the land.

THE SIN OF THE WORLD

In Grand'Maison's passionate denunciation of attitudes and structures that inflict suffering upon people and damage their lives, I hear the prophet denouncing the sin of society. I detect in Grand'Maison's writings an Augustinian sensitivity to the omnipresence of sin. He does not use the word 'sin' very often; with all Quebec Catholics he is aware that in the past a moralistic interpretation of sin was used by the clergy to regulate the culture of Quebec and control the behaviour of the people. Speaking of sin usually referred to matters of sexuality. Grand'Maison is also aware that the doctrine of original sin has been employed to undermine people's self-confidence and their hope that the struggle for a more just society will ever be successful. At the same time, our author is very conscious of the sinister side of all human achievements. He recognizes the potential of good ideas and good institutions to become instruments of domination, making people conform to an ideology and robbing them of their freedom. He realizes that truth can become a weapon to humiliate people who raise disturbing questions, hope can become a source of blindness making real threats invisible, and love can foster a practice of charity indifferent to social injustice.

All human achievements have a dark side; they have a potential for evil; they are liable to generate pride, create the desire to triumph over others, and produce contempt for the less gifted. While Fernand Dumont spoke with great respect of the first culture to which he belonged, Grand'Maison is more conscious of its ambiguity. Speaking of his French-Canadian working-class milieu, he remembers experiences of solidarity as well as brutal conflicts.[38] At the same time, Grand'Maison is no moralist. He recognizes that personal sins must be understood in their relation to structural sins. The interaction between these two produces the self-destructive current operative in every society. Few theologians recognize as clearly as Grand'Maison how deeply we are implicated, knowingly or unknowingly, in the structural sins of our society – its surrender to the demands of capital, its exploitative practices, its colonial domination, its military policies, and its production of weapons for sale. I think that our author would agree with the remarkable analysis made by Pope John Paul II of the part played by personal sin in the structural sin of society.

> There are the personal sins of those who cause or support evil or who exploit it; of those who are in a position to avoid, eliminate or at least limit certain social evils but who fail to do so out of laziness, fear or the conspiracy of silence, through secret complicity or indifference; of those who take refuge in the supposed impossibility of changing the world and also of those who sidestep the effort and sacrifice required, producing specious reasons of a higher order. The real responsibility, then, lies with individuals.[39]

Grand'Maison would agree that none of us can claim innocence. The reason that he does not despair, as I mentioned in a previous paragraph, is his faith in God's gracious and wholly unmerited presence in human life and human history, the mystery of redemption revealed in Jesus Christ. With Saint Augustine our author holds that the good is something marvelous, a gift of God, summoning forth joy and gratitude. Because of the divine presence made known by Jesus, Christians can never stop doing good, extending their friendship to others, and standing against injustice and domination. Grand'Maison holds that even in the worst conditions, Christians are called to be in solidarity with the victims of society, engage in critical thinking, plot reformist actions, and improve their world by loving their neighbours.

We have seen that Grand'Maison envisaged the future Church of Quebec as a relatively small community in a secular society, a community that does fight against the secular world, but engages in dialogue with it to foster co-operative action in the service of the common good. He now sees more clearly how the Church should define its mission in society: in solidarity with *les tiers*, the Church will remind society of its injustices, help the excluded to become recognized, and labour to make society more pleasing to God. In reminding society of its injustices, the Church raises ethical issues, laments the widespread emptiness of heart, and proclaims humanity's spiritual vocation. Our author never ceases to be grateful for the Good News.

5

Jesus Greater than the Church

When Christians are unhappy with their Church, they turn to Jesus to find enlightenment. They renew their faith by listening to him, reflect anew on his message of new life, and try to discover what they should think and how they should act in their present situation.

A well-known example is the book *Jesus Before Christianity*[1] published in 1976 by the South African Dominican priest Albert Nolan, who was deeply troubled by the reluctance of the Churches of his country to condemn the Apartheid regime as unethical and un-Christian. Rereading the New Testament and studying the ministry of Jesus among the people of the land convinced him that being Christian in South Africa demanded active resistance to Apartheid. His book persuaded many Christians in his country and the wide world that, despite the indifference of the Churches, God's Word in Jesus called them to stand up against this inhuman and soul-destroying legislation.

Theologians and exegetes in Quebec, troubled by the Church's authoritarian style in the past and the Vatican's resistance to dialogue in the present, have turned to Jesus Christ to be sustained in their faith and guided by his message. Reflecting on his words, his life, and his messianic promises, they see the world and appreciate the Church in a new light, and discover the form their faith commitment should take in the present situation. It is this turn to Jesus on the part of theologians and exegetes that I wish to illustrate in the present chapter. I realize that Christians in all parts of the world are turning to Jesus Christ with questions raised by contemporary culture. In fact, in their work Quebec theologians and exegetes are in dialogue with critical thinkers worldwide. Yet peculiar to Quebec was its recent entry into social-democratic and pluralistic modernity and the massive exodus from the Church.

For Fernand Dumont and Jacques Grand'Maison, as we saw in the preceding chapters, Jesus was the prophet who revealed God's Truth and was himself the Truth. In a few pages written with great passion, Grand'Maison presents Jesus as the redemptive mystery operative in human history, generating the Church and yet transcending it.[2] Grand'Maison makes these bold proposals: (1) Before Jesus was revealed, he was present in human history touching people's hearts. (2) When he became visible he summoned forth the ecclesial communities from below. (3) He always grants more than his followers expect. (4) In shaping his communities, he relies upon resources available in each place. (5) He promises not tranquility, but contradiction. (6) He asks us to anticipate in the present the kingdom promised for the future. (7) He wants us to build the Church together. (8) At the end he will judge us according to the measure of our humanity. According to Grand'Maison, the Church proclaims the revealed Truth and obscures it at the same time.

JEAN-PAUL AUDET

In 1968 Jean-Paul Audet, a Dominican scholar, the author of an original study of the Didaché,[3] was invited by the Institut pastoral de Montréal to address a gathering of Catholics eager for the renewal of their Church. His talks, published in the *Communauté chrétienne,* subsequently became part of a little book entitled *Le projet évangélique de Jésus*.[4] These Catholics were dissatisfied with the routine Catholicism of their parish. They complained that the ecclesiastical framework in which they lived had been defined by men in positions of authority who did not know them, did not listen to them, and were unaware of their spiritual aspirations.

Jean-Paul Audet believed that the time had come to rethink the Church's pastoral ministry. Biblical scholars, he said, have paid little attention to the pastoral project initiated by Jesus himself in his Palestinian mission. Yet an attentive reading of the synoptic gospels allows us to have a good idea of the pastoral practice introduced by him. He proclaimed the coming of God's reign, he introduced people to a new self-understanding as God's sons and daughters, and he called them to be converted to a new way of life, at odds with the ethos of their society, defined by confidence, humility, the love of neighbour, the respect for justice, and the practice of gentleness and peace. Jesus did not give them a set of beliefs to be held; instead he initiated them to a new way of life in community. They were to live as brothers and sisters, as a spiritual family, in expectation of the kingdom God was about to initiate.

Audet showed that fraternity remained the abiding mark of the Church in the apostolic writings after the death and resurrection of Jesus. The baptized referred to one another simply as brothers and sisters. Their intimate community was sealed in the celebration of the Eucharist. Jesus, their brother, though now with God, was not absent from their community: he was present to them, as he had promised. The Church as fraternity (brothers and sisters), Audet argued, was more fundamental than the Church as people of God. The latter term expresses the Church's universal dimension: it also had a special meaning for Christians acquainted with the vocation of Israel in the Old Testament. Yet more fundamental and closer to daily experience was the Church as fraternity.

> This conclusion, we believe, has many lasting consequences. It suggests an ecclesial way of life ... It also suggests a certain orientation of pastoral action and Christian life. Questions related to the practical meaning of "fraternity" will have to be resolved increasingly by the *base community*. This is the natural place where Christian community becomes visible, unfurled and fully lived. It would be naïve to image that Christians can do all this without the practice of meditation. The key for the authentic renewal of the Church lies today in the base community ... as the site of the birth and development of Christian fraternity.[5]

In his talks and in his book, Audet suggests in some detail what a base community could be like in the Quebec of his day, what membership would entail, how to combine the shared life with work and responsibility in society, and what relation the base community would have to the parish and the diocese. In the early 1970s, Audet's pastoral proposal exercised great influence among large numbers of dedicated Catholics, especially in Montreal. They gathered in groups to discuss the future of the Church, the evolution of their spirituality, and the creation of new institutions. Many of them formed base communities, convinced that Jesus was present in their midst. Their effort is remembered in the film *Tranquillement, pas vite – Communauté de base* that presents the achievements and difficulties of a base community in Montreal over a period of eight months. While most of these communities had a relatively short life, some of them continue to thrive in the present. One of the issues that produced internal divisions among them was the question whether their members should become politically engaged in the reconstruction of society.

TWO VOLUMES: *JÉSUS?* AND *APRÈS JÉSUS*

Because Catholics were increasingly turning to Jesus and submitting to him their unanswered questions, the biblical scholars of the theological faculty of the University of Montreal decided to offer public conferences on the relevance of Jesus, subsequently published in two volumes, *Jésus? De l'histoire à la foi*[6] and *Après Jésus: autorité et liberté dans le peuple de Dieu.*[7] In these books the authors examine the Scriptures and the early Christian writings to shed light on the theological issues that trouble Quebec Catholics who have embraced the culture produced by the Quiet Revolution. I shall comment on two articles of the first volume and three articles of the second volume.

Léonard Audet's article on the Reign of God[8] shows that its meaning is so rich and manifold that it cannot be reduced to a single concept. Jesus preferred to speak about it in parables. The author insists that divine revelation always transcends the categories we use to gain some insight into it. Many Catholics, the author writes, have a naïve understanding of doctrine; they think of it as a perfect expression of the truth and hence are troubled by biblical passages that seem to be at odds with it. At certain moments Jesus expected the full revelation of God's reign in the near future, yet at other moments he was more cautious. This uncertainty shows that Jesus embraced the entire human condition, including our finitude and fallibility. According to the article, the pastorally important meaning of God's Reign is the revelation of the redemptive purpose in human history, the locus of God's grace, a divine project in which believers are meant to be participants.

The article by André Myre, about whom more shall be said further on, deals with the Christological titles assigned to Jesus in the New Testament.[9] He distinguishes three different communities – the Aramaic-speaking Palestinian church, the Greek-speaking Judaeo-Christians, and the Christians of pagan origin – each having their own way of naming the risen Jesus. For the Judaeo-Christians of

Palestine, well acquainted with the Hebrew Scriptures, Jesus was the Messiah and the Son of Man predicted in the book of Daniel, whose return in glory is eagerly expected. For the Hellenistic Judaeo-Christians, Jesus became the Christ and more dramatically the Lord, the title the Old Testament assigned to God. The emphasis now shifted from the expectation of Christ's return to his redemptive presence in the Church. The Christian communities of pagan origin came to believe in the pre-existence of Jesus: he was already present at creation, and he became incarnate at a particular time. They focused not simply on the role of Jesus in the history of redemption, but on his very being, thus turning to a metaphysical vocabulary. André Myre insists that each of these communities engaged in its own Christological reflection. He rejects the idea that these were stages of a linear evolution that would eventually produce the creedal statements of the Church.

An article of the second volume deals with the pluralism in the early Church.[10] The author shows that while each Church had its own interpretation of Jesus Christ and its own way of celebrating his presence, the Churches were in solidarity with one another, united by what they regarded as their common faith. Theological understanding was contextual from the beginning, though without breaking the bond that united the different ecclesial communities as the one Church of Christ. The appreciation of the Church's internal pluralism faded in the Church of the West under the pressure of the papacy promoting an ever greater uniformity.

These three articles were relevant to Quebec Catholics because they documented freedom of thought and theological pluralism in the Church and showed that doctrine represents an effort to express a transcendent mystery in a concept: doctrine, though necessary, is always partial and never the last word.

Since Quebecers were participants in a cultural transformation, two articles in the second volume deal with the question of how social transformation is presented in the Scriptures.[11] The article on the Old Testament studies the passage of the people of Israel from a semi-nomadic to a sedentary way of life, a passage that produced conflicts and was resisted by many. The article by André Myre studies social transformation in the New Testament by focusing on the great debate over the reception of converts from paganism. Justifying the new practice involved rereading the Scriptures and reflecting anew on the words of Jesus.

In an article of the second volume[12] on authority in the Church, Jean-Louis d'Aragon shows that in the New Testament, authority is the prerogative of Jesus Christ in whom the Word God is revealed to humanity. Faith in Jesus Christ calls for obedience to the Gospel message. Like any human organization, the Church needs leaders that have authority and must be obeyed, yet the obedience to them is different from the unconditional obedience to the divine Word. Moreover, Jesus wanted governance in the Church to be qualitatively different from governance in the world. Governing in the Church is a service to the community, expresses paternal care, and is ready to forgive seventy-seven times (Mt 18:22). This was a very high ideal. From the beginning, ordained ministers in the Church have been tempted to adopt a worldly understanding of their power to rule. Jean-Louis d'Aragon notes that in the Western Church obedience to the ecclesiastical authorities was taken more seriously than fidelity to the Good News preached by Jesus. Catholics tended to understand the Christian life as conformity to a set of rules, rather than as following of Gospel.

JÉSUS: CHRIST UNIVERSEL?

In 1989 the annual conference of la Société canadienne de théologie dealt with questions Catholics in Quebec were asking about Jesus Christ. The fourteen papers given at that occasion, subsequently published in the book *Jésus: Christ Universel?*[13] show that to answer these questions theologians reread the Scriptures, rethink the tradition, and reflect on contemporary Christian experience, their own and that of their community.

The first article by Normand Provencher shows that the approach to Christology has changed in all regions of the contemporary Church.[14] Since Vatican Council II has made the reading of Scripture the starting point and the soul of theology, theologians now begin their Christology with the story of Jesus, recorded principally in the synoptic gospels. In the past, the article argues, Jesus was singular and had universal meaning because he was interpreted in metaphysical terms as God's eternal Word, addressing the whole of humanity. By contrast, today theologians and exegetes find the universal meaning of Jesus in his historical singularity: his mission, his struggles, and his relation to God reveal the life that Christians, wherever they live, are to lead in their particular context. The words of Jesus are universally relevant because they shed light on all historical situations and summon Christians, wherever they are, to obey the Father and serve God's approaching reign.

In a concluding article, Provencher confirms that this shift in Christological understanding has also taken place among the theologians of Quebec.[15] While there are significant differences among them, they move along converging lines. What preoccupies them is not the classical Christology or the ontology of the God-Man. For them the centre of attention is the concrete Jesus of Nazareth, his singular historical existence, his special relationship to God, his pastoral mission in Palestine, his attitude toward the Temple and the Law, and his critique of the religious establishment. Because his prophetic message, which provoked his persecution and death on the cross, was divinely confirmed in his resurrection, theologians are able to deal with questions that, at the time of Jesus, were not yet raised or were raised in a manner different from our own. Because the prophet, repudiated by temple and empire, was rehabilitated in the resurrection, he continues his prophetic mission in the Church.

The articles in this book thus deal with the light shed by Jesus Christ on the interrelation of men and women and on the Church's relation to the wide world – the world religions, dissidents and nonbelievers, pluralistic societies, the poor and the colonized. Louise Melançon shows that the promises of Jesus include the deliverance of women from patriarchal subordination; Achiel Peelman shows that Jesus is in solidarity with the Native peoples struggling against subjugation by the Christian colonizers; and Jean-Guy Nadeau relates the cross of Jesus Christ to the human suffering in this violent age. The articles written by Raymond Lemieux and Jean-Paul Michaud on the images of Jesus in secular culture persuaded Normand Provencher to conclude that Jesus has escaped the Church and become a guiding figure in other religious and even secular contexts, where his name is sometimes instrumentalized for ambiguous purposes.

The above-mentioned interpretations of God's revelation in Jesus make several points that respond to the concern of Quebec's Catholics. Jesus called his followers to form a church community, in which they live as brothers and sisters and participate in his mission, a church community that is pluralistic, obedient to God's Word, yet open to contextual interpretations. The divine truth is revealed in the symbolic discourse proper to the Bible, transcending the doctrinal formulations that have become pastorally necessary. As Christians enter a new cultural situation, they find answers to their questions by rereading and interpreting anew the biblical texts. Because the appointed church leaders remain part of the fraternity, their style of governance differs from the governance in secular society. The focus on the ministry of Jesus and the ministry in the early Christian communities helps Quebec Catholics to formulate their hope for the renewal of the Church.

OLIVETTE GENEST

Olivette Genest is a biblical scholar whose work has been appreciated by her colleagues. For the ceremony of her retirement from the University of Montreal, Alain Gignac edited a festschrift in her honour, in which he writes, "Her contribution was not only in the field of exegetical studies; her attentive and religiously sensitive reading [of the New Testament] actually unsettled and gave new life to the religious imagination of Western Christianity."[16] The reference is here to Genest's contribution to feminist theological reflection[17] and, in particular, to her exegetical study of the meaning of Christ's death. As a woman of faith she had been troubled by the widely held theory, the vulgarized version of St Anselm's soteriology, that the death of Jesus was the sacrifice demanded by God as satisfaction for the sins of humanity. Making God exact satisfaction, Genest felt, was at odds with the Gospel message of divine compassion.

In her book *Le discours du Nouveau Testament sur la mort de Jésus: Épîtres et Apocalypse*, she shows that the exegetes who followed the historical-critical method say very little about what the death of Jesus means theologically. They are more interested in the complex composition of the biblical accounts of Jesus' trial, condemnation, and death, asking which verses are historical and which are elaborations representing different theological concerns. Genest thus decides to turn to semiotics. Instead of going behind the text, searching for its historical *Sitz im Leben* and the author's intention, the semiotic approach remains in front of the text, trying to understand it by taking account of its internal structure and logic. Once a text has been written it becomes an object, like a poem or a painting: it now utters its own truth, independent of its original context, simply through the relationships of its various parts. Using this exegetical method to interpret the passages on the death of Jesus in the

Epistles and the Apocalypse, Olivette Genest finds that the death of Jesus is presented in different images, each one with a distinct theological meaning. These images do include Christ's death as expiatory sacrifice, yet other images present this death as part of the victorious struggle against the powers of darkness, as a payment for release from slavery, as a death to sin for a new humanity, as the dismantling of the wall of separation, and as the death of mortality, the end of the reign of death. This is how Genest concludes her study:

> In the various images of the death of Jesus, all starts in sin as a dead-end from which to free humanity. But all also starts from the gift of God, leading to the destruction of sin and the removal of barriers. Sin does not condition all in humanity's relationship to God in the renewal of creation. Despite its massive presence, sin is not the cohesive element in the discourse on the death of Jesus. Except in our unhealthy interpretive schemes, hypnotized as we were by hidden guilt. [18]

The last sentence refers to a complaint frequently made by Quebec Catholics that the clerical Catholicism imposed on them in the past put such an emphasis on sin, the violation of precepts, and divine punishment, that Catholics were made to think of God as a stern judge and feel the pain of guilt, instead of believing in God's love.

ANNE FORTIN

An entirely different focus on Jesus Christ is taken by Anne Fortin, professor of theology at Laval University. Her first field of research was the reformist hermeneutics of Jürgen Habermas, yet following her more recent pastoral experiences, she has embraced the semiotic approach to biblical interpretation and developed her own theological method, different from that of the majority of her colleagues. She now reads the Scriptures by remaining in front of the text, allowing herself to be addressed by the biblical Word. While Oliviette Genest tries to understand the text by attending to its internal pattern in an objective manner, Anne Fortin wants the reader to be personally challenged by the text and rethink his or her self-understanding. Instead of interpreting the text so that it makes sense to the reader's modern consciousness, she wants the reader to be unsettled by the strangeness of the text and question his or her self-perception and way of life. Her method relies on a linguistic theory developed by a group of French philosophers who argue that human consciousness is constituted by language.

In her book *L'annonce de la bonne nouvelle aux pauvres*[19] Fortin practices *lectio divina*, i.e. an attentive, faith-guided reading of the New Testament that invites readers to open themselves to God's Word, be challenged and converted by it, and be reconstituted as men and women of faith. I found the book puzzling. In his preface to the book, Jacques Racine writes that readers will be surprised that "les pauvres" mentioned in the title do not refer to people living in material poverty and that the author does not discuss the biblical texts denouncing the injustices of society. Anne Fortin makes it quite clear that she does not read the Gospel as a call for social change. She has in fact been criticized for presenting the Christian message in a manner that makes people indifferent to structured inequalities that damage human lives.[20]

I began to understand her book when I read her articles published in various reviews and collections.[21] In her pastoral work with people engaged in social work or the serving professions, she discovered that these Catholic Quebecers were totally alienated from the Church, the liturgy, and their parish. They suffered, Fortin believes, from a loss of roots and an absence of a clear sense of identity, products of today's individualistic culture. This applies especially to Quebec, she argues, because the secular and religious symbols that shaped people's self-understanding have undergone such rapid change. The *lectio divina* to which she introduces small groups of people is intended to reconstitute them as Christian believers. She sees this attentive reading as an extra-ecclesiastical sacrament, being addressed by a word uttered in power capable of transforming a person's self-definition. In this faith-guided reading of Scripture, Fortin brackets the world with its many problems because the people participating in her groups are already deeply involved in serving society. What they need is a *lectio divina* that converts them every day to Jesus Christ.

Anne Fortin regards her semiotic reading of Scripture as a scientific method because it is based on a rational linguistic theory that recognizes the self-constitution of human beings through language. Still, reading the Bible in this manner involves the response of the reader, a subjective reaction, open to everyone willing to be addressed by God's Word. In one of her articles, she applies her approach to the passage in Matthew 14, in which Jesus walks on the water and tells his frightened disciples not to be afraid. Instead of asking whether this really happened and how to understand miracles today, she wants the reader to listen to the text as addressed to them, to see Jesus walking on the insecure waters of their own lives and hear his grace-filled words "Do not be afraid," empowering them to march on.

German-speaking Catholics were taught to listen in this manner to the Gospel passages read at Mass by the Austrian liturgist Pius Parsch, who had great influence in the Catholic Church from the 1930s on.[22] He taught that in and through the words and images of the biblical text, Jesus now saves and sanctifies the attentive listener. Christ's utterances and gestures, especially his miracles, recorded in the biblical texts reveal how he now acts within us as we reflect on them in faith. Parsch defended his approach to reading the Scriptures with an appeal, not to a linguistic theory, but to Odo Casel's controversial theology of mystery. For this Benedictine, the liturgy and the biblical texts within it do more than recall what happened in the past; they render mysteriously present the redemptive work of Christ.

What Pius Parsch in his day did not see was that God's Word in Scripture addressed to me also expresses a judgment and a promise in regard to the society to which I belong – a message that unsettles me, that I would prefer to disregard, but that will not allow me to remain indifferent. I recall Karl Rahner's phrase, cited by Grand'Maison, "Divine revelation has not converted people as long as they have not reinterpreted their historical situation."[23]

RÉMI PARENT

Rémi Parent, a Redemptorist priest, professor of theology at the University of Montreal, was the author of numerous books that made Jesus Christ the norm and centre of Catholic ecclesiology. He produced theological studies and reflections that were, at the same time, spiritual reading for a readership beyond the academy. He believed that theology was relevant for all believers, professional and lay. When criticized for the passion with which he wrote about Jesus, he made this reply: "When people say that a book is passionate, they most likely suggest that it lacks intellectual rigour, as if passion and rigour were destined to cancel one another."[24] Rémi Parent was a pastor in communication with a wide circle of committed Catholics, to whom he listened, from whom he derived insights, and to whose concerns he addressed himself. I wish to mention three of his books.

In *L'Église c'est vous*[25] Parent demonstrates that the men and women who believe in Jesus Christ constitute the Church. While we often use the word "Church" to refer to the ecclesiastical hierarchy, in theological terms the Church refers to the Catholic people. In his preface to this book, Bishop Charles Valois of Saint-Jérôme writes the following paragraph.

> At a time when many men and women withhold their adhesion to the Church without rejecting, they say, their faith in Jesus Christ, Father Rémi Parent's brings lucid and convincing enlightenment. While demonstrating that "the Church is not an add-on to faith [in] Jesus Christ, and that we cannot do without the Church without affecting our faith" Father Parent puts belonging to the Church at the heart of the Christian communities, sign and symbol of the People of God.[26]

In this book Rémi Parent makes the point that faith in Jesus Christ does not remain a private event: believers are in fact summoned by their faith to form a fraternal community and become the Church. In Christ, believers are reconciled to God and to one another. That Jesus creates the Church from below, through faith and baptism, is a point – as we saw above – also made by Jean-Paul Audet and Jacques Grand'Maison. Parent insists that the Church is not an institution imposed upon believers by powerful administrators with a divine mission; in truth, the Church is summoned forth and gathered in Christ through the gift of faith, mediated by the Holy Spirit. Because believers constitute the Church, they are responsible for its mission in the world and for its spiritual and material well-being. The ordained ministers in the Church are not meant to remove this responsibility from the believing community; on the contrary, they are appointed to help believers to exercise their ecclesial responsibility more effectively.

In the Church of Quebec the ecclesial co-responsibility of lay people was not an abstract idea. Because of the shortage of priests, many bishops relied upon lay men and women to provide pastoral services in the parishes and fulfill various ecclesial tasks in the diocese as liturgists, teachers, and administrators. Bishop Charles Valois of Saint-Jérôme was well known for having assigned many ecclesial responsibilities to lay men and women. He believed that the texts of Vatican Council II entitled him to do so. In his autobiographical reflections published after his retirement,[27] he recounts that his integration of lay people into the ecclesial ministry was criticized by a

Roman Congregation, that he went to Rome to defend the practice of his diocese, but that the recommendations of Vatican Council II did not impress the Roman authorities.

Rémi Parent was keenly aware of the resentment against clerical domination that had come to pervade the public culture of Quebec. He believed that only a radical change in the self-understanding of bishops and priests could heal this wound. In his book *Une Église de baptisés: pour surmonter l'opposition clerc/laïcs*[28] he shows that faith and baptism produce a lived fraternity of brothers and sisters that no subsequent ecclesiastical appointment or ordination can interrupt. Through their baptism believers become priests and prophets; they are the mediators who make the Gospel present in society and hand on the faith to the next generation. Citing ecclesiastical texts of the past, Parent shows that the magisterium has been unwilling to recognize the ecclesial mission of the baptized: these texts refer to them simply as lay men and women, thus defining them by their relation to the clergy and not their baptismal relation to Christ. The task of the ordained ministers, Parent argues, is to make the baptized more effective mediators of the Gospel.

Since priests, bishops, and popes belong to the community of the baptized, they are brothers in the same family of faith. They have special authority in the Church, yet they will exercise their rule as brothers among their siblings, in dialogical fashion, careful not to appear as lords located above the family of faith. What symbols, Parent asks, have the ordained adopted to signify their authority? The ornate ceremonies at the Holy See do not signify that the ordained ministers think of themselves as brothers in the graced fraternity of Jesus. Parent calls for changes in the ecclesiastical apparatus.

The issue raised in his book by Rémi Parent has been examined in greater detail by the young Joseph Ratzinger in a book whose title in English translation is *The Meaning of Christian Brotherhood.*[29] Here Ratzinger reflects on the same biblical texts invoked decades later by Parent, especially the sayings of Jesus: "You must not allow yourselves to be called Rabbi, since you only have one Master and you are all brothers. You must not call any one on earth your father, since you have only one Father and he is in heaven" (Mt 23:8–9). Ratzinger argues that Jesus contrasted the proud hierarchism practiced in the religion of the temple with the undifferentiated brotherliness of the Christian community. Ratzinger then asks himself whether the Catholic reality does not resemble the temple hierarchism castigated by Jesus more than the Christian fraternity depicted in the New Testament.[30] The message of Jesus, the young Ratzinger argued, obliges the Church constantly to renew itself from within so that the spirit of brotherhood reigns among the Christian people and their ordained leaders.

Parent's conclusion is more radical. Good will and greater generosity on the part of the ordained are not enough: what is needed, he argues, is structural change, allowing the Christian people to speak, be listened to, and become co-responsible for the Church's collective life. Anything less, he argues, offends the dignity granted to the baptized. Focusing on Jesus of the New Testament, Parent concludes that something must have gone wrong in the self-organization of the Catholic Church. He realizes of course that his ecclesiastical proposal is utopian, an ideal inspired by Christ's messianic promises, unrealizable in the present historical conditions. Yet this utopia is not a useless daydream: it challenges the present order and may eventually bear spiritual fruit.

Suffering from a degenerative disease, Rémi Parent confronted the religious meaning of death with faith and courage. In his book, *La vie, un corps à corps avec la mort*,[31] he argued that all Christians, and not only he, must turn to the person of Jesus to discover for themselves the meaning of life and death. Already before the final death of the body, death is a dimension of human life. In failure, breakdown, illness, and daily vulnerability, we recognize that human life, though blessed by God, is carried on under the shadow of death. The vulnerability of the child Jesus and, later, his suffering caused by rejection, slander, and persecution are signs of Jesus' mortality, anticipating the cruel death inflicted on him at the end. With Jesus, Christians pray for faith and serenity in facing the signs of death. Parent sees the conservative opposition in the Church to the renewal proposed by Vatican Council II as the shadow of death which makes Christians suffer, yet over which they must not lose their serenity. Parent faces his own demise with tranquility and faith. Yet he is careful not to suggest that Christians who remain uncertain about eternal life are faithless doubters and should feel guilty. Doubting and living in hope go hand in hand.

MICHEL BEAUDIN

That Hans Urs von Balthasar focuses his Christology on the obedience of Jesus to the Father greatly impressed Michel Beaudin, professor of theology at the University of Montreal. Here divine revelation is not the making known of divine truths, but the drama of God's self-revelation in Jesus Christ that transforms all who believe in him. In his book *Obéissance et solidarité*[32] Beaudin offers a careful analysis of the complex theological thought developed by von Balthasar, putting the emphasis on God's love revealed in Jesus – which is the Father's love for the Son, the Son's love for the Father, and their unity in the love of the Holy Spirit. According to von Balthasar's theology of redemption, believers are empowered to participate in Jesus' surrender to the Father, thus becoming lovers themselves. The fruit of the Gospel is a new practice, a new way of life.

In the final section of his book, Beaudin shows that von Balthasar accounts for God's transformative self-revelation in Jesus in purely spiritual terms, which allows him to present his theology as a universal wisdom, meaningful in all parts of the world, independent of people's historical context. Beaudin appreciates the transformative thrust of von Balthasar's theology, even if he regrets its indifference to the suffering of the poor and oppressed. While the death of Jesus on the cross is of central significance for the Swiss theologian, he never discusses the historical reasons why Jesus was rejected by the religious authorities and condemned to die on a Roman cross. Still, Beaudin shows as unwarranted the effort of conservative Catholic circles to make von Balthasar an opponent of the Church's renewal initiated by Vatican II. Von Balthasar's dramatic understanding of divine revelation actually makes him think of the Church in developmental terms.

RICHARD BERGERON

Passionately engaged with Jesus and alienated from the hierarchical Church, some Catholic scholars have decided to cross the border and cease to define themselves as Catholic. They now claim to speak from outside the Church. In the special context of Quebec, this does not mean that they have left the Catholic community: they continue to attend Catholic theological meetings, publish their books with Catholic publishers, and be read by Catholics as guides for their spiritual journey. Because of their faith and dedication, the reader does not realize or forgets that the authors of the inspiring texts claim to have left the Catholic Church.

Richard Bergeron, a gifted writer and the author of many theological studies, has, throughout his entire academic life, focused his attention on Jesus Christ. Like Michel Beaudin, he was impressed by the focus of von Balthasar's Christology on the obedience of Jesus to the Father. In his book *Obéissance de Jésus et vérité de l'homme*[33] Bergeron tries to show that by participating in the surrender of Jesus to the Father, Christians are set free and become responsible agents in history. The reader notes the influence of existentialism: obedience to the Father is the entry into authentic human existence. In some situations, Bergeron insists, obedience to the Father demands disobedience to human authorities, even in the Church.

Bergeron eventually abandoned his early theology. In a presentation to la Société canadienne de théologie he rendered an account of his spiritual journey.[34] Deeply convinced of God's presence in the world religions, he came to deny the uniqueness of Jesus as universal saviour as proclaimed in the Church's creed. In his books Bergeron now accused the Church of suffocating the Spirit. A few years later, he loses confidence in all the religious traditions: they have become obsolete and no longer mediate the divine presence. He now observes signs of an emerging universal spirituality, independent of the religions, accessible to all men and women, whatever their cultural or religious background, if they are ready to look inward, move to the centre of their being, and discover their rootedness in a mystery that transcends them. Moving towards this centre, they become more truly themselves. The call to the mystical life, Bergeron argues, is universal, for God has created human nature and is the ground and horizon of each human being. Yet to say that "God dwells within us" is inadequate because this would imply an inadmissible dualism, seeing God and humans as two distinct entities. Our rootedness in God is so profound, Bergeron argues, that we can speak of it only in paradoxical terms, confessing that we are both one with God and distinct from God. In an article entitled "Pour une spiritualité du troisième millénaire," Bergeron mentions contemporary scientists, philosophers, and poets who have experienced this intimate call to the spiritual life.[35] They anticipate, our author believes, what will be taking place universally.

Bergeron's books have been critically reviewed by Quebec theologians. They have raised serious objections to his ideas, without insulting their friend, continuing to regard him as a brother in a common quest. They have been critical of his individualism, insisting that human beings constitute themselves through their encounters with others, with their language, their culture, and their religious inheritance. Humans turn inward, not as isolated monads, but in a manner made accessible to them by participating in a culture. In his review of Bergeron's book *Renaître à la spiritualité*,[36] Pierre Pelletier[37] even suggests that Bergeron's audacious proposal of a universal spirituality for the third millennium is based on the old Thomistic thesis that all humans, as created and sustained by God, have "a natural desire to see God" (*Summa Theologica*, part I, qu. 4).

I ask myself why a spiritual person as modest and gentle as Richard Bergeron chooses to object to the Catholic Church in principle, even though he sees the mystical life as in perfect keeping with the Catholic tradition. Behind his decision, I think, is a stance Fernand Dumont called "No monopoly, please!"[38] The Church's official discourse makes us forget that we are not better or wiser than others, that God the Spirit blows where God wills, and that one does not have to be a Catholic to follow the beatitudes of Jesus. The irony of the Gospel is that again and again we meet outsiders who are more trusting, more hopeful, and more loving than we are. "No monopoly, please!" also reminds us that in recent history the Catholic Church has discovered the ethical implications of the Gospel by listening to secular humanists. In the 1930s, the Catholic Church still rejected civil rights and liberties; it even flirted with fascism in several European countries. Nor is the ecclesiastical magisterium today a reliable ethical guide in all issues of personal ethics. I suggest that "No monopoly, please!" persuades Bergeron to define himself against the Church, even though this stance is not incompatible with the universal mediation of Jesus Christ rightly understood. Despite his post-Christian theology, our author remains deeply attached to Jesus. His most recent book *Et pourquoi pas Jésus?*[39] is a passionate presentation of Jesus as his unique and uncontested Master whom he, Richard Bergeron, follows on his journey into God.

ANDRÉ MYRE

Crossing the border in a quite different way happened to André Myre, a learned exegete whose books and articles have introduced Quebec Catholics to Jesus of Nazareth seen in the light of recent postcolonial studies. This reading of Jesus recognizes the colonial occupation of Palestine by the Roman Empire, the various ways the emperor imposed his rule, and the efforts of the temple hierarchy to assure the people's peaceful submission to Rome.[40] These studies have uncovered the political dimension implicit in Jesus' preaching: God's coming reign, differing from the reign of Caesar, will be a realm of love, justice, and peace, a new way of life anticipated in the beatitudes. Best known among the exegetes sensitive to postcolonial studies is the American scholar Richard Horsley, the author of many books on the New Testament.[41] In his own writings, André Myre insists that the Jews in Palestine did not look upon their relation to God and their relation to society as two distinct spheres: for them the spiritual had social meaning and the coming of God's reign promised their entry into a just society. In his books and articles, often written in a poetic and persuasive style, Myre interprets the significance of the New Testament, especially the synoptic gospels, for Catholics in Quebec in search of spiritual well-being and more just social relations.

Why has André Myre crossed the border? He belongs to the school of exegetes who think that the earliest texts of the New Testament are the most authentic ones. For him, the later texts, composed for theological reasons by the Christian community, are less reliable, and the post-biblical creeds, while enriching the tradition, have no binding force. Studying the authority structures of the Churches founded by the apostles, Myre shows that these structures were not uniform, that they were devised to serve specific local communities, and that they differed from the monarchical episcopate that came about several decades later. Myre holds that there is nothing divine in the ecclesiastical organization: it was set up by the believing communities for pragmatic purposes, a thesis at odds with the Catholic understanding of the Church's hierarchy of apostolic succession. Acknowledging that he has crossed the border, Myre sometimes polemicizes against the Church.

At the same time, Myre is passionately attached to Jesus and tries to follow his way in radical fashion. His book entitled *Lui* (*Him*) gives a poetic account of a man, very much like Jesus, who walks through the streets of Montreal, has life-giving sympathy for people in trouble, and denounces the conditions that make them suffer – until the police arrive to arrest him as a trouble-maker. Myre's interpretation of the New Testament stresses the human and social liberation brought by Jesus in a language full of spiritual meaning.

Still, careful attention to his texts reveals a secularizing reading of the Gospel: even resurrection has only a this-worldly meaning. Myre argues ingeniously that already in the later part of the Old Testament, the word "resurrection" was used as a slogan by people of faith: when discouraged by the defeat of Israel, they affirmed their belief in resurrection, meaning that God would mercifully lift up Israel again and restore it to its rightful place. "Jesus has risen," Myre argues, was the slogan uttered by the believing community to signify that the death of Jesus was not the end, for with God's help the cause to which he was committed – the human and social liberation of humanity – would go on. While I am unconvinced by Myre's purely secular interpretation of the New Testament, I read his writings with great spiritual pleasure: they correct the idea that main concern of the Gospel is the salvation of souls.

GUY CÔTÉ AND THE QUEBEC BISHOPS

At the end of this chapter I wish to refer to the Christology of Jesus as humanizer presented in a booklet published by the Catholic Bishops Conference of Quebec. Entitled *Jésus Christ, Chemin d'humanisation*, it was produced by a committee of bishops and theologians.[42] It was actually written by the theologian Guy Côté. This pastoral document on Jesus Christ is intended to guide all forms of religious instruction in the Church of Quebec. I wish to summarize briefly its main points because in this ecclesiastical document Jesus is proclaimed as greater than the Church, as destined to rescue humanity from its self-destructive potential and empower men and women and their societies to become authentically human.

At the beginning the booklet recalls the biblical message that Jesus is the Way, the Truth, and the Life (Jn 14:6). He is the New Man (Eph 2:15, 4:24), the New Adam (Rom 5:17), the faithful Servant delivered unto death and raised up by God, in whom humanity is delivered from sin and "renewed in the image of its Creator" (Col 3:10). Through Christ, men and women enter into their true humanity and reach its fullness, participating in the life of God (2 Pt 1:4). That in Jesus humanity is revealed unto itself, the booklet recalls, is a principal theme of *Gaudium et Spes*. We read in it that "Christ, the final Adam ... fully reveals man to man himself and makes his supreme vocation clear."[43] Also "[t]he human person deserves to be saved and human society deserves to be renewed. Hence the pivotal point of our total presentation will be man himself, whole and entire, body and soul, heart and conscience, mind and will."[44] The redemption brought by Jesus Christ is here interpreted as the humanization of men and women and the historical conditions in which they live.

Confirming and developing this teaching, John Paul II writes,

> Man is the way for the Church – a way that, in a sense, is the basis of all the other ways that the Church must walk – because man – every man without any exception whatever – has been redeemed by Christ, and because with man – with each man without any exception whatever – Christ is in a way united, even when man is unaware of it.[45]

To proclaim humanity's humanization in Jesus, the booklet continues, we must first have an understanding of the threats to human well-being, the destructive power of sin, the traps into which humans fall as persons and as collectivities. These threats are presented in four categories. What wounds humanity externally are (1) the domination that oppresses people and (2) the exploitation that destroys the natural environment, and what wounds humanity internally are (3) idolatry and (4) despair. This articulation of human evil avoids the temptation of preachers and theologians either to denounce personal sins without attention to social sins or to repudiate social sins without the recognition of personal sins. In an original way the booklet provides categories that point to the constant interaction between the personal and the social. Teachers and preachers of the Good News must show that Jesus promises to rescue humanity from these four threats, that his gifts enable believers to wrestle against the dehumanization produced by personal failures and oppressive structures. The booklet makes clear that good will cannot be taken for granted. It is the grace of a merciful God that allows men and women to resist the threats to their humanity and enter more fully upon their destiny as human beings. Since Jesus is greater than the Church or – in the words of John Paul II – since Jesus is in some way united to every human being, he, the saviour, is the humanizer of the entire human family. This proposal of Christian humanism is not an arrogant project of self-redemption; it is rather a way of life sustained by an unmerited divine gift.

6

Faith and Justice

In the 1970s and early 1980s, the Canadian Catholic bishops published a series of bold pastoral statements, based on the prophetic spirit of the Gospel, that summoned Catholics to become radical critics of society and ardent agents of social change. The bishops did not influence the majority of Canadian Catholics: most of them probably never had occasion to read the pastoral statements. Yet these texts had a profound influence upon a minority of Catholics, especially members of religious congregations, persons related to community development, and theologians teaching ethics and social justice in schools and universities. It is impossible to understand the evolution of practical theology in Quebec without attention to these episcopal documents.

THE OPTION FOR THE POOR

Because these documents are not widely known and because they no longer represent the teaching of the Canadian Catholic bishops, I wish to mention two statements that deserve to be remembered. The first one, published by the bishops in 1976, is entitled "From Words to Action: On Christian Political and Social Responsibilities." It contains this paragraph:

> As disciples of Christ, all of us have the responsibility to play a role in the creation of the social order based on justice. We stand in the biblical tradition of the prophets of Israel (Amos, Jeremiah, Isaiah) for whom to know God is to seek justice for the disinherited, the poor and the oppressed. The same Spirit of God that came upon the prophets filled Jesus of Nazareth ... In the light of

> that Spirit he announced that he was the message of the prophets come true – "the good news to the poor" and "liberty to the oppressed" (Lk 4:18, 19) … For the Christian community this struggle for justice is not an optional activity. It is integral to bringing the Gospel to the world.[1]

In the same statement, the bishops recognize that many Catholics are socially engaged as workers, thinkers, teachers, and activists. Then they add,

> Unfortunately, those who are committed to this Christian way of life are presently a minority in the life of the Catholic community. Yet this minority is significant because it is challenging the whole Church to live the Gospel message by serving the needs of the people.[2]

The statement then proposes six guidelines for an evangelical way of being socially engaged: (1) recognizing the Gospel's call for social justice, (2) modifying our affluent lifestyle, (3) listening to the victims of injustice, (4) denouncing injustice in our communities, (5) collaborating to change the causes of injustice, and (6) assisting the poor and oppressed.

My second example is the bishops' statement "Ethical Reflections on the Economic Crisis," published in 1982, when Canada was experiencing an economic recession. Again, the bishops refer to the Gospel as the principle that guides their critical social message.

> The principle … has to do with the preferential option for the poor, the afflicted and the oppressed. In the tradition of the prophets, Jesus dedicated his ministry to bringing "good news to the poor" and "liberty to the oppressed." As Christians we are called to follow Jesus by identifying with the victims of injustice, by analyzing the dominant attitudes and structures that cause human suffering and by actively supporting the poor and oppressed in their struggles to transform society.[3]

One of the conclusions reached by the bishops is the following:

> This option calls for economic policies which realize that the needs of the poor have priority over the wants of the rich; that the rights of workers are more important than the maximization

of profits; that the participation of marginalized groups has precedence over the preservation of a system that excludes them.[4]

Readers of chapter 4 on Jacques Grand'Maison may have been startled by the bold criticism of society made by this theologian in the name of Christian faith, yet in the light of the bishops' radical social teaching, neither the content nor the tone of Grand'Maison's polemical writings is surprising.

From where did the Canadian bishops get these radical ideas? It was not from Vatican Council II. The Council had advocated a liberal reformism. The influential bishops and theologians at the Council came from the industrialized Western societies that were prospering, thanks to the success of regulated capitalism and the welfare state. Implicit in the conciliar document *Gaudium et Spes* was the hope that the system that had made these societies wealthy could be extended to other continents and help the poor nations to prosper economically.

This perspective was not shared by the bishops of Latin America. In 1968, three years after the end of the Council, the Latin American bishops, assembled at Medellin, Colombia, produced a set of documents that looked upon the global economic system from the margin, from the perspective of the poor nations, and found it gravely wanting. The bishops defined the "the option for the poor," founded upon the Gospel, as the twofold commitment (1) to look upon society and culture from the perspective of the poor and the powerless and (2) to give public witness in support of their struggle for freedom and participation.[5] Rereading the Gospel in dialogue with liberation theology, the bishops extended their solidarity to the masses of the poor and looked upon the Latin American continent from their perspective. According to their analysis, Latin America was caught in a global economic system that enriched the centre in the North at the expense of the periphery in the South. The bishops offered support to the poor and powerless in their struggle for greater justice.[6]

The teaching of the Latin America bishops at Medellin had considerable influence in the Catholic Church. It made more specific the message of Paul VI in his encyclical *Populorum Progressio* of 1967, it affected the statement "Justice in the World" made in 1971 by the World Synod of Bishops held in Rome,[7] and it found expression in John Paul II's encyclical *Laborem Exercens* of 1981, announcing the

Church's solidarity with workers and the poor struggling for justice. This is what he wrote:

> To achieve social justice ... there is need for ever new movements of solidarity of workers and with workers ... whenever it is called for by the social degrading ... or exploitation of workers and by growing areas of poverty and even hunger. The Church is firmly committed to this cause, for it considers it to be its mission, its service, a proof of fidelity to Christ, so that it can truly be "the Church of the poor."[8]

Before reporting how "the option for the poor" was interpreted by activists and theologians in Quebec, I wish to mention the interruption this principle produced in my own life. In the 1970s, while I was studying sociology, I began to look at Canada and the world from the perspective of the poor, the unemployed, the Native peoples, and other groups suffering discrimination. I began to realize that the dominant culture reconciles people with society as it is and makes the marginalized groups almost invisible. The ideology that blesses the present order and hides its victims appears to most people simply as common sense. To discover the truth, to decipher the cover-up, to recognize the sinister side of our world is a troubling experience. Yet the option for the poor, as I mentioned above, is not simply a new *blick* on the world; it is also an activist principle calling for solidarity with the people pushed to the bottom. The option for the poor demands that one resituate oneself in society and in the Church.

In a small book I wrote in the 1980s, *Compassion and Solidarity*,[9] I showed that this option was based on a new religious experience and fostered a new spirituality. I recognized that prayer, piety, and theology are vulnerable to the dominant ideology that renders the victims of society invisible. Even the great Catholic mystics who yearned to be united to God were not greatly troubled by the suffering inflicted upon the people by oppression and wars.[10] The dark night of the soul they went through was the recognition of their unworthiness and their distance from God. For many Christians today, the option for the poor produces a different dark night of the soul: their faith in God is shaken by the endless suffering of others, the genocides, the wars, the manipulated famines, and the structured inequalities that damage innocent people. Can God be trusted when innocent children are bombed and burned? Many of us prefer to live restlessly, disturbed by this troubling question, rather than find rest in a facile answer. The option for the poor does not allow us to find peace in God while others are starving, humiliated, and dying young. In this dark night, some Christians lose their faith. Moving into the light of day demands a new spirituality, the quest for a blessed restlessness, a worship of praise and lamentation, a religious experience of peace and perplexity. I have called this "dancing with a wounded leg." God consoles and hurts us at the same time: God consoles us by embracing us in love and hurts us by reminding us of the affliction imposed upon our brothers and sisters. The more firmly we believe that God is love, the more troubled we are in our faith by the killing fields of the world.

I have made these brief observations because the option for the poor has occasionally been accused of being a political commitment, unrelated to the spiritual message of Jesus. While this option does involve a particular approach to the political order, it is grounded in the life and the words of Jesus and sustained by a spiritual yearning. Catholics in Quebec, as we shall see, have developed this topic in their own way.

What the option for the poor means for the theological self-understanding of women we shall see in the next chapter.

The option for the poor became part of Catholic social teaching in Canada and other parts during the 1970s and the early 1980s. After that date, the Quebec bishops continued to endorse it every year in their Labour Day statements on the first of May.[11] Yet from the 1980s on, Catholic social teaching became reformist, as it had been prior to 1970, providing Catholics with universal ethical principles, such as the dignity of the human person and the priority of the common good, to help them make a critical evaluation of their society and take an active part in reforming it. The debate between the option for the poor and the reformist approach to justice has been most lively among Quebec Catholics.

PLURAL RESPONSES IN QUEBEC

In the document "A Society to be Transformed" of 1977, Canadian bishops point to three different ways in which Canadian Catholics, and Quebecers in particular, actively involve themselves for social justice.

> Some will choose to continue reforming our present capitalist system in the light of the Gospel. Others will choose to participate in socialist movements, trying to reconcile them with the teachings of Jesus. And still others, rejecting these options, will become involved in searching for some alternative socio-economic order based on Gospel principles.[12]

(1) The first group refers to Catholics who favour a regulated capitalist economy, framed by government policy, welfare legislation, and public respect for labour unions. In Quebec of the 1960s and 1970s, social democracy of this kind was the aim of the Liberal Party and, after its foundation, the Parti Québécois. Because the Quebec government initiated and supported economic development, Quebecers referred to their economy as Québec, Inc. Social democracy of this kind corresponded to the teaching of *Mater et Magistra*, Pope John XXIII's encyclical of 1961. Many Catholics, urged by their faith and the love of justice, supported the reform policies of either one of these two political parties. Well-known among them was Claude Ryan, a brilliant layman, at one time a leader of Catholic Action, who joined the Liberal Party and became its leader from 1978 to 1982. Other prominent Catholics supported the Parti Québécois. Louis O'Neill, a learned Catholic priest, joined this political party, became an elected member of the National Assembly, and officiated as Minister of Cultural Affairs between 1976 and 1981. He was a well-known personality: in 1956, he and Gérard Dion, also a priest, had published the manifesto "L'immoralité politique dans la Province de Québec," that denounced the authoritarian style of the Duplessis regime.[13] Jacques Couture, a Jesuit, was elected as a member of the National Assembly for the Parti Québécois and became Minister of Labour and subsequently of Immigration between 1976 and 1980. After some hesitation, unsure of whether political life was part of his vocation, Fernand Dumont accepted the invitation of the Parti Québécois to become Deputy Minister of Cultural Affairs, responsible for *le Livre blanc* on Quebec's linguistic policy, known as Bill 101.

Claude Ryan and Louis O'Neill published important theological reflections on the relation of faith and justice. On a subsequent page I shall make a few observations on Claude Ryan's book *Mon testament spirituel*, published shortly before his death.

(2) The second group mentioned by the bishops was Catholics committed to socialism. In the 1970s Marxism had a strong cultural

presence in Quebec: it was taught in high schools and colleges, and many young people became members of radical political organizations. Radical Catholics involved in political action joined the Christian-Marxist network “Politisés chrétiens,” the purpose of which was to sustain the members in their Christian faith and root their activities in the Gospel.[14] According to Yves Vaillancourt, one of the founders of the network, they regarded Marxism simply as a sociology of oppression and thus a scientific guide for political action, while they rejected the Marxist deterministic theory of history and instead put their trust in God’s liberating presence to humanity.

The network was founded in 1974 and closed down in 1982. It had been challenged by Catholic groups committed to the option for the poor. These Catholics argued that Marxism focused exclusively on the struggle of the working class, thus paying no attention to the subjugation of women and the plight of the poor, the unemployed, and the racially despised, such as the Native peoples. These Catholic groups wanted the Church to become “l’Église populaire,” extending its solidarity to the poor and marginalized.[15]

(3) This takes us to the third group mention by the bishops. These Catholics thought that justice was not served by capitalism nor by any known form of socialism. What was needed was a cultural and societal transformation that would allow all people to work, live in dignity, and share the goods they produced. Since such a global social project was out of reach, urgently needed in the present was creative activity of people on the community level, devising self-help institutions, setting up offices to assist minorities, engaging in projects to satisfy local needs, and creating alternative models of economic development. These Catholics supported *le mouvement communautaire*, a term used in Quebec to refer to the movement of people involved in community development and the social economy. These Catholics believed that, at this time, social change must be promoted from the bottom up.

To clarify the intellectual and theological dimensions of the struggle for greater justice, the theological faculty of Laval University, assisted by CAPMO (Carrefour de pastorale en monde ouvrier), organized a conference in 1991 to commemorate the centennial of Leo XIII’s encyclical *Rerum Novarum*. At this occasion 700 persons from all parts of Quebec came together to reflect theologically on their society, which in the late 1980s had been increasingly invaded by economic and cultural neo-liberalism.[16] The participants agreed that they had to give more thought to the relation of faith to economic life. A group of them set up the network "Les journées sociales" to organize meetings held over a long weekend every two years, bringing together Catholic activists from all over Quebec to discuss the economic challenges of their society in the light of the Catholic faith. We shall deal with this more radical current further on.

CLAUDE RYAN

Outstanding among the reform-minded Catholics was Claude Ryan, a gifted intellectual who regarded his entry into politics as a vocation. He wanted government to promote social justice, from the top down as it were. Among public personalities in Quebec he was altogether unusual: he was a man of prayer, and whenever possible, went to daily Mass. In his political life he sought to apply Catholic social teaching. He was an enigma to English Canadians because he was a federalist and a nationalist at the same time: he wanted Canada to reform its Constitution, making it recognize the people of Quebec as a nation. Pierre Elliot Trudeau opposed him because he was a nationalist; and the Quebec sovereignists opposed him because he was a federalist. Since Ryan proposed his political ideas in a very moral tone, unusual in public life, he was often caricatured as a priest. He was actually a great gentleman, respectful of people with whom he did not see eye to eye. We occasionally met as speakers on the same panel, and even though I politely disagreed with him, there was a warm feeling between us as brothers in the same faith.

Claude Ryan was well educated in theology: he had read the great authors such as Congar, de Lubac, and Rahner who had prepared the theological renewal of Vatican Council II. Yet the theologian and spiritual guide he appreciated above all was the nineteenth-century English sage John Henry Newman, made a cardinal late in his life. When Ryan retired from political life, he taught a course on Catholic social thought at McGill University; he was also invited by various Catholic groups to lecture on the relation of religion and politics and the decline of the Catholic Church in Quebec. Before he died, he published a selection of these lectures in *Mon testament spirituel.*[17] I wish to review what he says about the relation between Christian faith and political involvement.

According to the traditional distinction, which Ryan accepts, the Church deals with matters spiritual and the State with matters temporal: the two institutions belong to different spheres. In the regime of Christendom, which, according to Ryan, remained operative in Quebec until the Quiet Revolution, the bishops had the authority to intervene in the political sphere. Today, thanks to a progressive historical evolution, in keeping with the teaching of Jesus, the bishops, deprived of their political authority, have learnt to respect the freedom of society to regulate itself. Today the Catholic hierarchy stays out of politics. Yet this does not mean, Ryan continues, that Christian faith no longer makes a contribution to the well-being of society. Whether they be professional politicians or not, Christian men and women are committed by their faith to an ethical vision of society and a political effort to reform society accordingly. In this engagement they are helped by the Church's social teaching. In a secular society such as Quebec, marked as it is by a hostile memory of the past, Catholics, including Catholic politicians, do not mention in public that their political convictions are guided by their faith. Ryan remarks that only after his death did Canadians discover that Pierre Elliot Trudeau had been deeply attached to his Catholic faith. In his public speeches he had never said a word of his religious commitment. Ryan argues that in a political democracy a Catholic in government may have to pass laws contrary to the Church's teaching, if they correspond to the ethical reasoning of the majority. The Catholic politician may not impose his religious convictions upon society.

Ryan holds that the political order as part of God's creation deserves respect and that becoming professionally involved in politics is, for some Christians, a vocation, a calling to be of service to the common good. He strongly opposes the widespread cynicism in regard to politicians. In every society, he argues, one finds two distinct political currents, one inclined to protect the orderly achievements of the past and oppose social reforms, and the other eager to improve the institutions of society and welcome social change. In both of these currents are Christians working for social justice. Ryan thinks that the traditional British two-party system, inherited by Canada and Quebec (but challenged in both), provides stability and an opening to gradual reform that avoids the political splintering that paralyses a number of other societies. Catholics in both of these parties will do their best so that the universal ethical principles of Catholic social teaching will be respected by their society.

These universal principles include the high dignity of the human person, the priority of the common good, respect for the environment, the equality of citizens before the law, and the principle of solidarity. From these and other universal principles, political thinkers derive concrete institutional proposals that would make these ethical norms operative in the lives of the people. Catholic politicians will do their best to move society closer these ideals. Ryan is aware that even with the best of intentions, governments are heirs to conditions created in the past and that their *marge de manœuvre* is limited. Relying on the same principles, Catholics as conscientious citizens will take part in the public debate, try to influence public opinion, and, in many cases, support or even join the political party that they trust.

The recent statements made by the Quebec bishops, Ryan argues, had little public influence because they were formulated in general terms and did not speak to the debate actually taking place among politicians. Uncomfortable with the option for the poor endorsed by the Canadian bishops in the 1970s and early 1980s, Ryan offers a liberal interpretation of this principle. The option for the poor, he argues, reminds governments of their duty to take care of the people in need. He interprets the option for the poor articulated by the Medellin Conference of 1968 as a principle that obliges the rich countries of the North to come to the aid of the poorer countries of the South.[18] Ryan was unwilling to recognize that at the Medellin Conference the Latin American bishops challenged the unregulated free market system with its centre in the North. Ryan had no sympathy for the radical social ethics emerging in the Church at that time. Yet he does mention that as a member of a government committee investigating the conditions of poverty in Quebec, he had been impressed by the help offered to the poor by engaged Catholics, including sisters, brothers, and priests of religious congregations.

JUSTICE FROM THE BOTTOM UP

Ryan was an admirable witness of the mainstream of Catholic social teaching. Yet his approach was quite different from that followed by the Canadian bishops in their pastoral statement on economic justice of 1983. In it they started their critical reflection, not by naming universal ethical principles, but by listening to the victims of their society. This is how they presented the steps of their methodology:[19]

1 Being present with and listening to the experiences of the poor, the marginalized, the oppressed in our society (e.g. the unemployed,

the working poor, the welfare poor, exploited workers, native peoples ... racial and cultural minorities, etc.);
2 Developing a critical analysis of the economic, political and social structures that cause this human suffering;
3 Making judgments in the light of Gospel principles and the social teachings of the Church concerning social values and practices;
4 Stimulating creative thought and action regarding alternative visions and models for social and economic development; and
5 Acting in solidarity with popular groups in their struggles to transform economic, political and social structures that cause social and economic injustices.

The Canadian bishops had become acquainted with this methodology through their dialogue with Catholic groups and centres committed to the option for the poor. This methodology was applied by Development and Peace, an organization founded by the Canadian bishops in 1969, in response to Paul VI's encyclical *Populorum Progressio*, to offer assistance to the self-development of the poor populations in the South. The same methodology was applied by Montreal's Centre pastoral en milieu ouvrier (CPMO) that listened to working people, helped them to analyze the cause of their frustrations, and supported them in their struggle for greater justice. The educational centre l'Entraide missionnaire in Montreal introduced religious congregations and their missionaries to this methodology, helping them to attain a critical understanding of the poor regions of the world, in which they practiced their ministry. The institute of popular education in Montreal, le Centre St Pierre, explored in conversation with its participants what the social message of the Gospel meant for their lives and for society as a whole. Le Centre justice et foi, listening attentively to the suffering of people, engaged in social analysis of the troubled world in the light of faith and reason: it published the review *Relations* to promote a critical culture in Quebec, and the bulletin *Vivre ensemble* concerned with justice for immigrants and refugees.

In their pastoral statement of 1983 the Canadian bishops made the interesting observation that to restrict the ethical debate on the economy to a choice between capitalism and socialism is to stifle the social imagination.[20] Because at this time no power on Earth is capable of setting up a humane economic system on the global scale, groups of imaginative people involve themselves in making society more just from the bottom up. The bishops refer to these efforts as creating "alternative models of economic development."

I wish to offer a description, however brief, of what Quebecers call *le mouvement communautaire* – in English, community development and community economic development.[21] This social engagement reveals the creativity of people belonging to the third sector of society: the unemployed, part-time workers, occasional workers, and underpaid workers – men and women pushed to the margin of society. The co-operative effort to improve the conditions of their lives is at the same time a protest against the existing economic order that has no place for them.

Community development produces an ever-expanding network of self-help groups, co-operatives, and non-profit organizations. Some of these groups have a political purpose: they are formed to exert pressure on city hall to protect a neighbourhood park or to stage protest marches against government policies harmful to the poor, destructive of the environment, or indifferent to international justice. Other groups have a social purpose: responding to local needs, they set up daycare centres, shelters for abused women, educational opportunities for the unemployed, or storefront offices counselling refugees and new immigrants. Some other groups have an economic purpose: responding to the needs of the community, they set up co-operatives and loan associations, and jointly run stores, community kitchens, backyard gardens, and other collective initiatives. Some of these co-operative enterprises become very large and employ many people.

In Quebec, community economic development (also called the social economy or *l'économie solidaire*) has become an extensive network of enterprises that produce goods and services for society and provide paid employment, yet operate according to democratic principles, at odds with capitalist practice.[22] Because of a long history of co-operatism and the support of the provincial government, the social economy in Quebec constitutes a significant sector of the economy. According to an estimate in 2006, it includes 6,000 enterprises, provides between 7 and 8 percent of the Gross National Product, and employs 120,000 people.[23] While the social economy is unable to transform society as a whole, it transforms the lives of a vast number of people. It fosters a culture of critical thinking and innovative practices that may lay the foundation for a new political movement.

Professional and lay theologians have reflected on this socio-economic movement in society. In the 1990s, the theological faculty of the University of Montreal introduced a course leading to a Certificat en pratiques sociales, to create leaders that promote and facilitate social involvement and economic co-operation. The faculty also set up le Centre de théologie et d'éthique contextuelles québécoises, which makes the option for the poor the starting point of scholarly research and reflection. The first team of professors responsible for it included Lise Baroni, Michel Beaudin, Denise Couture, and Jean-François Roussel. In this context I also wish to mention Vivian Labrie, an intellectual turned activist, an heir of social Catholicism, and the organizer and spokesperson of le Collectif pour un Quebec sans pauvreté, located in Quebec City, an organization that has an impact on political life in Quebec.[24]

In their pastoral statement of 1983 the Canadian bishops supported the social engagement of Catholic groups and centres critical of capitalist society. While in subsequent years, the bishops dropped their radical social teaching, Catholics committed to the option for the poor continued their public engagement and their theological reflection. In Quebec, their activities constituted a vital movement. In the cities, towns, and rural areas, many Catholics supported *le mouvement communautaire*, either by participating in it, by offering financial support, by recommending it to the Church, or by demonstrating its importance for society. Militant Catholics from all over the province attended "Les journées sociales," mentioned in a previous paragraph. This movement in the Church was often called the Catholic Left. Associated with it were Protestant Christians who shared the same perspective.

MICHEL BEAUDIN

Michel Beaudin is a theologian mentioned in the previous chapter as the author of a book on Christology. His subsequent research and a series of articles offer critical examination of classical liberalism and today's neo-liberal societies in the light of the Christian message.[25] That he never had the time to collect and edit these articles as a book is regrettable.

The first point Beaudin makes in his investigations is that Christian theology is obliged by its principles to concern itself with economics, even if this has rarely been the case. Because implicit in the Gospel is an anthropology, theologians must test whether or to what extent this concept of human life is in harmony with the anthropology implicit in the present economic system. Even if many economists believe that their science is independent of any philosophical presuppositions, it is hard to deny that the free market system presupposes that humans are independent actors, each inclined to promote his or her own advantage. Many scientists believe that increasing one's wealth and consumption is as natural as hunger for food and thirst for water, even though anthropological studies comparing different cultures have shown that this is not the case. Tribal cultures, traditional societies, and capitalist economies define humanity in different ways. The theologian is therefore obliged, Beaudin argues, to test whether the concept of the human revealed in the Gospel is in keeping with that operative in contemporary society.

Beaudin's second point is not obvious to most observers. He argues, as we shall see, that economic liberalism, the theory underlying the unregulated market system, has acquired something like a sacred character: it is revered as the truth and the power that will enrich the world and rescue people from poverty.

Studying the origins of economic liberalism in Great Britain, Beaudin finds that its advocates, most famous among them Adam Smith, praised individualism and utilitarianism and sought to undermine the institution of social solidarity proper to the traditional society. They regarded the market as the humanizing institution that transformed the selfishness of its participants into a power favouring the common good. Market competition obliges factory and store owners to keep the price of their goods low enough so that customers will come to buy them; the same self-interest also obliges them to pay their workers a subsistence wage to keep them healthy and their arms strong. The law of supply and demand works like "a hidden hand" producing an equilibrium of wealth in society.

I read Adam Smith many years ago. I remember a remark of his that confirms Beaudin's idea that economic liberalism exercises an anti-solidarity power. If the owner of a clothing store, visited by a cousin, offers to sell him the coat he needs at a reduced price for family reasons, the owner thinks he is doing a good thing, while in fact he harms society by interrupting the logic of the market system.

Beaudin is acquainted with the work of Karl Polanyi. At one time he was associated with the Karl Polanyi Institute of Montreal. From Polanyi's *The Great Transformation,* Beaudin adopts two far-reaching theses. First, in pre-modern society, the economy was not a system distinct from people's social relations; it was in fact a society-building activity. People were motivated to work not to increase their profit, but to confirm their bond to their community and preserve their respected place in it. Here work was embedded in social relations. The capitalist market, Polanyi has shown, rips the worker out of his community; his work no longer confirms his social relations; his new location estranges him from the inherited values that gave meaning to his life. The free market system, Polanyi writes, "disembeds" workers from their social matrix. That they were exploited by the industrial owner, Marx already recognized; what Marx overlooked, Polanyi argues, is the human loss, the disruption of social solidarity. As the free market expanded, society lost its autonomy and became increasingly dependent on an economy that had no intrinsic bond to it.

Polanyi's second thesis is that from the second part of the nineteenth century on, a counter-movement started in Britain that sought to safeguard the integrity of society through the institution of new laws. This movement supported laws that protected the land, the health of the people, and the workers employed in the industries, as well as providing help for the poor. Polanyi describes in great detail the movement that eventually aspired to social democracy, in part in response to the political pressure of working people. Polanyi published his famous book in 1942, predicting that this countermovement would produce social democracy in Britain and the West after the war. The movement was supported by the economic ideas of John Maynard Keynes. This great economist recognized with Marx that capitalism was an unstable system, moving from boom to bust; yet he differed from Marx by proposing that government stabilize the economy and guide the market so that it becomes an instrument serving the common good of society. Polanyi was right: after the war Keynesian capitalism and the welfare state flourished in Western societies. What Polanyi did not foresee was the turn to neoliberalism at the end of the 1970s that quickly became the single global system, promoting its profit-oriented individualism and undermining the traditions and institutions of solidarity worldwide.

Beaudin insists that the Gospel, calling humanity to love, justice, and joint responsibility, stands against the anti-solidarity thrust of economic and cultural neo-liberalism. Because the anthropologies of the Gospel and of neo-liberalism are incompatible, Beaudin argues, Christians must practice resistance in contemporary society. This resistance implies support for social movements that try to change society from below, *le mouvement communautaire*, the social economy, the efforts to protect the environment, the world social forums, and many other social endeavours. Again, following an inspiration of Polanyi, Beaudin recognizes the beneficent cultural impact of the social economy: in it, people's daily work re-embeds them in their social relations, creating a strong sense of belonging. The social economy and the other social movements promote a critical culture and generate circles of social solidarity that may one day allow the construction of a movement to transform the whole of society.

Since the neo-liberal economy widens the gap between rich and poor on the global and the local levels, since this economy produced the financial crisis of 2008 that cost tax-payers billions of dollars, and since this economy causes a shrinking of the middle classes, it is not easy to explain why governments support this irrational economic system and why ordinary people re-elect governments that damage their own material well-being. Gilles Dostaler, a Quebec economist and historian of economics, related the option for neo-liberalism to the death wish that, according to Freud, dwells in the unconscious of humanity.[26] The prominent Quebec scientist and humanist, Pierre Dansereau, lamented the blindness of the policy-makers at the top.

> Like many of my colleagues, I am compelled to be pessimistic. What is happening now, particularly with the emphasis on privatization, is a loosening of controls. And without controls, we will not be able to clean up the environment ... nor re-establish greater justice in the distribution of the most basic resources ... Thinking only in terms of the needs of production moves in a direction contrary to evolution.[27]

The scientist and humanist Riccardo Petrella, a frequent visitor in Quebec, tells his audiences that the continuing commitment to neo-liberal policies, despite the economic and ecological crises they generate, is the product of stupidity.[28]

Michel Beaudin offers a different explanation. To gain a better understanding of industrialists and businessmen he has interviewed about thirty francophone members of the economic elite in the area of Montreal, asking them how they relate their ethical values to the competitive world of the economy.[29] These businessmen recognize that they do not apply the ethics they practice in their families to their daily activities to make their firms more successful. Beaudin reports that a few of these men are uneasy about the ethics implicit in their competitive struggles, while the great majority firmly believes that the competitive race made possible by the free market system is the force that increases the wealth of the world, makes human life more healthy and more comfortable, and will in the long run eliminate poverty. These men think of themselves as privileged actors in support of human evolution.

The interviews with these leaders in business convinced Beaudin that their trust in the free market had a sacred character: it gave meaning to their lives, summoned forth their best energies, and could not be shaken by any counter-evidence. They recognized that the competitive market damages some people and excludes others from the necessities of life, yet they interpreted these by-products as sacrifices necessary to move the world forward in the direction of progress. The commitment to neo-liberal policies, Beaudin concluded, was a faith, a belief system, a sacred trust in a better future, even though it undermined human solidarity and produced masses of victims. Beaudin's analysis offers an explanation of why capitalism has such a long life, why, after each depression and the brief recognition of its cause – the detachment of the market system from ethical norms – this recognition is soon forgotten and society re-embraces liberal capitalism. A religious conviction, even if idolatrous, cannot be easily shaken. Beaudin's analysis also explains why low-income people, the unemployed, and the poor often vote for governments that remain indifferent to their plight: they believe that the rich have the sacred key for resolving the economic crises; the rich know how to succeed in business and will therefore be able to make society succeed.

If this analysis is correct, then all people committed to social justice can do, be they religious or secular, is to practice resistance. For this reason Beaudin involved himself in Les journées sociales, the above-mentioned network of the Catholic Left. The talks given at these biennial meetings and the debates that follow them have been published in a series of small books, bearing witness to the closeness of theology to people's daily problems and concerns.[30]

GUY PAIEMENT

A gifted spiritual leader of the Catholic Left, the Jesuit Guy Paiement, a doctor of theology, chose not to become a university professor, but to become identified with *le mouvement communautaire* and reflect on the meaning of the Christian message from that location. He was an original thinker, capable of expressing in persuasive prose the redemptive power of the Gospel for people struggling for respect and social justice in their society. He was an inventive activist who devised ever new collective projects to give public witness to the social message of divine revelation.

In this chapter I wish to mention only one of Guy Paiement's projects. When Cardinal Archbishop Marc Ouellet held the International Eucharistic Congress of 2008 in Quebec City, many socially engaged Catholics felt that this celebration of the Eucharist's ritual dimension, designed to revive the traditional Catholic identity, failed to recognize that this ritual had lost its relevance in Quebec society. To promote an alternative approach, Guy Paiement asked several groups of engaged Catholics to write a text giving the reasons why the Eucharist was of importance to them, texts he subsequently published in the form of a booklet. In his introduction he wrote that the Christian identity is not so much a treasure that has been lost and must be recovered, as a way of life initiated by the self-giving of Jesus, a way of life of his followers that, ever new, leads the Church into the future. For our groups, he wrote, the Eucharist is like a birth, giving new life, making us walk along a new path. He entitled the booklet *Témoins d'une naissance*.[31]

The booklet is filled with ideas, traditional and new, that see the Eucharist as the celebration of the Church's social mission. We are reminded that for St Thomas the consecrated bread was a step toward the *res*, the completion of the sacrament, the presence of Christ in the assembled community. The Eucharist is the sacrament of inclusion, we read in the booklet, a message overlooked in canon law, preventing as it does some Catholics from receiving communion and excluding women altogether from the priesthood. Even though Jesus instituted the Eucharist at a round table, a symbol of the Church as a fraternal community, the Church eventually decided to celebrate the Eucharist as a symbol of its hierarchical division, with the laity in the nave and the clergy in the apse. According to some texts, the Eucharist celebrates human labour, the production of bread and wine, correcting the class structure of society that put labour at the bottom. Other texts note that the Eucharistic liturgy invites everyone to join the meal with Jesus, a judgment on the sinful world where vast numbers of people go hungry. Since the fourth gospel replaces the bread and wine at the last supper by the washing of the feet, many believers associate the Eucharist with the service to the poor. Since Jesus has told us that he is present in the poor, some authors writing in the booklet confess that their work with and for the poor for greater justice has Eucharistic meaning for them. Others see in the Eucharist an eschatological sign, anticipating the banquet of the promised future, that reconciles the entire human family in the Spirit. Celebrating the Mass is for some a judgment on exclusion, hatred, and wars and a proclamation of God's universal solidarity. These rich theological interpretations make it hard to understand why the Catholic Church from the late Middle Ages on has made the mode of Christ's presence, transubstantiation, the all-important issue of the Eucharist.

ANDRÉ BEAUCHAMP

Theologians who made an option for the poor have debated among themselves how to relate their theology to the issue of ecology. They are troubled by some ecological movements that focus on the efforts of individuals to protect their natural environment by recycling their garbage, monitoring their use of water, and avoiding the employment of non-degradable utensils, without any analysis of the major political and industrial policies that destroy the natural environment. Personal discipline is useful and has an important cultural meaning, yet without a critical look at the larger picture, ecological concern can distract people from attention to the sources of the environmental crisis. Added to these unresolved problems is the political tension between Red and Green, between socialists eager for jobs and industrial growth and greens opposed to industrial development harmful to the environment or even supporting limits to growth. In Canada, the labour-oriented New Democratic Party does not see eye to eye with the Green Party, which is preoccupied with protecting the environment.

An important researcher who tries to resolve this conflict is André Beauchamp, a Catholic priest and a scholar, who has worked for many years in the Ministry of the Environment of the Quebec government. In this capacity he has co-operated with natural scientists and produced reports recommending ecological policies to the Ministry. He is the author of many books, some explaining the environmental problems to ordinary people[32] and others, in a theological vein, developing an ethics and a spirituality for the ecological movement.[33] Beauchamp started very early to warn the government and the public of the impending environmental crisis.

The Church has been slow in acknowledging the ecological concern. Beauchamp notes that John XXIII's encyclical *Pacem in Terris* of 1963 did not mention it. It was his successor, Paul VI, who first raised the issue. The subsequent popes, John Paul II and Benedict XVI, made several important statements on the threat to the natural environment and the ecological responsibility of the human community. Still, Beauchamp argues that the ecclesiastical magisterium has never made a profound study of the present crisis, nor faced the theological issues raised by it.[34] He gives three examples of this reluctance. First, official Church teaching has refused to rethink the biblical story in Genesis that presents divine creation as complete and final. Second, this teaching has not questioned the anthropocentric interpretation of Genesis nor recognized that humans are also part of nature, borne by it and respectful of its integrity. Third, this teaching has never taken seriously the explosion of the world population beyond the capacity of the world's natural resources, hiding behind its prohibition of birth control.

Important in the context of this chapter is that as Beauchamp continued his research, he arrived at the conclusion that the ecological movement must go hand in hand with the struggle for social justice. He reminds people who find this difficult to accept that this is not a totally new discovery. The Brundtland Report produced for the United Nations in 1987 recognizes the interrelation between the ecological crisis and the present orientation of industrial development.

> Until recently, the planet was a large world in which human activities and their effects were neatly compartmentalized within nations, within sectors (energy, agriculture, trade), and within broad areas of concern (environment, economics, social). These compartments have begun to dissolve. This applies in particular to the various global 'crises' that have seized public concern, particularly over the past decade. These are not separate crises: an environmental crisis, a development crisis, an energy crisis. They are all one.[35]

André Beauchamp insists that over twenty years later the need for collaboration between Green and Red has become more urgent. At Les journées sociales of 2011 on the interrelation between social justice and ecological responsibility, Beauchamp, the invited main speaker, offered a series of reflections to show that the two concerns belong together.[36] The limited natural resources of the earth have been unjustly distributed almost from the beginning: the powerful have always taken more than their share. The poor people living on the land were able to survive thanks to their agricultural labour. Yet their subsistence economy was destroyed by the arrival of capitalist production. Now entrepreneurs bought stretches of land to produce food for profit. The people were chased from the land; they drifted into the cities where they became the exploited proletariat devoid of any rights. Since the logic of capitalism demands the constant increase of production, it had a destructive impact on the natural environment: it destroyed the forests, it polluted rivers, and it exhausted the soil. Yet it took a long time before the destructive effect became a dramatic threat and an even longer time before people realized what was happening. Beauchamp said,

> What humans have done to nature by dominating it in despotic and violent fashion, man has done to woman, rich to poor, capitalist to workers, white to black or Aboriginal, north to south, etc. In this regard, the ecological cause and the social cause are one and the same. What is different is the level of analysis.

Capitalism is not the only force that damages the environment. The communist regimes of the Soviet bloc, which had the power to control production, lacked the necessary ecological consciousness. Their industries devastated the earth. In other parts of the world, poor people struggling to survive spoil and deforest their environment. Leonardo Boff, Beauchamp recalled, spoke of two cries to which the world must listen: the cry of the poor and the cry of the earth.

As there are economists who think that the world's economic problems can be solved by the sole application of scientific reason, so there are ecologists who hold that resolving the ecological crisis is a purely scientific project. Beauchamp regards this as total blindness. In his books, he shows that our relationship to nature is an ethical and a spiritual challenge. The sciences are necessary to deal with the means to be employed, but the goal of the ecological movement, the motivation for engaging in it, and the virtues required for it to succeed involve a commitment to ethical values and an appropriate spiritual approach to the natural universe. To these issues theology has much to say.[37] Beauchamp recognizes that the emphasis of Christian preaching on human redemption or even the saving of souls tended to place the human at the centre and look upon the natural environment simply as a resource for human survival. Having neglected reflection on God's creation in the past, the Christian community must now renew its theology, recognize in nature a reflection of God's beauty, and develop a spirituality that prompts us to be disciplined and make the sacrifices needed to make the Earth flourish.

I was present at a lecture Beauchamp gave at le Centre justice et foi on the threats to the natural environment and the possibility of the extinction of the human race. After the lecture an anxious listener asked him whether God's promise made to humanity in Jesus Christ rules out the possibility of humanity's self-inflicted death. Without the slightest hesitation, Beauchamp said no: the Scriptures do not guarantee our collective survival.

LISE BARONI AND YVONNE BERGERON

The movement of the World Social Forum, started in 2001, encouraged the holding of regional social forums to bring together local groups and individuals engaged in alternative social practices. Inspired by this model, le Centre de théologie et d'éthique contextuelles québécoises and le Réseau œcuménique Justice et paix organized in November 2006 the first Forum québécois: théologie et solidarité, attended by 150 engaged Catholic and Protestant Christians. The participants discussed their common concerns. They spoke of their faith and their loss of faith; they talked about how they perceived their mission and how they related themselves to their Church. Some submitted their thoughts in writing. This collection of personal testimonies became the starting point of theological research and reflection that eventually led to the publication of a substantial book, *L'utopie de la solidarité au Québec*, edited by a committee of five: Lise Baroni, Michel Beaudin, Céline Beaulieu, Yvonne Bergeron, and Guy Côté.[38] One section of the book analyzes the ways in which these Christians related themselves to their Church, a spectrum moving from identification to aloofness. Another section, written by Michel Beaudin, offers the history of the Catholic involvement in social justice movements in Quebec since 1891, the year Leo XIII published his encyclical *Rerum Novarum*. The section I wish to discuss in the following pages deals with the questions

"Where is God?" and "Who is Jesus?"[39] It was authored by Lise Baroni and Yvonne Bergeron.

Baroni and Bergeron, both retired professors of theology, begin their inquiry by reflecting on the experiences of the participants. God had become a problem to most of them. Since the world is moving towards a major crisis and ever greater sectors of the population are made to suffer, words such as divine omnipotence and divine providence are losing their meaning. Many of these Christians are suspicious of theology: the words that sound interesting in the classroom are unrelated to the painful reality of every day. In my own writings I have called this experience "the breakdown of trust": it sends believers into the dark night of the soul where faith is turned into a question mark.[40]

Still, Baroni and Bergeron are able to discern in the experiences of these Christians references to a transcendent dimension. First, they are troubled by the suffering of others, lament the forces that damage human beings, and remain unreconciled to the world as it is. They are inhabited by the conviction that the world should be different; they are haunted by the utopia of a just and egalitarian society, marked by mutuality, the sharing of goods, and the respect for the earth. The outrage over the way things are and the dream of what they ought to be, raises them up to transcend self-seeking and the headaches caused by their personal problems. Second, these Christians find in themselves the energy to repair the world on a level to which they have access. They act, plan, organize, help, teach, or preach to change social conditions so that people will be able to live a life of dignity and discover their creativity. Here again these Christians are lifted out of themselves and their yearning focuses on others. These experiences, Baroni and Bergeron argue, reveal a transcendent dimension in the lives of these Christians. They find themselves internally gripped by a concern of which they are not the authors and which transcends the desire for their own well-being. God is present in their lives.

I wish to add to this that Christians and other people who have this double experience – being deeply disturbed by the suffering of others and driven to act on their behalf – are well aware that this is not a universal experience: a great many people are not moved or touched in the same way. Many good people see poor Amerindians stumbling on the streets of their city without feeling a sting in their heart, without being hurt by the troubling memory of colonial oppression. That some people have the double experience described by Baroni and

Bergeron is not simply due to intelligence and good will; it is due to a gift, granted to some and not to others; it is God's doing.

Who is this God present in human life, the two theologians continue to ask. It is not a heavenly king ruling the world from above, made in the image of human kings, rulers, or presidents. It is the triune God, they argue, the God revealed by Jesus, the caring Originator of history, whose hidden face is revealed in the man of Nazareth and who, as Spirit, touches human minds and hearts throughout the world. God is not the powerful Outsider, but the gracious Insider. The freedom and humility of Jesus teach us to bracket the old ideas of divine omnipotence and divine providence. Human history is not mapped out in the divine mind; on the contrary, because God is present to humans, they are free to create their history. The triune God is the template of human becoming.

The reasons why the two theologians turn to the triune God implicated in human history are the same that prompted theologians like Blondel and Dumont to rethink traditional theism and opt for panentheism, as I put forward in chapter 2.

Baroni and Bergeron also raise the question, "Who is this Jesus?" The testimonies gathered at the *Forum québécois* all referred to him. These Christians had doubts about God, but no doubts about Jesus. They believe that by his words, his life, his death, and his risen presence, Jesus announces a utopia of solidarity, the coming reconciliation of humanity in peace and justice. Believing his messianic promises, these Christians become critics of society as it is and actors against the stream. Baroni and Bergeron show that the faith of these Christians is indeed scriptural: they study the mission of Jesus recorded in the synoptic gospels, following the post-colonial exegesis that situates Jesus in occupied Palestine. I referred to this exegesis in the preceding chapter. The two theologians present Jesus as prophet, as having authority to forgive sins, as humble and silent about himself, as obedient to God's will and therefore free to disobey humans, and as identified with the simple people, caring for them, healing the sick and feeding the hungry, and challenging the religious elites and secular powers, knowing that this will lead to his death. Relying on the fourth gospel, the two theologians affirm that in this concrete lived humanity is made present the invisible God whose name is Love.

In the past, Baroni and Bergeron remark, Christians committed to the option for the poor avoided the word "spirituality"; they were suspicious of the vocabulary of piety, fearing that it would lock them into the old Catholicism from which they wanted to escape. Today this is changing. Discovering the Spirit in their lives, many of them become grateful, rely on God's presence, listen to God's voice and respond to it, developing a spirituality of their own.

7

In Christ neither Male nor Female

The 1960s saw the emergence of a new wave of feminism in North America that had an effect on the Christian Churches, including the Catholic Church. In 1966 two movements of Catholic women were founded in Quebec: Le mouvement des femmes chrétiennes and L'association féminine d'éducation et d'action sociale. In 1967 the Canadian government created the Royal Commission on the Status of Women, which submitted its report, over 500 pages long, to the Canadian parliament in 1970. Among the briefs submitted to the Commission was a statement prepared by the theologian Élisabeth Lacelle in collaboration with her class on women in the Christian tradition at the University of Ottawa.[1] Lacelle was the first professional theologian in French Canada who wrestled with the questions raised by critical feminist reflection in regard to religion in general and Catholicism in particular. In her writings she acknowledges the inspiration she received from the work of American Catholic feminist scholars, in particular the theologian Rosemary Radford Ruether and the exegete Elisabeth Schüssler Fiorenza.

THE EFFORTS OF THE CANADIAN BISHOPS

The reactions of the Canadian bishops to the women's movement have been carefully recorded by Élisabeth Lacelle. As the bishops were preparing their recommendations for the Roman World Synod of 1971, they received a statement from a Catholic women's group in Edmonton, asking them to demand that the Synod make a solemn declaration that men and women were fully members of the Church with equal rights and that the barriers limiting the participation of women in the Church's ministries should be removed. The Canadian bishops were ready to listen to these voices. They invited sixty women, thirty anglophone and thirty francophone, to come to Ottawa for a conference and to write a statement – in fact, two statements, one in English and the other in French – expressing their expectations and aspirations.

Since the bishops wanted to use these statements in their report to the Synod, there was not much time. The statement of the francophone group, chaired by Élisabeth Lacelle, simply posed four questions and expressed three wishes. (1) How will the Church translate the equality of men and women into its teaching on family life and social structures? (2) How will gender equality affect the organization of the diocese and the parish? (3) Can the Church modify the present limitation of ordained priesthood to celibate males? (4) Will the Church recognize the conscience of married couples, especially of women, and modify the rules that currently exclude many Catholics from the Eucharistic liturgy? The three wishes simply expressed in concrete terms how the francophone group would like to see the Church reply to the above questions. The report of the anglophone group formulated its proposals in a different manner, yet the content was the same. Both reports insisted that introducing relations of equality between men and women, even if understood as complementary, would make the Catholic Church more faithful to the Gospel, give it a more radiant public image, and increase its beneficent impact on society as a whole.

At the plenary meeting of the Canadian Catholic Bishops Conference (CCCB) in September of 1971, the bishops received five recommendations summarizing the proposals made by the sixty women: that the Synod declare unequivocally that men and women are full members of the Church with the same rights and privileges, that canon law exclude all barriers against women, that women be able to qualify as ministers in the Church, that the presence of women be encouraged in all church organizations, and that priests be urged to respect the dignity of women when dealing with issues of sexuality and married life. The CCCB almost unanimously accepted the proposal that the delegates to the Synod ask the pope to create a mixed commission, including bishops, priests, and lay and religious men and women, to examine the issue of the place of women in the Church's ministry. At the World Synod in October 1971 Cardinal George Flahiff, archbishop of Winnipeg, delivered the message of the

CCCB. He denounced the discrimination inflicted upon women in the Church, asked the assembled bishops to listen to the "signs of the times," and argued that the traditional arguments against the ordination of women in the Church's ministries had lost their validity.[2]

After 1971 the Canadian bishops continued their dialogue with the two groups of women; they also continued to remind the subsequent World Synods of the need to acknowledge sexist discrimination in the Church and rethink and reform the status of women in the Church. An ardent Canadian spokesman at the Synod of 1983 was Cardinal Louis-Albert Vachon, archbishop of Quebec City. During those years some dioceses in Quebec appointed women to a variety of pastoral positions. A woman became the general secretary of the Assembly of Quebec Bishops. Women were named chancellor, vicar general, chaplain of hospitals and prisons, in charge of parishes, in charge of faith education in dioceses, and so forth. Many women were convinced that Church would come to honour the feminist movement, repent of its inheritance of prejudice and discrimination, and recognize in its teaching and its practice the equality of male and female in Jesus Christ.

The Canadian Catholic women were deeply disappointed that the process of dialogue and reform came to an end. The papal commission on the place of women in the Church's ministry did include four women, yet they were not theologically trained and thus relied on the inherited categories. The conservative stance of the Vatican persuaded some Canadian bishops to become more cautious. In 1983 the Vatican published the new code of canon law confirming the exclusion of women from ordained ministries in the Church. In Quebec progressive bishops continued to appoint women to many pastoral tasks, yet their employment was not the result of an institutional change; it was simply a temporary measure initiated by the good will of the bishop or the parish priest, thus leaving the women in a vulnerable position.

Catholic feminists have reacted to the Church's refusal to listen to them in various ways. In the lecture on feminism in the North American Churches given by Élisabeth Lacelle at le Centre Sèvres, the Jesuit theological faculty in Paris, she distinguished between three different reactions.[3] Some women are leaving the Catholic Church; they may still be believers, yet they see themselves as outsiders. Other women remain Catholics on their own terms, purging the tradition of the symbols of male domination. A third group of women is remaining in the Catholic Church as it is, frustrated by the institutional sexism, yet hoping that feminist insight will eventually lead to the reform of the institution. Despite these different options, the three groups of women respect one another and remain in an ongoing dialogue.

MOVEMENTS AND INSTITUTIONS

Troubled by the vulnerability of the feminist struggle, Lacelle turned to sociological literature to gain a better understanding of social movements. According to Max Weber, reformist movements are started by a leader with prophetic insight, are sometimes supported by great numbers of people, and, under certain conditions, even gain the power to transform the dominant social institutions. Reformist movements disappear when they have successfully effected institutional change.[4] A contemporary Italian social thinker, Francesco Alberino, has expanded Weber's relatively brief proposals in an original manner. Alberino explores in particular the impact of the prophetic insight, the starting point of the movement. Lacelle quotes this paragraph from Alberino's study.

> The starting point is not a simple intuitive act, an extraordinary emotion which lasts a minute, an hour, or a day … Instead, it makes us discover that our life is founded on an error, that the world is not as we believed it to be, and that we are capable of transforming it. The starting point is the renunciation of what is known, the leap into the unknown: it is both death and rebirth, an irreversible mutation that influences all future behaviour.[5]

Alberino tries to show that this emerging insight attracts and transforms people: it generates a commitment resembling falling in love and thus creates a communion among the followers. The reformers have the experience of belonging to the same family. The emerging insight may well have a lasting effect, transforming the dominant institution. Yet when this happens, the original insight, now institutionalized, loses something of its power: it becomes bureaucratized and ceases to be a driving force.

This analysis sheds light on the feminist movement. Since the originating feminist insight has not succeeded in modifying the structures of the Church, the feminist movement within it is vulnerable and may even disappear. By contrast, the feminist movement has successfully changed the structure of modern society, making the equality of men and women a matter of public law. Yet through this success, following Alberino's argument, feminism has ceased to be a driving force in society. Lise Baroni and Yvonne Bergeron have offered their own description of this phenomenon.[6] Feminism, they argue, embraces three dimensions: (1) the joyful affirmation of woman's identity, (2) the struggle against the powers that put women down, and (3) the conviction that gender equality is a universal principle destined to affect the whole of humanity. Baroni and Bergeron argue that what has remained in contemporary Quebec is the first dimension: in reliance on the law, women confidently affirm their identity as women. Yet empirical studies have shown that women have lost the other two dimensions: they no longer see themselves engaged in a struggle, nor are they disturbed by the absence of women's rights in other parts of the world. By contrast, the failure of feminism to transform the ecclesiastical institution keeps feminism alive within the Church, despite its vulnerability.

Lacelle insists that to foster the movement toward gender equality in the Church, it is absolutely necessary to create centres of feminist research and reflection. One cannot rely on the universities, she thinks, because university departments often entertain a positivistic understanding of the social sciences and demand that research and teaching be value-free activities. Such departments are irritated by feminist scholarship, guided as it is by an emancipatory commitment.[7] What women have to do, Lacelle argues, is organize conferences and set up centres. In 1978 she herself co-ordinated a conference on women and religion in French Canada,[8] to which were invited theologians as well as historians and social scientists. In 1988, at Ottawa University, she created le Centre canadien de recherche sur les femmes et la religion.

Let me mention three other organizations promoting feminist concerns in the Church of Quebec. The collective L'autre Parole was founded in 1976 to foster theological reflection respecting the experience of women and take actions in favour of the full participation of women in the Church.[9] The collective was the idea of Monique Dumais; it was strongly supported by Marie-Andrée Roy and Louise Melançon.[10] Members of L'autre Parole became professional theologians, women scholars in other fields, women working for the Church as catechists, pastoral agents, or in other capacities, and –

more generally – Catholic women troubled by sexism in the Church. The collective had chapters in various cities of Quebec. Its review *L'autre Parole* published theological reflections and reactions to current events in church and society as well as expressions of personal faith. At the celebration of the collective's thirty-fifth anniversary in August 2011, it was announced that from then on the review would be published on the internet.

1982 saw the founding of le Réseau femmes et ministères, a network of women engaged in various ministries and other capacities in the ecclesiastical institutions.[11] They want to discuss their experiences, learn from one another, study theological texts, and advocate the full participation of women in the ministries of the Church. Over the years the network has organized public meetings and published books on feminist religious thought.[12] In 1986 a group of sisters belonging to various religious congregations founded l'Association des religieuses pour la promotion de la femme (ARPF). The religious engaged in this association want to raise the awareness of women in regard to their subjugation in church and society, promote egalitarian relations between men and women, and build a Church and a society where the dignity and autonomy of women are respected.

Feminist theological literature has become very rich in Quebec. The prominent theologians, the authors of books and articles, include Élisabeth Lacelle, Lise Baroni, Yvonne Bergeron, Monique Dumais, Louise Melançon, and Marie-Andrée Roy, all professors of theology or religious studies. Many other women – theologians, historians, and sociologists – have made important contributions to the literature supporting the struggle for the equal partnership of men and women in the Church. Names that come to my mind are Anita Caron, Denise Couture, Olivette Genest, and Marie Gratton. Significant texts have also been produced by Catholic women outside of the academy. Marie-Andrée Roy published an analytical bibliography in 2001 listing the studies on religion and women produced by researchers in Quebec since the Quiet Revolution.[13] She published an even more extensive account of feminist theological and religious literature in Quebec in 2007.[14] Her account was published in *Franchir le miroir patriarcal*, edited by Monique Dumais, which presents the multiple facets of feminist exegesis, theology, and religious reflection in French Canada.

The present chapter does not intend to present an analysis of this vast literature; it only presents a few introductory remarks. I will mention a number of issues that have preoccupied feminist theologians and religious thinkers in Quebec.

THE TASKS OF FEMINIST THEOLOGY

In a paper given in 1978, Monique Dumais describes the two tasks of feminist theology: to struggle against male domination and to reflect creatively on women's experiences.[15] The first task involves exploring and deploring the subjugation of women in church and society and denouncing the ideologies, especially the religious ones, that legitimate the inferior status assigned to women. The second task is to make the experiences of women the starting point for theological reflection. The experiences of women include first of all their feelings, their spiritual aspirations, and their frustration in the Church – experiences whose cognitive content deserves to be made explicit. Second, the experiences of women also include their reading of religious texts, which differs from men's reading of them. According to the sociology of knowledge, the interpretation of a text and an event depends in part upon the historical situation of the reader: women read sacred texts and religious events differently, not because they are different from men, but because their social location in church and society is different from that of men.

Some feminist theologians recognize an affinity between their theological effort and liberation theology.[16] Both are carried by an emancipatory commitment; both have the double task of revealing and denouncing domination and of taking seriously the experiences of the dominated. Yet there is a substantial difference between Latin American liberation theology and feminist theology: while the former aims at lifting up the poor and the hungry, making them disappear, the latter aims at a just equilibrium between men and women, under conditions of freedom, mutual respect, and co-operation. The Latin American authors of liberation theology were actually heirs of the dominant culture inasmuch as they overlooked the marginalization of women in their society. Thanks to the protest of women, these authors have begun to support the struggle of women in Latin America for justice, equality, and participation.

Some feminist theologians insist that their commitment to liberation includes solidarity with the poor and oppressed wherever they may be located. Monique Dumais tells us that the collective L'autre Parole has opted from the very beginning for solidarity with women as well as men who in their daily lives experience injustice, poverty, misery, or oppression.[17] This commitment is shared by the women associated with the Catholic Left and is expressed in theological terms in the book *L'utopie de la solidarité au Quebec*, discussed in the preceding chapter.

WHO IS GOD?

According to the dominant discourse in Bible and liturgy, God is lord, father, and king, the male ruler of the universe. Feminists read this discourse as an ideology assigning predominance to males. The Church's official teaching is that God is not gendered, that the divinity is neither "he" nor "she," that the Creator is beyond the distinction between male and female. Still, in the Bible this God is depicted as male. It is possible to transcend this inheritance, Monique Dumais argues, because there are some biblical texts that refer to God with female images. Dumais calls this "rescuing God from the male ghetto."[18] Theologically more significant is the feminist malaise with the traditional theism that assumes God to be the supreme being above history, the omnipotent ruler of the world, intervening from on high in human affairs and cosmic happenings. We have seen in chapter 2 that, beginning with Maurice Blondel, many contemporary theologians, women among them, have turned to panentheism, thinking of God as the matrix of human becoming.

Christian feminists refer to God spontaneously as a mystery present in human life. Here is a free translation of a short text in which Élisabeth Lacelle refers to God.

> Men and women in the various religions report that they experience in their history, as a component of their historical being, a relation to a Reality other than themselves or, at least, a Reality present to their experience in a relational dialectic, like a double movement both immanent and transcendent. This Reality is experienced by them as Other and yet as grounding the Same in a manner that renews their humanity and creates a relationship to the cosmic order.[19]

In the review *L'autre Parole*, women sometimes express their religious experiences by rewriting biblical or liturgical texts in an imaginative manner, replacing the patriarchal discourse by the poetry of egalitarian humanity. These texts are all panentheistic. Here are in English translation two short samples from a long list of texts, many of which are beautiful.

In the beginning was love
And love was immanent in life
From its shattering
Emerged the human: man and women came forth;
Autonomy of each.
In the beginning was harmony:
Relationship, not subordination,
Equality and responsibility.
And then came the chaos.[20]

I believe in the Being in the heart of my being
I believe in the life at the heart of my life.
I believe in the Word which gives me my name.
I believe in Life coming forth from the depths of time,
Bursting forth and fertile like the first morning.
I believe in the love which opens me to beings,
Enriches and deprives me simultaneously.
I believe in love which reveals to me the best of
Myself, speaks to my heart, warms me and
Welcomes me, in both my strengths and weaknesses.[21]

To correct the male image of God taken from the Bible, some anglophone feminists prefer to speak of Goddess. Their francophone sisters prefer not to translate this as "déesse," but to invent the word "Dieue," adding an "e" at the end. Women do this to make a point, not to suggest that God is gendered. Important for both women and men is the introduction of inclusive language in the liturgy and in the translation of biblical texts. Because French is a strongly gendered language, this adaptation demands a greater effort in French than in English. If you translate the word *Canadians*, you have to say *les canadiens et les canadiennes*; a welcome to all must be translated as *le bienvenu à tous et toutes*; asking whether a person is happy becomes *êtes-vous heureux?* for a man, and *êtes-vous heureuse?* for a woman. Because making the language inclusive is cumbersome in French, conservative churchmen have a strong argument against it. Still, linguistic inclusiveness is a matter of justice.

WHO IS JESUS?

Since patriarchy is part and parcel of biblical religion, Christian feminists ask themselves whether to leave this tradition or make an effort to rethink and reform it.[22] Is there an authority, they ask, that allows them challenge the inherited teaching? For many feminists, that authority is Jesus, the prophet of God, the saviour of humanity, who denounces the ideologies and structures that produce oppression and who promises the coming of God's grace, breaking down the walls of separation, reconciling humanity in a single community of friends. As we saw in the previous chapter, Lise Baroni and Yvonne Bergeron refer to this promise as "the utopia of solidarity." In an exegetical essay,[23] Élisabeth Lacelle confirms this interpretation of Christ's messianic promises. She shows (1) that Jesus initiated *koinonia*, a loving community of equals among his disciples; (2) that he proclaimed *koinonia* as the destiny of the entire human family; and (3) that while many structures of division and inequality still stand, his message invalidates their foundation and inspires social movements to abolish them. Baroni and Bergeron in *L'utopie de la solidarité au Québec*[24] and Bergeron in a separate article[25] offer a more radical interpretation of the redemptive mission of Jesus, putting greater emphasis on its political dimension. But they agree with Lacelle that Jesus Christ initiated a new order of the world that includes equal sharing between men and women.

We saw in the last chapter that over the last decades biblical exegesis has recognized Christ's emancipatory promises. In the book *Les femmes aussi faisaient route avec lui*, published in Quebec in 1995 and in English translation in the United States in 2000, a group of biblical scholars and theologians, men and women, follow the same exegetical approach to the study of Christ's innovative relationship to women and the egalitarian implications of his redemptive message.[26]

Catholic men and women attached to Christ's promises regret that the celebration of the Eucharist stresses the hierarchical inequality in the Church, using distinctive rites and vestments for different grades, rather than symbolizing the final reconciliation in Jesus Christ, the human community liberated from the master/servant and male/female inequalities.

RETHINKING ECCLESIOLOGY

Participating in the dialogue with the Canadian bishops, Élisabeth Lacelle had great hope for the future, while – as we saw above – the final outcome of this exchange made her sad. Reflecting on the debate among the bishops, she noticed that it had brought to light the conflict between two distinct visions of the Church: on the one hand, the Church as the people of God, guided by ordained leaders in dialogue with their brothers and sisters, and on the other, the Church as an hierarchical society, made up of the few who teach and command and the many who listen and obey.[27] Both concepts are present in *Lumen Gentium*, the former in chapter 2 on the People of God, and the latter in chapter 3 on the Church's hierarchical structure. Can the two concepts be brought together? We saw in chapter 1 that the Dumont Report proposed that the Church's papal-episcopal constitution is in principle no obstacle to the dialogical exercise of ecclesiastical authority. What is needed is the hierarchy's willingness to consent to constitutional limits on its authority.

Feminist theologians hold that dialogue between the believing community and the ordained ministers belongs to the essence of the Church. They are encouraged by the words of Vatican Council II that "lay people share in the priestly, prophetic and royal office of Christ, and therefore have their own role to play ... in the Church's mission."[28] According to the Council's ecclesiology,

> The Church's mission requires in the first place that we foster within the Church itself a mutual esteem, reverence and harmony, through the full recognition of lawful diversity. All those who compose the one People of God, both pastors and the general faithful, should engage in dialogue with ever abounding fruitfulness.[29]

After the Council, the bishops of Canada and many other countries started to engage in dialogue with their people and with women in particular. Women were greatly encouraged by this. Since the equality of men and women had, in the wake of the Quiet Revolution, become a value constitutive of Quebec's collective identity, many Catholic women in Quebec believed that the Church was about to change its teaching. This is what Fernande Saint-Martin wrote in 1976.

> Without a doubt Catholicism will soon allow women to choose freely the form and conditions within which they exercise their maternity. More important still is that Catholicism recognizes the freedom of women ... in the exercise of a vaster maternity, their concern with the problems of the children they bring into the

> world, their participation in the philosophical, scientific, artistic and technical spheres, and their engagement for a civilization that corresponds to their respect for the life and joy of humanity.[30]

These expectations came to naught. Conservative signals coming from the Holy See interrupted the dialogue between women and their bishops. The Vatican, as we shall see in chapter 9, wanted a return to traditional clerical rule, the ecclesiastical system that reserves all decision-making power to the clergy and expects of lay men and women nothing but obedience. The effort of restoration frustrated vast number of Catholics: they felt that the believing community, women and men, were not being heard and did not receive answers to their legitimate questions.

In the 1970s the ordination of women to the priesthood had become a hotly debated issue in the Catholic Church in North America. The Women's Ordination Conference, founded in the United States in 1976, promoted a renewal of the Catholic Church that would make its government inclusive, accountable, and transparent. The Conference demanded justice and equality for Catholic women and wanted women-centred theologies to be incorporated into everyday Catholicism. Many Canadians participated in this organization. As mentioned earlier in this chapter, in 1982 Catholic women in Quebec founded le Réseau femmes et ministère, which defined its mission in terms similar to those used by the Women's Ordination Conference. The Réseau holds conferences, encourages theological research, and publishes articles and statements of various kinds on its website.

On 22 May 1994, John Paul II published the apostolic letter *Ordinatio Sacerdotalis* "on reserving priestly ordination to men alone." The pope declared that divine revelation did not authorize the Church to change its ancient tradition and ordain women to the priesthood. He did not mention that the Catholic Biblical Commission had published a long report in 1977 showing that biblical teaching poses no obstacles to the ordination of women.[31] John Paul II demanded that this issue be no longer debated, using such strong terms that some churchmen believed that his decision involved papal infallibility. In actual fact, *Ordinatio Sacredotalis* provoked a critical debate in many parts of the Church. In Quebec le Réseau femmes et ministère wrote a letter to the bishops, later published in the newspapers, that expressed their disagreement with the papal teaching.[32] This letter was subsequently signed by 2,000 Catholics. The collective

L'autre Parole refuted the arguments of the pope and asked the Quebec bishops to make a prophetic gesture by ordaining a woman well prepared for this task.

WOMEN WORKING FOR THE CHURCH

In a paper given at Élisabeth Lacelle's 1978 conference, the historian Michèle Jean analyzed the paradoxical dimension of the place of women in Quebec society.[33] After the revolt of the patriots in 1836 and the new pastoral directives coming from Rome in 1840, the Catholic clergy assumed an ever greater control of the national culture. Women were urged to assure the survival of the nation, giving birth to many children and educating them in the Catholic faith. Women were to be spouses-and-mothers at home or spouses-virgins-and-mothers in the convent. Bishops and priests held that women did not have sufficient intelligence to take part in public life. At the same time, they founded religious congregations for women, assigning them the tasks of teaching, caring for the sick, and offering social assistance. While official prejudice excluded women from public life, they actually offered essential services for the well-being of society. The sisters did their important work under the control of the clergy.

At the same conference, Michèle Jean, a historian of religion in Quebec, told the story of the achievements and creativity of the religious congregations. Here is one paragraph:

> In my research I came to recognize that the women in religious communities were at the forefront in all domains of society. They grew like mushrooms in difficult moments of our history; they shot up during the stirrings of nationalism, especially after the Act of Union (1840) when the Church wanted to protect the country from the encroaching Anglicization and Protestantism, and after Confederation (1867) when the people needed protection against the secularizing nationalization of services and the state provision of education and social welfare.[34]

The place of women in the contemporary Church is marked by a similar paradoxical dimension. While the official teaching denies women's capacity to be ministers, they are in fact employed by the Church to render the services that keep it alive. As I mentioned above, women are working in parishes and diocesan offices: they are engaged in pastoral activities, administrative duties, catechetical teaching, chaplaincy services, and coordinating liturgical worship. Some of these women belong to religious congregations, while others are part of the laity. The acute shortage of ordained priests has made the functioning of the Church dependent upon the female helpers.

Feminist scholars have studied the experiences of the female employees of the Church. Anita Caron[35] and Marie-Andrée Roy[36] have examined their work from a sociological perspective, revealing the vulnerability in which these women live. They do not have an official status protected by canon law; they are hired as temporary substitutes; they depend on the good will of the clergy; they enjoy no freedom, but have to do what they are told. The financial remuneration of lay women is minimal.

The problematic situation of women employed by the Church has also been studied from an anthropological perspective, based on extensive interviews with women involved in various tasks.[37] The study reports the difficulties experienced by these women in their work and records their frustration and complaints. The study also shows that implicit in their religious aspirations is a theological vision of the Church, an ecclesiology based on Christ's promises to summon forth a community of believers, united by faith and baptism and equipped with ministries of various kinds, from which no one is excluded in principle. These women dedicated to serving the Church are also frustrated by it, especially after John Paul II's apostolic letter of 1994 made the exclusion of women from the priesthood almost a dogma.

On 15 August 1997, several Roman Congregations and the Pontifical Council of the Laity published jointly an Instruction on Collaboration of Non-ordained Faithful in the Sacred Ministry of Priests.[38] The Instruction praises the participation of lay people in the Church's liturgical and pastoral ministry, yet it reprimands a series of practices that are seen as having negative consequences. Avoided must be gestures and terminology that disguise the essential difference between the ordained and the baptismal priesthood. It is therefore illegitimate to say that lay people exercise "a ministry" in the Church; they simply perform functions assigned to them by the priest or bishop. Lay people may not be referred to as pastors, chaplains, co-ordinators, or moderators: these titles apply only to the ordained. Lay people may be assigned posts with decision-making authority in the diocese only under special circumstances, such as a shortage of ordained priests. This Instruction signals a return to the pre-conciliar Catholic ecclesiology.

WHO IS MARY?

Catholic women in Quebec have had difficulties with the image of Mary in popular religion. Beatrice Gothscheck, a theologian and former director of la Société de la Bible, has analyzed the image of Mary in Marian associations, the prayers offered on pilgrimages, the literature supplied at Marian shrines, and the paintings and statues of Mary in chapels and churches.[39] Several images of Mary predominate. She is the perfect women, virtuous, compassionate, humble, and obedient, enjoying a sanctity that is unreachable. She is also the Queen of the World reigning in heaven, the Mother of the Church and all the faithful, spreading her blue mantle over the poor and vulnerable. Gothscheck detects in these images the desire of women to be helped by a powerful woman who understands them better than men do, including their husband and their priest. Gothscheck also shows that certain aspects of these images are designed by the clergy to foster the obedience of women and their fidelity to the Church. The veneration of Mary as Virgin and Mother, Gothscheck argues, has given women the sacrificial ideal of becoming the mother of many children and at the same time renouncing their sexuality as much as possible. The author concludes that today Catholic women reject these images of Mary; reflecting on the Gospel, they want to define their identity as disciples of Jesus.

In 1978 a Quebec poet, Denise Boucher, who confessed to being a believing Catholic, produced a play, *Les fées ont soif*, that caused an uproar in the Catholic community.[40] In the play the statue of the Blessed Virgin Mary engages in conversation with two women also called Mary, one submissive to her husband and her priest, and the other a prostitute who despises all men. Affected by the story of these two women, Mary, the mother of Jesus, steps out of her niche in the wall and declares that she will define herself anew, be proudly alive, not submissive, and be sensual, yet without losing her dignity. The statue speaks to God:

And here I am before you
Ready to love you anew
New woman ready to be loved.
Here I am in the flesh
And full of celebration.

The play provoked strong opposition. Protesters marched in front of the theatre in which it was performed. While public opinion in the

Church regarded the play as blasphemous, Monique Dumais and other women associated with L'autre Parole offered a more positive interpretation. They saw in it a critical reaction to the image of womanhood imposed upon Quebecers by the Catholic clergy. The mother of Jesus whom the women of L'autre Parole admired and welcomed was the biblical Mary of the Magnificat who praised God for his goodness and his promise to liberate humanity from oppression.

AN ETHICS FOR WOMEN

In an article entitled "Une morale imposée à une éthique autodéterminée,"[41] Monique Dumais offers a series of quotations showing that in the past priests and lay leaders in Quebec used to define what it meant to be a woman and what her moral ideals were to be. Women, it was generally taught, were destined by nature to be mothers. What this implied in practical terms was spelled out in the public statements of men who opposed granting women the right to vote. After a long struggle, women in Quebec obtained their suffrage on 25 April 1940.

In 1923 an Oblate priest writes,

> The woman is meant to be a mother. If the right to vote risks making her less a mother, less a woman, then forget about suffrage. The question is not whether the woman is intelligent enough to vote ... but rather whether, however intelligent and well-intentioned she may be, she is made – save for rare exceptions – to exercise her heart and soul in the public arena and not only the home. Her restriction to the home seems to us to be the natural order ... suffrage for woman ... goes against the legitimate instincts of the female nature.[42]

In 1927 Henri Bourassa, influential politician and founder of *Le Devoir*, proposed these ideas:

> The "right to vote" is one of the ... social responsibilities that fall upon the man, due to his physical and mental make-up and, more especially, due to his role and responsibility as head of the family. The main role of the woman is, and will remain, despite what suffragettes now say and do, motherhood, holy and fertile motherhood ... Make no mistake, a bitter, violent and general

battle between the two sexes is approaching. The insanity of feminism has already troubled the minds of many men and women, awakening in a crowd of women bizarre and perverse instincts and morbid appetites.[43]

In 1945, Pius XII still taught that women were essentially mothers:

> The role of woman seems clearly determined by her traits, her aptitudes, by the particular qualities of her sex. She collaborates with man, but in her own way, following the natural tendency. So, the role of woman, her native inclination, is maternity.[44]

The vocation of maternity also included the duty of submission to the husband. Les Semaines sociales of 1923 explain this quite explicitly:

> As a natural society the family is still essentially a hierarchical society. According to both natural law and divine law, its members are not equal; they do not form some sort of democracy in miniature. Instead, they constitute an unequal society where some, due to nature and its Author, must command, and others obey; where the father and the mother have their proper roles … The role of the mother is not compatible with feminist claims.[45]

Dumais presents many other quotations to demonstrate that the clergy defined the nature and the role of women, pretending that their design was in fact God's design. These men defined the essence of womanhood without ever asking women how they saw themselves or what their human and religious aspirations were. Women were treated like subjects without a voice, destined to be told what to think and what to do. The clergy invoked the Creator to prove that the superior power of men was divinely ordained and could not be questioned. In Quebec, Dumais writes, women, taught who they were by the clergy, were prevented from moving towards an authentic realization of themselves. She concludes that after the experience of imposed submission to men and exclusion from responsible citizenship, women in Quebec, actors in the Quiet Revolution, now refuse to believe men who tell them what is right and wrong for them. They now receive the Church's ethical teaching with a grain of salt.

The bishops of Quebec have become aware of the harm their teaching has inflicted upon women. In 1989, they published the document "Violence en héritage," expressing regret that their teaching in the past has made women vulnerable to violence in the home. In the past priests were taught to tell women beaten by their husbands to be patient, forgiving, and submissive. Today, the bishops write, priests are instructed to urge a woman beaten by her husband to tell him that if he threatens her again, she will inform the police. In November 1990, the fiftieth anniversary of the law granting women the right to vote, the bishops published a formal apology to women, regretting that fifty years ago the bishops had campaigned against this law.[46] These two gestures were well received in the Church of Quebec.

On 21 November 2007, Cardinal Marc Ouellet, then the archbishop of Quebec City, published a letter out of the blue, without having consulted his brother bishops, in which he regretted that in Quebec prior to the Quiet Revolution, many Catholics, including priests, held prejudiced opinions, such as anti-Semitism, racism, indifference to Aboriginals, and discrimination against women and homosexuals. These attitudes and abuses of power, the cardinal wrote, tarnished the image of the clergy and undermined its moral authority. "Mothers were rebuffed by priests with no consideration for the family obligations they had already assumed." These abuses, the cardinal continued, "shook people's confidence in religious authorities, and we understand! Forgive us for all this harm!" This letter blamed prejudiced Catholics for these conditions and accused some priests of the abuse of power, without admitting that these attitudes were related to the bishops' official teaching. For this reason the letter was not well received in the Quebec Church. Women as well as homosexuals reminded the cardinal that discrimination continues to be practiced in the Church today.

From the experiences of women in Quebec, Monique Dumais concludes that women will have to do their own ethical reflection; they cannot risk once again putting their trust in the teaching of men. As Christian believers, women will listen to Scripture and the Christian tradition, wrestle with the meaning of these texts, and apply their message to the life they lead in present-day society. After the culture of imposed alienation, women have to repossess and assume responsibility for their own bodies. Dumais refers to this as an autonomous ethics. She does not mean "autonomous" in the secular sense, signifying independence of God. She holds instead that believers are sustained by God as they wrestle to discover what is the right thing for them to do. Dumais recognizes that in this wrestling, Catholics are likely to arrive at different conclusions and that the Church will have to tolerate a certain ethical pluralism among its members. Such a pluralism is not foreign to the Catholic tradition: for instance, some Catholics are pacifists, while others defend the just-war theory. What this pluralism implies for the ecclesiastical magisterium we shall see in a subsequent chapter.

The thoughts of feminist thinkers presented in this chapter demonstrate that feminist theology is not only for women; it helps all believers to see more clearly the nature of men and women, the vocation and mission of the Church, and the practical implications of God's revelation in Jesus Christ.

8

Catholic Faith and Cultural Catholicism

Until now we have studied the theological ideas and pastoral proposals of intellectuals in the Quebec Church. In chapters 1 and 2 we saw what Vatican Council II said about the contextual character of theology and what the Dumont Report proposed in regard to dialogue and pluralism in the Church. In the subsequent chapters I presented the theological proposals of Quebec religious thinkers and theologians, beginning with Fernand Dumont and Jacques Grand'Maison and continuing with a series of theologians and exegetes, men and women, who try to articulate what the Gospel means in contemporary society.

In this chapter I wish to do something different. I shall consult authors who have examined how the Catholic people of Quebec have reacted to these theological developments. Theologians and sociologists in the 1980s have drawn a portrait of Quebec Catholicism that revealed its decline, its confusion, and its contradictions. What has remained stable, some observers claim, is a purely cultural Catholicism. Since the Catholic community continues to shrink, the bishops appointed the Larochelle Commission in 1990 to study the Church's perilous condition and come up with a set of pastoral policies to give it new life. In the present chapter we shall examine the Larochelle Report and analyze the intense theological debate produced by this document, involving lay men and women, bishops, and priests.

In 1968 when the Dumont Commission held hearings in the various regions of Quebec, people were eager to speak about their faith and participate in the pastoral renewal of the Church. Yet when the Dumont Report was published in 1971, the enthusiasm had disappeared. A recent book, *Modernité et religion au Québec,* has shed some light on this development.[1] Shortly after the beginning of the Quiet Revolution, in 1962, the Dominican review *Maintenant* supported the political modernization of society with theological arguments.[2] It called for the declericalization of Quebec and the democratization of the Church. With Vatican Council II *Maintenant* saw no conflict, in principle, between modernity and the Christian faith. While this message was well received among the reading public, the bishops themselves were as yet not on the same wavelength. Gilles Routhier, theologian and church historian, argues that in their pastoral planning in the1960s the bishops tried to make the Church's bureaucratic structures more efficient, following the example of the provincial government, ignoring the teaching of Vatican Council II on the priesthood of the baptized and the need for intra-ecclesial dialogue.[3] Because of their silence, he argues, the conciliar message did not reach the ordinary church-going Catholics. In the late 1960s these conciliar themes were taken up by the Dumont Commission and acknowledged by the bishops, but this was late. Vast numbers of Catholics were turning their backs on the Church.

The rapid decline of the Quebec Church, as we saw in chapter 1, has puzzled sociologists and been explained by them in various ways. Yet their studies did not examine the beliefs and practices of the Catholics who remained in the Church. The surviving Catholicism became the object of pastoral and sociological studies later.

QUEBEC CATHOLICISM STUDIED BY THEOLOGIANS

At the end of the 1970s Fernand Dumont and Jacques Racine, engaged in conversation, revealed their impression that the majority of church-going Catholics were greatly confused. These Catholics recognized that something had changed in the Church, but they did not know what this meant in their personal lives of faith. The two scholars decided to sponsor a research project that would examine the practices and religious ideas of the Catholic people. The result was published in two volumes, *Milieux et témoignages* and *Entre le temple et l'exil*, in 1982.[4] The purpose of these books was pastoral. The contributing authors were not sociologists, but theologians in dialogue with people in the parishes. They hoped that their study would create a bridge between the faithful and the circles that promoted the new thinking in the Church.

The first volume presented studies of the religious ideas entertained in different sectors of society, such as farmers, workers, middle-class people, youth, and parish workers. The second volume offered critical reflections on the results of these empirical investigations. Two of these critical reflections were written by Dumont and Racine respectively. Both authors painted a dark picture of Quebec's Catholic community. People were perplexed; they knew something had changed, but they had no clear idea of the teaching of Vatican II, nor were they affected by the teaching of the Quebec theologians. Some Catholics were clinging to the religious practices they had inherited, while others interpreted the new emphasis on personal freedom as permission to take their faith less seriously and adopt an increasingly secular outlook.

Fernand Dumont recognized that seeing the Church as "un héritage et un projet" is a challenging task. What is demanded is an openness to the new that remains faithful to one's inheritance, and a turn to critical reason that preserves trust in the power of the Gospel. Dumont acknowledged that theologians tend to detach themselves from the piety of their families and express their religious convictions in terms that their families don't understand. Dumont's theory of the first and second culture insists that the second culture – in this case, the theological expression of the faith – needs to revitalize itself by repeated returns to the first culture – in this case, the lived piety of the people. At the same time, he argues, religious life that is indifferent to theological interpretations and has no living contact with the public culture becomes sectarian and fosters the Church's departure from society.

To explain the confused response of Catholics to the renewal of Vatican II, Jacques Racine pointed to the heavy cultural weight of traditional Catholicism in the historical conditions of Quebec. The Christian message that became glued to our hearts, he writes, was not the beatitudes announced by Jesus, nor the wisdom of the Church Fathers, nor the insights that led to Vatican II, but the catechesis of the Counter-Reformation, the definition of papal infallibility, and the social doctrine of Leo XIII that remained normative until John XXIII's *Pacem in Terris*. Many Quebecers got stuck in this legacy, while others revolted against it, opting for the freedom to define their own faith.

The contributors to these two volumes observe that Quebecers are, on the whole, unable to speak about their religion. Even in the home, parents now find it almost impossible to communicate their Catholic faith because the children in school follow the new catechetical teaching that emphasizes the love of God and uses poetic language that differs from the doctrinal discourse learnt by the parents. What is urgently needed, the authors feel, is not new ideas, but the creation of contexts in which Catholics learn to speak – *prendre la parole*.

The concluding chapter offers a brief summary of how the authors in this book see the evolution of the Church's self-understanding initiated by Vatican II and the Dumont Commission.

> A move from a clerical Church to the Church, People of God,
> From a Church of Christendom to a Church with a mission in society,
> From a Church of rituals to a Church of the Word,
> From a Church of rules to a Church of spiritual experience,
> From a uniform Church to a pluralistic Church,
> From a Church adapted to the world to a Church that participates in changing the world,
> From a Church that legitimates the social order to a Church in solidarity with the poor.[5]

QUEBEC CATHOLICISM STUDIED BY SOCIOLOGISTS

A number of sociologists have made empirical investigations of Quebec Catholicism. I wish to mention two studies frequently cited, Raymond Lemieux's published in 1998 and Martin Meunier's published in 2010.

In a widely cited article,[6] Lemieux begins his study of Quebec Catholicism by investigating measurable data such as attendance at Sunday worship, the sacramental practice of baptism and marriage, and the assistance of a priest at death and burial. He finds here a dramatic decline of Quebec's traditional religion. In Montreal the withdrawal from the Church is greater than in the towns and villages of the regions, yet even in Montreal – surprisingly and inconsistently – a high percentage of parents still want their babies to be baptized. Relying on interviews and questionnaires, Lemieux examines what Catholics actually believe. He discovers that vast numbers of them, unaware of the Church's official teaching, have their own religious ideas. Even those who know the official teaching make up their own minds. The great majority of Quebecers believe in God, but when asked who or what this God is, their answers vary greatly. This pervasive ambiguity is carefully documented by Lemieux. He explains this phenomenon by recalling that Catholicism was at one time a constitutive dimension of the French-Canadian identity. Just as Jews and Mennonites, after losing their faith, remain rooted in their respective traditions and continue to see themselves as Jews or Mennonites, Quebecers, after turning away from the Church, also remain attached to their Catholic identity. They no longer go to church and decide for themselves what to believe, yet they think of themselves as Catholics and want their children to be baptized. Lemieux refers to this inconsistency as "being Catholic without the Church" or as "cultural Catholicism."

In the same article Lemieux also presents the movements in the contemporary Church that betray vitality and imagination, information usually overlooked in sociological studies. He mentions in particular the catechetical movement, the network of base communities, the charismatic movement, the groups of social solidarity, and the educational milieu created by the study of theology and the Bible.

Twenty years later Martin Meunier and his colleagues published the chapter "Permanence et recomposition de la 'religion culturelle,'"[7] a major empirical study of the evolution of Quebec's Catholicism from 1970 to 2006. The study confirms the results of Lemieux's investigation, showing that since 1970, the departures from the Church have multiplied and the inconsistencies have become ever more startling. Instead of presenting the figures and tables provided in Meunier's study, I shall simply summarize the conclusion which he draws from them. His investigation demonstrates the existence of a misalignment or incoherence among three aspects of Quebec Catholicism: (1) a growing mistrust of the Church as an institution, revealed in the dramatic drop in Sunday church attendance and marriages blessed in church; (2) an almost unchanged identification with Catholicism and only a slight decline of infant baptism; and (3) an absence of unanimity of religious beliefs among Catholics, indifferent as they are to the Church's official teaching. Meunier and his colleagues ask themselves whether a religion marked by such contradictory attitudes has a future.

THE LAROCHELLE REPORT[8]

The Catholic bishops recognized that the Church of Quebec continued to shrink. In 1990, twenty years after the Dumont Report, they appointed another commission, this time a small research committee chaired by Jean-Louis Larochelle, a Dominican priest, to investigate the decline of the Church and come up with new pastoral recommendations. The Larochelle Report, entitled *Risquer l'avenir*,[9] published in 1992, explains the methodology adopted by the committee. It differed strikingly from the approach followed by the Dumont Commission, which, as we saw in chapter 1, had held public hearings in the various parts of Quebec. The Larochelle Commission relied on the co-operation of a large number of parishes, carefully chosen to represent different regions of Quebec; different environments, urban and rural; and different economic conditions, affluent and indigent. The participants were asked to set up groups to study the development of their parishes over the two decades between 1970 and 1990. These groups were then requested to respond to a detailed questionnaire, after which they were interviewed by the committee. The members of these groups were largely drawn from parish workers, that is, lay men and women employed by the parish for various pastoral tasks.

The radical conclusion of the Larochelle Report was that the Catholic Church in Quebec is dying. The report documents the continuing decline of membership in the parishes, the ageing of these communities, the almost complete disaffection of the young, the shrinking number of priests, the gradual disappearance of religious congregations, and the shattered self-image of parishes overwhelmed by a feeling of powerlessness.[10] There is evidence that even the Catholics who continue to go to church have only a vague idea of what being Catholic means and that they are unable to put into words what they believe. The Report concludes that unless the Quebec Church introduces a new pastoral approach, it will disappear altogether. With its back against the wall, the Church must "risquer l'avenir," risk its future by embarking upon a radically new path.

While the Dumont Report looked with favour upon the humanistic dimension of modernity – personal freedom, democratization, pluralism, and tolerance – the Larochelle Report analyses the secularizing consequences of modernization in a highly critical fashion. The Report fully accepts the sociological theory of secularization. It cites with approval the work of Peter Berger, who had argued in the 1960s that the rational and scientific discourse dominant in modern society produces an approach to the world that leaves no room for divine transcendence.[11] Berger echoes here the conclusion of Max Weber that the instrumental rationality dominant in modern society inevitably leads to the disenchantment of the world and thus the waning of religion. This is how the Larochelle Report puts it:

> Every type of society fashions the personality of its members. Through the process of secularization people interiorize the ways of doing, thinking and feeling proper to their society; thus the ways of their culture become their own personal way. When persons are socially integrated there is neither opposition nor rupture between them and their society, but rather continuity and interpenetration.[12]

Even Christian believers in modern society, the Report continues, discover that the place religion occupies in their personal consciousness has changed. From celebrating a total vision embodied in their society, religion becomes a freely chosen personal journey. The only religion that can survive, the Report goes on, is one that is freely chosen and capable of defining its identity against society. The Report recognizes the relative success in the modern world of "the sects," emphasizing as they do personal conversion, opposition to the dominant culture, and the willingness to define themselves as marginal. The sects expose their members to a counter-socialization. Catholics in Quebec, the Report argues, will have to learn from the sects.

These sociological reflections guide the Report in its positive recommendations. If the Catholic Church wants to survive in Quebec, it must communicate a voluntary, experiential, and well-informed Christian faith and adopt a counter-stance to society, not by looking away from society as do many sects, but by critically engaging society in solidarity with the poor and the weak. These two points were already made in the Dumont Report, which had recommended teaching religion to adults so that they could acquire a personal faith and urging Catholics to work for justice in society. Yet the Larochelle Report offers a more radical interpretation of these pastoral objectives. Three proposals are especially startling.

First, the Church should concentrate its teaching on adults. At present, great energy and resources are spent on the education of children. Behind this effort stands the idea that if children are brought up as well catechized, practicing Catholics, they will remain active members of the Church when they grow up. This idea may have had some validity in the past, the Report argues, yet in the present it has become an illusion. There is no empirical evidence whatsoever for the notion that Quebec children brought up as good Catholics remain Catholic as they enter adolescence and adulthood.[13] Putting great effort into giving religious education to children is not a realistic pastoral policy. The Church should apply its resources, the Report argues, to the education of adult Catholics, improving their understanding of the Bible, sustaining their personal engagement, and teaching them the practical meaning of Christian faith in modern society. The Church must foster voluntaristic religion based on spiritual experience and profound conviction.

Second, the Report suggests that the Church should abandon large parishes and instead organize Catholics in "primary groups," that is to say, groups small enough to allow members to enjoy face-to-face acquaintance. In such communities, the members learn to speak to one another about their religious convictions, express their doubts, and discuss possible answers to their spiritual problems. Here Catholics would find support for their personal faith, threatened as it is by secular society. Here they would develop a critical sense in regard to the social order and discover how they can become agents of social change. In large parishes, priests teach the faith in doctrinal terms and the people remain silent, while in small communities, people learn to talk about what they believe in their own vocabulary and thus become capable of communicating their faith to others. If primary groups are of the essence and secondary groups, such as large parishes, are to be abandoned, then the giant church buildings that decorate Montreal and other cities in Quebec will lose their function. These large church buildings, impressive and beautiful though they be, should be abandoned and sold. The financial investment in keeping these buildings in good repair and heating them in the winter could then be used to expand the Church's educational ministry and strengthen its social witness in society. Moreover, these enormous churches misrepresent the historical reality of today's Church. At one time these large edifices symbolized the spiritual and cultural unity of the local community and Quebec as a whole, in solidarity with worldwide Catholicism. Yet today, these massive buildings, largely empty on Sunday, confuse the parishioners and prevent them from accepting who they are, a small religious community in a secular society.

Third, the Report recommends that the Church turn its back on "cultural Catholicism." Catholicism can survive in Quebec only if it understands itself as a voluntaristic religion. In the New Testament, the Report reminds the reader, the Church was a community of disciples, men and women personally committed to Jesus Christ. Repudiating cultural Catholicism means, in practical terms, that priests should refuse requests made by couples to be married in church or have their babies baptized, if these couples are not active members of a Christian community. Similarly, priests should refuse to give Christian burial to people who have not been active Christians. This was a radical proposal since the majority of Quebecers (as we saw above), while detached from their parishes, still wanted their babies baptized and a church funeral for themselves. The Report argues that cultural Catholicism is a form of superstition that damages the Church since it undermines the true meaning of Catholic identity and obscures the dividing line between the believing community and the secular society. Cultural Catholicism tempts the Church to delude itself about its historical reality, assume that it still represents society as a whole, and cling to the illusion that its continued presence is guaranteed.

While the Dumont Report was guided by a Durkheimian imagination, the Larochelle Report had a certain affinity with Weberian sociology. It accepted Weber's theory of secularization. Weber also looked upon religion as voluntaristic, rather than as the product of a community. For Weber, moreover, society was conflictive, not organic: it was held together not by a set of common values, but by a government with a big stick demanding obedience and conformity. For him, society was shaped by the dominant institutions and their cultural impact and, at the same time, seriously challenged by countervailing currents expressing the frustrations of people at the margins.[14] The Larochelle Report argues that the Church can only survive if it becomes a countervailing movement.

The Larochelle Report provoked a lively debate in the Quebec Church. After its publication in 1992, a large assembly was held in Montreal to discuss and vote on its recommendations. The assembly gathered 570 people, among whom were 333 lay people, 51 religious women, 2 deacons, 128 priests, and 25 bishops, plus representatives of theological faculties and pastoral centres. The Report was admired for its brilliance, yet the discussion revealed that the great majority of participants had objections to its pastoral recommendations. An account of this assembly, accompanied by theological commentaries, was published in the book *L'avenir des communautés chrétiennes*.[15] The most thoughtful critiques were offered by André Charron, a pastoral theologian known for his generous interpretation of cultural

Catholicism.[16] In my opinion, the great value of the Larochelle Report was that it forced the Catholic community to think theologically. While sociological investigations are important, they are not the grounds upon which the Church adopts its pastoral policies. The ultimate judgment will have be justified in theological terms.

Let me present a brief summary of the debate. Some participants argued that the Report did not take into account the unpredictable action of the Holy Spirit in the Church and, for this reason, allowed itself to adopt a pessimistic stance, insensitive to the vital movements existing within the Church. Others argued that the Report had an ecclesiocentric understanding of God's redemptive presence in history: it assumed that divine grace is largely confined to the Church, while Catholic teaching after Vatican Council II recognizes God's redemptive presence in the world. They argued that all personal manifestations of love and selflessness and all social transformations towards greater peace and justice are signs of God's gracious presence, and that it is the Church's task to read the signs of the times, discover God's work in the world, and support the divinely initiated currents in history. Still other participants complained that the Report had an excessively negative image of the modern world, characteristic of pre-conciliar Catholicism. Since then the Church has learnt a great deal from the modern world, beginning with religious liberty and human rights. Even the process of secularization, the argument went on, has a positive side: it dispenses the Church from legitimating the established order and thus allows it to define itself as the defender of the vulnerable and excluded.

Another objection accused the Report of relying uncritically on the sociological theory of secularization, which has never been demonstrated. In fact, in the 1990s Peter Berger published a book that refuted the theory of secularization he had vigorously proposed in the 1960s.[17] By putting all the blame for the decline of the Church upon the secularization of society, the Report overlooks the Church's own responsibility for the loss of its members. The Church's authoritarian style, its triumphalist symbols and discourse, the absence of institutions for dialogue between its members and their leaders, the Church's inflexible sexual ethics, and its outmoded attitude towards women – all these are factors opposed to the spirit of the Gospel and reasons why so many Catholics leave their parishes and turn their backs on the Church. By looking away from these disturbing phenomena, the objection continues, the Report lacks humility.

Another complaint dealt with the Report's negative view of cultural Catholicism. People who are heirs of a Catholic culture often retain, even if they are no longer practicing Catholics, a good number of Catholic symbols, customs, and virtues, such as a sense of the spiritual, resistance to materialism, loyalty to the family, engagement in charities, the cultivation of neighbourliness, the practice of hospitality, and social solidarity with the poor and the sick. When such people ask to have their infants baptized or to have a Catholic burial, they may not be moved by sentimentality or superstition; they may desire to express in meaningful symbols the inherited Catholic values they continue to hold. It also happens that people who have lost the Catholic faith but cherish its cultural and ethical inheritance may at times of sickness or personal turmoil experience the revival of faith and become believers again.

The radical proposals of the Larochelle Report were rejected by the majority of the voters. Catholics believe that the Church is the home of saints and sinners and hence hesitate to set up moral criteria for membership. Some participants at the assembly argued, correctly I think, that the Report was based on the testimony of religious professionals working in the parishes and hence reflected the convictions of highly motivated believers who desired all Catholics to be equally committed. The Dumont Report, as we saw in chapter 1, recognized the need for pluralism within the Church, symbolized traditionally by the two ways, life in the world and life in a religious community, and expressed at Vatican Council II by the acknowledgment of different vocations in the one Church. Still, the Larochelle Report, while rejected by the Catholic community, deserves to be remembered. It contains a radical theological truth that Catholics were unwilling to recognize, but that will haunt the Church of the future.

THE PLURALISTIC SOCIETY

The Larochelle Report recognizes no affinity between the Gospel and the values proposed by modern society. Its judgment of the present is negative without qualifications. This evaluation is echoed in statements made by Cardinal Ratzinger/Benedict XVI that see present-day society as dominated by relativism. He laments "the dictatorship of relativism"[18] that produces contempt for people committed to or in search of an abiding truth. Yet, as we shall see, there are also statements of Benedict XVI that recognizes the pluralism of modern society.

People who call themselves non-believers entertain different visions of human life and follow different currents of thought. It would be a mistake to make rapid generalizations about secular people and draw a neat line between believers aided by God's grace and non-believers imprisoned in relativism. Among the men and women unable to believe in God are many who are deeply committed to truth and justice, even if they do not raise metaphysical questions. Being ethically concerned and thinking deeply constitute a graced way of being, quite different from "the unexamined life," the immersion in daily work and the struggle of existence without reflecting on the meaning of life, which, according to Socrates, is not worth living.[19]

Popes and other clergymen often lump all non-believers together as selfish persons dwelling in darkness. In his encyclical *Caritas in Veritate* of 2009, Benedict XVI even writes, "A humanism which excludes God is an inhuman humanism."[20] Yet rethinking this harsh judgment two years later, in the fall of 2011, the pope invited non-believing humanists to participate in the interreligious celebration at Assisi. In his speech at that occasion, he acknowledged the wisdom among agnostics.

> In addition to the two phenomena of religion and anti-religion, a further basic orientation is found in the growing world of agnosticism: people to whom the gift of faith has not been given, but who are nevertheless on the lookout for truth, searching for God. Such people do not simply assert: "There is no God". They suffer from his absence and yet are inwardly making their way towards him, inasmuch as they seek truth and goodness. They are "pilgrims of truth, pilgrims of peace". They ask questions of both sides. They take away from militant atheists the false certainty by which they claim to know that there is no God and invite them to leave polemics aside and become seekers who do not give up hope in the existence of truth and in the possibility and necessity of living by it. But they also challenge the followers of religions not to consider God as their own property, as if he belonged to them, in such a way that they feel vindicated in using force against others. These agnostics are seeking the truth, they are seeking the true God, whose image is frequently concealed in the religions because of the ways in which they are often practiced.[21]

Respect for non-believers committed to truth and justice is not new in the Catholic Church. What is new is a respect unaccompanied by the wish to convert them to Christianity. In chapter 3 we saw that this was the attitude adopted by Fernand Dumont. He wanted to dialogue with his non-believing colleagues; he wished to understand them and be understood by them. His expression "No monopoly, please!" reminded the Church that there is wisdom and holiness among outsiders, deserving recognition and gratitude.

The purely negative evaluation of Quebec society implicit in the Larochelle Report overlooks the presence of non-believers committed to truth and justice. In a review of Charles Taylor's *A Secular Age* I wrote the following lines:

> I am surrounded by secular men and women dedicated to human rights, justice and peace, people who live simple lives, have families, enjoy friendship and do not hunt after material success. They belong to social movements, support social democracy, defend human rights and gender equality, actively oppose racism, demand justice for the global South and respect the claims of the Native peoples. I heard the well-known Quebec journalist Michel Venne say in an interview that he was a non-believer committed to the promotion of human rights. His wife is a Catholic, he said, and because there are no rituals to celebrate dedication to human rights, he sometimes accompanies his wife to church. When Françoise David, co-founder of the left-wing political party Québec Solidaire, was asked by reporter what she believed in, she replied, "The values I endorse are equal rights and equal chances, social solidarity, constructing a culture of peace and respect for nature."[22]

In Quebec many men and women who grew up Catholic and later became non-believers continue to appreciate elements of their Catholic past. A typical case is the filmmaker and writer Bernard Émond who presents himself as an agnostic, yet insists that to make sense of the drama of human life and the responses of people to its tragic dimension, he draws upon the ideas and images of the Catholic tradition, such as fidelity, sin, compassion, love, and sacrifice.[23] The films he produces remind the viewers that there is a difference between the surface and the depth of life and that access to the depth is mediated by certain human experiences, often associated with suffering.

To show that the wisdom of unbelievers often appreciates aspects of religion, I wish to quote a thoughtful text written by the Canadian author Nancy Huston, who has lived in Paris since 1970 and writes her novels in French.

> Coming home at nightfall the other evening, walking past Saint-Médard Church (15th century) and, right afterwards, the Great Mosque gently lighted by the full moon, I realized how important these sites are to me in the city landscape, built by and for people who are not like me, people who believe in God. I often go into them. I would miss them if they were one day to disappear.
>
> My generation (I was born in the 1950s) is very special in this respect: nearly all of our parents were practicing believers, almost none of our children are. We are the tipping point. This is a big thing. And yet we never talk about it. How did this disenchantment of the world occur in our minds and bodies. What are its advantages ... and disadvantages? We have become so vehemently critical of religion – it controlled our bodies and sexuality, drove people into passivity, and distracted them from their real problems by hanging before them an illusory heaven. We have so hastily replaced religious beliefs by scientific and political certitudes that we often forget the more positive side of religion, for which we have found no substitute ... the ability to withdraw from our daily routine to renew our strength; the sense of the existence of another world, not useful nor defined in economic terms; the great joy of feeling that we belong to something.[24]

At this point I recall that Fernand Dumont recognized that the significant division in human society – an ever shifting boundary – is not between believers and non-believers, but between people committed to truth and justice and people imprisoned in their private purposes. He had a generous perception of cultural Catholicism, believing that it taught respect for truth, generosity, and social concern to many Quebecers. It was not his intention, as we saw in chapter 3, to foster the conversion of non-believing Quebecers to the Catholic faith. He thought that the Church's task was to foster mutual respect and understanding among Quebecers and promote their reconciliation in a joint effort to create a more just and more humane society.

9

Faith and the Magisterium

The Dumont Report recognized the need for an ecclesiastical authority to teach and legislate. In fact, every society requires a decision-making centre with the power to rule. In present-day culture, the Dumont Report argues, the stability of a society requires an ongoing communication between the ruler and the ruled. An absence of conversation between the two is experienced as oppressive by the latter and, for this reason, provokes disloyalty and disobedience. To enable ecclesiastical authority to teach and rule wisely and be respected by the community, the Dumont Report recommends the creation of spaces for public dialogue between the Catholic people and their leaders – in the parish, the diocese, the national Church, and the Church universal. The right of Catholics to speak and be heard is not in contradiction with the authority of the hierarchy; on the contrary, such a dialogue allows popes, bishops, and priests to promote the Gospel more effectively.

The Church is not a democracy; nor is it a monarchy or an oligarchy. As an organization the Church is not modelled on any secular institution. The Church is a community of believers; it is united by faith and baptism; and it is governed by ordained ministers in dialogue with the baptized. Vatican Council II has recognized the participation of the baptized in Christ's priestly and prophetic office.

> In the Church there is diversity of service but unity of purpose. Christ conferred on the apostles and their successors the duty of teaching, sanctifying and ruling, in his name and power. But lay people also share in the priestly, prophetic and royal office of Christ and therefore have their own role to play in the mission of the Church.[1]

In *Lumen Gentium* we are told that the Church is guided by "hierarchical and charismatic gifts,"[2] the former referring to the teaching of popes and bishops and the latter to the insights and initiatives of the baptized.

The Dumont Report looked upon Vatican Council II as an extraordinary occasion of intra-ecclesial dialogue. Before the Council, the bishops produced recommendations worked out in conversation with their priests and their people. At the Council, the bishops were in conversation with each other and the appointed theologians; they also engaged in dialogue with the pope. This multiple dialogue was so fruitful, so sensitive to the guidance of the Holy Spirit, that Paul VI wrote the encyclical *Ecclesiam Suam* in 1964, designating dialogue as the pastoral method of the future. The pope called for dialogue with the world and dialogue within the Church, a dialogue to which he himself was open.

> We greatly desire that this dialogue with our own children be conducted with the fullness of faith, with charity, and with dynamic holiness. May it be of frequent occurrence and on an intimate level. May it be open and responsive to all truth, every virtue, every spiritual value that goes to make up the heritage of Christian teaching ... We want this dialogue ... to be ready to listen to the variety of views which are expressed in the world today. We want it to be the sort of dialogue that will make Catholics virtuous, wise, unfettered, fair-minded and strong.[3]

Paul VI made it clear that popes and bishops keep their authority and the Catholic people have to obey them, yet he wanted this authority to be practiced in the spirit of dialogue. The Dumont Report fully recognizes this. I mentioned in chapter 1 that the Report specifically states that its understanding of dialogue was in keeping with the Church's papal-episcopal structure. Yet, as I mentioned in the same chapter, the Report also asserts that respectful dissent plays a significant role in the evolution of the Church's official teaching.

The Dumont Report was published in 1971, a time when the respect for dissenting voices had a special relevance. In 1968 Paul VI had published the encyclical *Humanae Vitae*, reaffirming the prohibition of artificial methods of birth control. He had published this encyclical without consulting the bishops of the Church and in disagreement with the study commission he himself had appointed.

This was a clear signal that he had lost his enthusiasm for dialogue and was returning to a monarchical understanding of the papacy. Yet empirical research has shown that his teaching has not been received by the majority of Catholics in the societies of the West.

The Quebec theologians follow the proposals of the Dumont Report: they see themselves in respectful dialogue with the ecclesiastical magisterium and acknowledge that in some situations dissenting voices play a significant role in the evolution of Catholic teaching. According to Fernand Dumont, as we noted in chapter 3, the evolution of Catholic teaching in the Church's history depends upon three factors in constant interaction: (1) the religious experiences of believers, (2) the reflection of theologians, and (3) the discernment of the episcopal and papal magisterium. He holds that the dialogue among these three groups, occasionally interrupted by conflict, allows the magisterium to formulate the norms of belief in a given context.

Very few Quebec theologians offer theological reflections on the exercise of the Church's magisterium. Most of them do not deal with the question raised for them and for educated Catholics in general by the undisputed fact that at Vatican Council II the magisterium changed its mind on a number of issues, in particular on religious liberty, human rights, the ecumenical movement, the respect for Judaism, and the presence of God's grace in the whole of human history.

AN UNRESOLVED QUESTION

In 1998 the meeting of la Société canadienne de théologie asked for papers dealing with topics that for pastoral reasons deserve urgent attention. In the paper I gave at this meeting, I showed that ordinary Catholics have questions regarding the magisterium that need to be taken seriously. Their parents were brought up with the idea that the Church's official teaching never changes, while at Vatican Council II and afterwards, the Church did change its teaching on faith and morals.

Well known to Catholics of the past was the teaching *extra ecclesiam nulla salus*, no salvation outside of the Church. In 1442 the Council of Florence declared, "No one existing outside of the Catholic Church, neither pagans, nor Jews, heretics or schismatics, can participate in eternal life; instead they will go into the eternal fire 'prepared for the devil and his angels' (Mt 25:41) unless they have become members of the Church before the end of their life."[4] This teaching had practical consequences: Catholics avoided contacts with dissident Christians and the followers of other religions, believing them to be deprived of God's grace. As late as 1943, Pius XII still taught that non-Catholic Christians were deprived of the Holy Spirit.[5] Yet rereading the Scriptures and the Catholic tradition, and being attentive to new spiritual experiences, the bishops at Vatican Council II arrived at the conclusion that revealed in Jesus Christ is the presence of God's grace in the whole of human history. "Since Christ died for all humans and since the ultimate vocation of humans is in fact one and divine, we must hold that the Holy Spirit in a manner known only to God offers every human being the possibility of being associated with the Pascal Mystery."[6] Despite the universality of sin, God is graciously at work in the human family, summoning humans to trust, hope, and love – and yearn for freedom and justice for all. For Catholics living in a pluralistic society, the conciliar teaching makes them look upon their neighbours in a different way, respecting them, listening to them, and being open to co-operating with them to make society more just.

The new teaching also led to the elimination of limbo, a teaching that Catholics had been taught to accept. Assuming that God's grace was confined to the Church, the traditional teaching was obliged to deny the entry into heaven of babies who had died unbaptized. Since putting them into hell would have been too severe, the Church invented a place for them, called *limbus infantium* or limbo, in which the suffering imposed on these infants was simply their exclusion from intimacy with God. After recognizing that revealed in Jesus Christ is God's loving embrace of the whole human family, including newborn babies, Catholics stopped worrying about their fate in the case of death, assured that they were safely in God's arms. In 2007 the International Theological Commission produced a report, subsequently recognized by Benedict XVI, that laid to rest the old teaching of the *limbus infantium*.[7]

Despite these changes, the new teaching on the universality of God's grace is, on a deeper level, in continuity with the Church's traditional teaching confessing Jesus as universal saviour, his death and resurrection as the beginning of a new era, and the limitlessness of God's love of humanity. In changing its teaching, the magisterium remained faithful to the core of the Christian message.

What is missing is a theology of the magisterium that accounts for its evolution in time, including moments of discontinuity. When I learnt that the International Theological Commission, instituted by the Holy See in 1969, was preparing a theological statement on the ecclesiastical magisterium, I expected that this group of theologians would provide some answers. Their statement, entitled "The Interpretation of Dogma," published in 2007, offers only a few paragraphs on the changes in the Church's teaching. It briefly recognizes that in the encounter with modernity, the magisterium has modified its attitude towards the sciences; towards human rights, especially religious liberty; towards the ecumenical movement; and towards several other issues. This is how the declaration accounts for these changes.

> In a world which is increasingly pluralistic and in a Church where differences are more pronounced, the magisterium fulfills its mission in having more and more recourse to discussion. In such circumstances, the heritage of faith cannot be passed on except by the willingness on the part of the magisterium and others with pastoral and theological responsibility to engage in a common dialogue.[8]

The Commission was unwilling to explore the new situation and the new functioning of the magisterium in any detail. It offered no answer to Catholics who are puzzled by the doctrinal evolution that has occurred, including reversals of previous positions. Was the Council of Florence right or wrong when it solemnly declared that people outside the Catholic Church went to hell when they died? How do we reconcile the repeated condemnations of religious liberty by the popes of the nineteenth century with the Declaration of Religious Liberty promulgated by Vatican Council II?

CARDINAL RATZINGER'S ANSWER

To my knowledge, the only attempt of the magisterium to answer this question has been a *nota* of Cardinal Joseph Ratzinger, published in *Osservatore Romano* of 1 and 2 July 2001,[9] that applies the historical-critical method to the interpretation of the Church's official teaching. The *nota* lifts the condemnation of forty propositions drawn from the philosophical work of Antonio Rosmini that were pronounced in 1887 – and then explains how the magisterium can do this without involving itself in an internal contradiction.

Antonio Rosmini (1797–1855) was an Italian philosopher and ardent Catholic whose holy life was widely acknowledged in his day. Rosmini's famous book, *The Five Wounds of the Church*, written in 1832, contained a program for the reform of the Church. Among several proposals, Rosmini suggested that the clergy and laity of a diocese be involved in the selection of their bishop. This book as well as another one written by him were put on the Index of Forbidden Books in 1849, yet in 1854, one year before his death, Rosmini's entire work was declared above suspicion. A few years later, in 1887, the decree *Post Obitum* of the Holy Office condemned as erroneous forty propositions drawn from his writings, some of which were published posthumously. The *nota* of July 2001 now declares that these propositions are not erroneous. This switch, Cardinal Ratzinger writes in the *nota*, can be explained.

A superficial reading of these events, the cardinal writes, suggests an intrinsic and objective contradiction. Yet an attentive reading of these events, taking into consideration their historical context, reveals that this change is appropriate and non-contradictory. The cardinal reminds us of the historical situation in 1887 when the forty propositions were condemned. In 1879, Leo XIII's encyclical *Aeterni Patris* had tried to unify the theological education of the clergy by making neo-Thomism the Church's official philosophy, which meant that philosophical pluralism was no longer welcome. Moreover, many passages in Rosmini's writings were ambiguous and, if read from a neo-Thomistic perspective, clearly erroneous and deserving of ecclesiastical censure. The situation was urgent, the cardinal continues, because at the time non-Catholic philosophers were interpreting Rosmini in line with their own orientation. Hence the decree *Post Obitum* was fully justified. According to the cardinal, the present situation is quite different. First, serious research has shown that if Rosmini's ambiguous and obscure passages are interpreted in the light of his own philosophical work, their meaning is not contrary to Catholic teaching. Second, in his encyclical *Faith and Reason* of 1998, John Paul II has welcomed philosophical pluralism in the Church and actually mentioned with great respect Antonio Rosmini among several Catholic thinkers of the nineteenth century. That is why, at the present time, lifting the condemnations decreed in 1887 is fully justified. The magisterium was right in 1887 and in 2001, protecting the truth in two different historical situations.

The *nota* of July 2001 is an important ecclesiastical document, for it applies the historical-critical method (which is commonly used today for interpreting the Scriptures) to the interpretation of the Church's official teaching. Cardinal Ratzinger's approach opens the door to a new field of research.

A brief look at the historical context of the Council of Florence, famed for its exclusivist discourse, reveals that it took place at a time when the Council of Basle, though dissolved by the pope, was still in session, promoting a conciliar theory that stipulated the superiority of the Council over the pope. Because the Council of Florence defended the papacy against a powerful competing ecclesiastical institution, it denounced all outsiders, even if they were Christians leading holy lives, as hostile to God and worthy of hell. In other historical contexts, the Church offered a more generous ecclesiology.

Cardinal Ratzinger's approach also encourages us to read the papal condemnation of religious liberty in its historical context. In the European Middle Ages, the Christian faith was shared by the king and his people and constituted an important dimension of the common good of society. This inheritance was reconfirmed after the wars of religions by the Peace of Westphalia in 1648, which decided that to protect the religious peace of Europe the religion of the prince should determine the religion of his people (*cuius regio, eius religio*). The separation of Church and State introduced by the liberal societies emerging in the late eighteenth century undermined this legal inheritance and, in the eyes of conservatives, including the popes, threatened the common good of society. The popes believed that in this situation, the Gospel demanded that Catholics defend the old order, protecting as it did the Church's well-being. Over a century later, reflecting on the Gospel in a pluralistic society persuaded the magisterium to change its teaching and recognize people's religious liberty.

Cardinal Ratzinger's application of the historical-critical method also helps me to understand why, on issues of human sexuality and the man-woman relationship, the majority of Catholics in the societies of the West do not accept the Church's official teaching. The Church's discourse on these topics, reflecting the values of a culture that no longer exists, sounds like a foreign language to many contemporary Catholics. The absence of consent in Quebec has been documented in the above-mentioned studies of Raymond Lemieux and Martin Meunier. Detailed research of the beliefs of Catholics in the USA, published in November 2011,[10] shows that the majority of

American Catholics are faithful to the Church's central teaching on God and Jesus Christ, yet that in matters of personal morality they rely on their own conscience, not on the magisterium. In Quebec, women theologians have been most emphatic in rejecting the official Catholic teaching on the man-woman relationship and human sexuality. Louise Melançon reports in an article how her work as a theologian led her to disagree with the official teaching on these issues.[11] Sophie Tremblay also reports in an article that the members of the network *Culture et foi* live an intense life of faith, while rejecting the official teaching on these issues.[12] The conservative argument that these Catholics give in to the hedonistic current of contemporary culture is not convincing. The major Protestant Churches offer a reading of the Bible and theological reflections that allow them to be more open to contemporary values. What the Catholic magisterium does not realize is that the passage from a culture marked by patriarchy to a culture aspiring to gender equality produces profound changes in the self-understanding of men and women and affects even their sexual lives.

The development of doctrine, Dumont has shown, depends on three factors: (1) the religious experience of believers, (2) the reflection of theologians, and (3) the discernment of the magisterium. The dialogue among these three groups, occasionally interrupted by conflict, allows the magisterium to formulate the norms of belief in a given context. Yet Dumont also puts forth that the Church's emphasis on "orthodoxy" has problematic pastoral consequences. It suggests that faith in God's Word is belief in a series of doctrines, forgetting that in fact faith is the entry into a new way of life and of seeing the world.

ANDRÉ NAUD AND ARMAND VEILLEUX

A bold proposal regarding the magisterium has been made by André Naud. In his book *Les dogmes et le respect de l'intelligence*[13] Naud allows himself to be inspired by theological reflections offered by Simone Weil, the French philosopher well-known for her wholehearted commitment to faith and justice. Naud presents a careful reading of the passages in which Simone Weil reveals her faith in Jesus Christ and at the same time explains why she is unable to become a member of the Catholic Church. She fully embraces Catholic doctrine on the Incarnation, the Trinity, and the Eucharist, yet finds it impossible to be baptized and become a Catholic. The great obstacle for her is the Church's power to say *anathema sit*, i.e. to condemn and exclude a person unable to accept an official dogma. Weil believes that this power violates both the freedom and the intelligence of believers. Persons of faith, she argues, accept a dogma taught by the Church when it confirms their faith and offers a deeper insight into it. Belief in a dogma is not an act of obedience, nor can it be produced by willpower; it is rather the emergence of a deep conviction. Believers accept a dogma of the Church when it sheds light on what they believe and thus increases the intelligibility of their faith.

At the same time, Weil wants the Church to teach with authority; she trusts that in doing so, the Church is guided by the Holy Spirit, offering ever greater insight into God's revelation. Catholics, she argues, are obliged to listen attentively to the Church's authoritative teaching. Paying attention, it must be noted, has an important meaning in Weil's philosophy. Listening carefully, becoming sensitive to the hidden meaning of what is said, recognizing the pain in the words of the other, being ready to learn, to hear the new, to be surprised, and if need be, to be corrected or converted – are all attitudes implied in what Weil means by paying attention. Catholics, she holds, are obliged to pay attention to the Church's teaching and try to be convinced by it, yet in doing so they remain free. If their attention does not lead to an enlightenment of their faith and they find themselves unable to embrace a particular dogma, Catholic believers must be free to express this unbelief in public. For Simone Weil, the dissenting person merits respect, not excommunication.

André Naud fully agrees with Simone Weil. He tells us that the discovery of her thought has made him happy. After anguishing over certain Catholic dogmas, he has found the freedom to reveal his thought and to be at peace in the Church.

The proposal of Simone Weil, seconded by André Naud, deals with belief in dogmas, i.e. doctrines defined by the Church as belonging to the substance of the Christian faith. Most dogmas were defined in antiquity. The Church's contemporary magisterium deals with a wide spectrum of doctrines and moral norms that it does not claim are dogmas to be believed, but simply require an obedient acceptance – a topic not dealt with by Weil and Naud.

Critical reflections on the Church's contemporary magisterium are offered by a Quebec Cistercian, Dom Armand Veilleux, currently the abbot of Scourmont Abbey in Belgium. This thoughtful monk, engaged in many pastoral functions in his Order and his Church, offers his theological reflections in public lectures given in Europe and North America, all of which are available on his website. In the following pages I wish to present the ideas expressed in a lecture on the present crisis in the Church that he gave at Louvain University on 8 February 2010.[14]

Societies in the West have changed, Veilleux argues. We live in a new pluralistic situation, shoulder to shoulder with people of different religions and of no religion and surrounded by images and proposals of alternative ways of life. We no longer belong to walled communities with members sharing the same philosophy of life. The family, the parish, the village, and the neighbourhood have acquired porous walls. People now have to decide for themselves whether to become and remain believers. They are no longer urged to believe by a tightly woven community to which they belong. In the West, wall-to-wall religion has disappeared. This point, I wish to add, is strongly made by Charles Taylor when, in his recent book *The Secular Age*, he defines contemporary secularity as the culture in which people have to decide individually how to define the good and whether to be believers or non-believers.

Dom Veilleux argues that the conservative movement currently fostered by the Vatican does not take into account the cultural transformation produced by the new pluralism, the dissolution of all protected communities, and the need of people to rely on their own judgment in matters of religion and ethics. Until now, Veilleux continues, the magisterium assumed that Catholic societies or fenced-in Catholic minorities in non-Catholic countries are able to transmit the faith to the next generation. Catholics used to obey the authoritative teaching and remain loyal to their parish and the wider Catholic community. Popes and bishops addressed Catholics to strengthen their communities, demanding unanimity and denouncing non-conformity. Dom Veilleux argues that this pastoral policy does not work anymore. In this secular, pluralistic society, people choose to be Catholics based on their own judgment. As members of the Church, they respect ecclesiastical authority and are willing to listen and learn, yet since trusting their personal judgment has led them into the Church, they continue as Catholics to rely on their own conscience. In fact, Veilleux adds, Catholics now want to speak and be heard in the Church. The abbot thinks that the Vatican still offers its teaching as if Catholics lived in stable communities with clearly defined boundaries, clinging to doctrinal unanimity and refusing to dialogue with outsiders. According to the abbot, "the Church tries to be present to a world that no longer exists."

Veilleux proposes an alternate way of teaching. He thinks the Church should promote a humanism in keeping with the Gospel, in which there is room for pluralism. Many people in the West, he notes, still have religious concerns. A great number of Catholics have left the Church because they disagree with certain teachings or find the organization oppressive, yet they often continue to believe in the Gospel and are engaged in works of love, justice, and peace. Veilleux also appreciates the widespread longing for spirituality: people want to be in touch with their own depth to survive and be well in today's troubled and conflictive world. People who call themselves agnostic, he continues, often interpret the human struggle of existence in images drawn from the Christian faith, such as love, forgiveness, compassion, service, and sacrifice. Secular people committed to justice and peace often appreciate the Church's social teaching and advocate co-operation between believers and non-believers in a common effort to make society more just and more humane. There is, moreover, a spiritual dimension in the social movements for justice and peace, for human rights, for the protection of the environment, for a moral economy, for equality between men and women, for the protection of refugees, for the respect of gays and lesbians, and for solidarity with the peoples of the global South. Among these people and in these movements, Veilleux holds, the Spirit is at work. In a new evangelization, the Church must find words to encourage and support all the people touched by God's Spirit, telling them that the Church respects them and wants to co-operate with them and that its hope for the future is grounded in God's self-revelation in Jesus Christ. Such a proclamation of the Good News involves dialogue, disagreement, and pluralism: its aim is not to create a unanimous Church, but to serve and encourage the wider movement in society touched by the Spirit of Jesus.

We should not be surprised that this new mode of proclamation is proposed by an abbot. Today many monasteries have become centres of prayer and reflection, attracting believers and agnostics, that communicate the wisdom of the Gospel, helping each person to pursue his or her own path to God. Here the Gospel does not divide, but gathers.

The cultural impact of the new pluralism and its influence on believing Christians presented by Veilleux is also offered in the writing of Peter Berger,[15] Charles Taylor,[16] and Fernand Dumont. For the latter, the new pluralism belongs to the second culture in which Christians have to live their faith. Since the secular culture obliges people to decide for themselves whether to become or remain believers, the task of the magisterium is to protect the Church's unity in what is essential, respect the consciences of Catholic believers, and recognize the pluralism of convictions as a sign of the Church's vitality.[17] To rescue believers from spiritual individualism, the magisterium must emphasize the convictions and practices held in common, especially the Scriptures and the sacramental liturgy, with respect for the pluralism of interpretation.

In an article of mine on the Church of tomorrow, influenced by Dom Armand Veilleux's analysis, I show that Karl Rahner described the present phase of the Church's history in similar fashion: its existence as a minority in countries where it exists and its openness to cultural and theological pluralism.[18] He writes that we will be a Diaspora Church, an international network of minorities.

This is how I have summarized his ideas:

> In the present age ecclesiastical pluralism will be greater than in antiquity. Vatican centralism and enforced unanimity will not survive. Catholics will be encouraged to think for themselves, be in conversation with their bishop and make their own contribution to the life of the Church. Catholics will have to learn … to live with diversity and remain brothers and sisters in Christ, even as they disagree with one another in matters related to their diverse cultures. [19]

As a sociologist Fernand Dumont recognizes that every organization, including every Church, is in need of a governing authority. He is grateful for the early ecumenical councils that defined the doctrines of Incarnation and Trinity, yet he regrets that after the Reformation, especially since the nineteenth century, the papacy has multiplied doctrinal norms without an ongoing conversation with the various Catholic communities and without taking into account the rich pluralism within the Church.

10

The Challenge of Pluralism

In his book *A Secular Age*, the Montreal-based Canadian philosopher Charles Taylor argues that the starting point for the secularization of European culture was the emergence in the seventeenth century of a humanistic philosophy that criticized the exclusiveness of Christianity and advocated instead universal justice. Christian charity stopped at the borders of the Church; it did not embrace schismatics, heretics, Jews, or pagans. The philosophers Justus Lipsius († 1606) and Hugo Grotius († 1645) wanted an ethic of universal solidarity. They believed that human beings have a God-given intelligence that allows them to sit around the table, engage in dialogue, and together define the ethical norms for a society in which people live together in peace and justice, excluding no one.[1] This, Taylor argues, provided a dignified alternative to Christianity.

It was only after the horrors committed during World War II, especially the Holocaust, that the Christian Churches were willing to question their relationship to outsiders – to Jews, dissenting Christians, and members of the world religions. Recognizing that contempt for outsiders has grave social and political consequences, Christians, listening anew to the biblical message of love, justice, and peace, heard a summons to extend their solidarity to all human beings. The bishops gathered at Vatican Council II decided to change the Church's official teaching. The Decree on Ecumenism acknowledged dissident Christians as brothers and sisters in Christ, and the Declaration *Nostra Aetate* acknowledged the ongoing validity of God's ancient covenant with the children of Israel. *Nostra Aetate* also expressed the Church's respect for the world religions, recognizing that many of their ideas and values are shared by Christian believers.

In this chapter I shall discuss the theological and pastoral questions which the new openness to religious pluralism raised for the Church of Quebec. In recent decades Quebec society has changed. The Asian and African immigrants who have come to Quebec in great numbers introduced this society to a religious pluralism it had not known before. Followers of the different world religions became our neighbours. This obliged the bishops, in dialogue with theologians, to clarify the attitude that Catholics should adopt in regard to their new neighbours. Since the new religious and cultural pluralism also produced a debate in the secular society, the Church found itself obliged to join this debate, spelling out the social implications of the love of neighbour. There were historical reasons why, in the climate of the new openness, the Native peoples strengthened their movement of protest, demanding their release from the colonial institutions imposed on them. The loud voice of the Natives prompted the Canadian Churches to repent of their past blindness and made theologians in Quebec reflect on the evil of colonialism.

THE CHURCH AND RELIGIOUS PLURALISM

The bishops and theologians of Quebec fully endorsed the teaching of the Decree on Ecumenism and the Declaration *Nostra Aetate*. Two francophone Canadian theologians, Bernard Lambert[2] and Jean-Marie Tillard,[3] had made major contributions to the ecumenical movement. In Montreal, Irénée Beaubien was an ardent promoter of ecumenism, and Stéphane Valiquette started dialogue with Jews prior to Vatican Council II. In 1963 Robert Vachon and Jacques Langlais founded le Centre Monchanin, soon to become le Centre interculturel de Montréal, fostering interreligious dialogue and honouring the spirituality of the Native peoples. Eventually ecumenism and interreligious dialogue were fostered by Quebec's faculties of theology.

The Church's new openness to the world religions raised many questions for ordinary Catholics who had been taught that there was no salvation outside the Church. Does the new teaching mean that all religions are equally true? What should be the attitude of Catholics to the non-Christian immigrants who have become their neighbours? Vatican Council II had not resolved the theological question raised by *Nostra Aetate*. The Council did not explain how to reconcile interreligious dialogue and co-operation with the Church's mission to proclaim the Good News. The conciliar documents mention three distinctive vocations of the Church. The decree *Ad Gentes* confirms the Church's mission to convert non-Christians to the Christian faith; *Gaudium et Spes* recognizes the Church's vocation to promote justice and peace in the world; and *Nostra Aetate* calls for interreligious dialogue and co-operation. The social engagement for justice and peace and the practice of interreligious dialogue go together very well, yet how to relate these two activities to the missionary proclamation of the Gospel is not clear.

The ecclesiastical magisterium has not resolved this question. In the instruction *Dominus Jesus,* issued in 2000 by the Congregation of the Doctrine of the Faith and signed by its president, Cardinal Ratzinger, we were told that interreligious dialogue weakened the Church's mission to convert the world and that Catholics taking part in this dialogue should never forget that the ultimate purpose of their participation in dialogue is the conversion of their partners to the Catholic truth.[4] As pope, Joseph Ratzinger eventually changed his mind. Benedict XVI, speaking in Jerusalem on 9 May 2009, recognized that the purpose of interreligious dialogue was to promote mutual understanding and co-operation among the various religious communities, supporting the social peace in pluralistic societies. Speaking in England on 17 September 2010, Benedict even admitted that what believers in the various traditions, including Roman Catholics, have in common is that they are seekers, each trying to enter more deeply into the truth of their own tradition. More remarkable still is Pope Benedict's speech delivered on 18 November 2011 in Benin, Africa, that honoured the religious and cultural pluralism of the African continent and praised the efforts to achieve interreligious reconciliation. He said, "I would like to use the image of a hand. There are five fingers on it and each one is quite different. Each one is also essential and their unity makes a hand."[5] Mutual understanding among cultures and religions, appreciation for each other without condescension, and respect for the rights of each one, he said, are moral obligations that must be taught to the faithful of all religions. It is not clear whether this means that the African Church should stop its mission to convert non-believers to the Christian faith.

Since *Nostra Aetate* raises urgent pastoral problems, the Quebec bishops appointed a theological committee in 2000 to study how the new teaching affects the relation of Catholics to the Native peoples and to non-Christian religious believers living in Quebec. In

June 2005, relying on the work of this committee, the bishops published the theological note "Est-ce que toutes les religions se valent?"[6] The note explains that the new openness to the world religions does not mean that all religions are equally true, for as Christians we believe that God's truth is wholly and uniquely revealed in Jesus Christ. The note rejects religious relativism; at the same time, it also repudiates religious absolutism, i.e. the refusal to recognize any truth outside of one's own religious tradition. The authors of this theological note arrive at a positive interpretation of religious pluralism. They explore the implications of a sentence from John Paul II's encyclical *Redemptoris Missio*:

> Other religions constitute a positive challenge for the Church: they stimulate her both to discover and acknowledge the signs of Christ's presence and of the working of the Spirit, as well as to examine more deeply her own identity and to bear witness to the fullness of Revelation which she has received for the good of all.[7]

In the instruction *Dominus Jesus* of the year 2000, Cardinal Ratzinger still held that religious pluralism existed only in fact (*de facto*), while in principle (*de jure*) there was only one religion, Roman Catholicism. At that time he still believed that religious pluralism was an unhappy condition to be overcome eventually by the triumphant spread of Catholicism. By contrast, the Quebec bishops, following hints made by John Paul II, attribute the plurality of religions to divine providence. Engaging in interreligious dialogue, the bishops argue, Catholics acquire a deeper understanding of their own faith, give witness of this their faith before the world, and discover God's redemptive action in other religious traditions. The new openness to the plurality of religions allows the Church to become more truly itself and fully realize its destiny. It is an enlightening paradox, the note suggests, that the commitment of Christians to the One Truth is the very reason why they love and respect outsiders and engage in dialogue with them.

Because this teaching is so new and has many pastoral implications, the Quebec bishops believed that more has to be said. They enlarged their appointed committee, asking it to clarify the meaning of interreligious dialogue for Quebec and help the Church to redefine its attitude towards the spirituality of the Native peoples. The report of this committee was published in 2007 as the booklet *Le dialogue interreligieux dans un Québec pluraliste*.[8] It contains a summary of the conciliar teaching on the Church's relation to the world religions, a careful survey of religious pluralism in Quebec, an appreciation of Native spirituality, and pastoral advice for interreligious activities in Quebec. Following the suggestion of the Pontifical Council of Interreligious Dialogue, the booklet recommends interreligious dialogue on different levels: (1) dialogue of the street among neighbours, (2) dialogue in view of common action in society, (3) dialogue on prayer and meditation, and (4) dialogue on matters of theology.

Recommending friendly relations between the Catholic population and the recent non-Christian immigrants also contains a social message that we shall examine in a subsequent section. Some priests are able to communicate the new teaching to their parishioners, while others find it unsettling and prefer to remain silent. Montrealers driving past the Holy Family Church on rue Lajeunesse see over its entrance two large placards in French and English, saying "Respect the religion of your neighbour."

The booklet of the Quebec bishops tried to resolve the conflict between dialogue and proclamation, an issue the Roman magisterium has left up in the air. In *Redemptoris Missio*, John Paul II recognized dialogue and proclamation as two distinctive activities, each following its own guiding principles.

> Dialogue does not originate from tactical concerns or self-interest, but is an activity with its own guiding principles, requirements and dignity. It is demanded by deep respect for everything that has been brought about in human beings by the Spirit who blows where he wills.
>
> Interreligious dialogue is a part of the Church's evangelizing mission. Understood as a method and means of mutual knowledge and enrichment, dialogue is not in opposition to the mission [of proclamation]; indeed, it has special links with that mission and is one of its expressions.[9]

What the teaching of John Paul does not do is to help a Church or a parish to decide whether to engage in dialogue with its non-Christian neighbours or whether to invite them to accept the Christian message. The Quebec bishops give an answer to this question. Their booklet argues that the Church in Quebec makes no effort to convert non-Christian immigrants to the Christian faith. What the bishops want Catholics to do is to welcome the newcomers, respect their traditions, protect them against popular prejudice, and help them to feel at home in their new society.

> The Catholic Church in Quebec, founded upon the population of this land, today welcomes people of all world religions ... The Church carries with society the responsibility of their future together with that [of the established population] ... This future cannot blossom harmoniously without a special sensibility to interreligious dialogue aimed at mutual understanding and respect for difference. In certain concrete situations, directly targeting conversion of people of other religious traditions can be inappropriate and constitute a lack of respect and a barrier to proclamation.[10]

The major Churches of Europe and North America refuse to evangelize the non-Christian immigrants in their society, even if they do not offer theological arguments for their decision. The Islam-in-Europe Committee, set up in the 1990s by the European Churches, Catholic and Protestant, recommended that the Churches ask their members to welcome and respect the new immigrants and help them to integrate in their new home.[11] The Quebec bishops do not hesitate to combine admiration of the plurality of religions with the confession of the unique mediatorship of Jesus Christ. Here is a text from the booklet *Proposer aujourd'hui Jésus Christ* published in 2003 by the archdiocese of Montreal.

> The religious pluralism in Montreal, a chorus of seekers of God, elicits the wish to know the score and understand the multiple languages of the Spirit. This first fruit of interreligious dialogue is to lead the communities to the best of themselves, to highlight that which is humanizing in their tradition and downplay that which is intransigent. In the practice of cordiality the Spirit welcomes us. As they help human persons to grow, the different religions can be considered as authentic manifestations of God's care. Still, the mission of proclaiming the Gospel remains.[12]

When the government after a long public debate decided in 2005 to secularize the school system of Quebec, the bishops regretted that Catholic religious knowledge would no longer be taught in the public schools. Yet their appreciation of religious pluralism made them react favourably to the new course, Ethics and Religious Culture, introduced by the Ministry of Education for all students without exception. In a communiqué of 17 February 2012, the bishops write, "We accept the decision of the government of Quebec to introduce a single course on ethics and religious culture for all students and recognize the value of its aim and purpose: the respectful recognition of 'the other' and the promotion of the common good."[13] At the same time, the bishops remain vigilant: they will follow the impact of this course on the Catholic students.

The difficult question in regard to the Church's mission – when to proclaim the Gospel and when to engage in interreligious dialogue – has preoccupied me in my own theological writings.[14] I have argued that at the present time, troubled by the memory of European colonialism and the ongoing violent conflicts in the name of religion, the Church renounces its mission to convert to the Christian faith believers settled in their inherited religious tradition and supported by it in their pursuit of the good life. With such believers the Church engages in dialogue and co-operates, serving the common good of society. The Church is sent to preach the Gospel to people who are unsettled seekers, who are confused or thoughtless, who are prisoners of a destructive ideology or caught in a religious current that generates hatred for outsiders.

SOCIETY AND CULTURAL PLURALISM

The cultural pluralism created by the arrival of immigrants from all parts of the world has produced reactions in Quebec that are different from those in English-speaking Canada. In Quebec the heated debate on this topic does not allow Christians to remain silent. Catholic social justice centres, religious congregations, and the bishops themselves have commented on this issue in the light of the Christian message. To make this debate comprehensible, I shall present a brief summary of the evolution of Quebec society and its ongoing insecurities.[15]

The descendants of the French settlers in North America thought of themselves as *les Canadiens*, the French-Canadian nation, the core and centre of which was Lower Canada, later the province of Quebec. A vigorous sense of national identity, supported by the Catholic Church, enabled them to define themselves in a manner at odds with the dominant North American culture produced by Protestant values and secular modernization. Because French-Canadian nationalism was rooted in a common religious culture, it was open to the integration of the people of other origins, in particular the Aboriginals and the nineteenth-century Irish immigrants. Yet since the financial and educational elites concentrated in Montreal were English-speaking, the immigrants arriving from the late nineteenth century to the 1960s tended to join the Anglo minority, allowing the French-Canadian majority to remain undisturbed. Still, beginning in the 1930s, the desire to catch up with modernity became strong in certain sectors of Quebec society, including the movement of Catholic Action. This trend came to a climax on 22 June 1960, when the Liberal Party under Jean Lesage was elected to form the provincial government, replacing the conservative Union Nationale. What took place was a major political and cultural upheaval, the Quiet Revolution, briefly described in chapter 1 of this book. Quebecers had multiple aspirations: to catch up with North America's technological and democratic developments; to replace the Anglo economic elite and become the masters of their own province; to preserve a strong sense of social solidarity, inherited from the past; and to elect a government that would support economic development and redistribute the wealth of society in favour of workers and the poor.

At this time, Quebecers started to see themselves as a nation. They thought of themselves as a people settled on a territory with clearly defined boundaries, enjoying a common cultural heritage, a democratic political organization, a sound economy, and the capacity to welcome people of other origins. They referred to themselves no longer as *les Canadiens*, but as *les Québécois*. They saw themselves as a nation within the Canadian confederation. Responding to the Quebec's emerging pluralistic self-understanding, the Quebec government adopted a Charter of Human Rights and Freedoms in 1975; and to reinforce the internal cohesion of the pluralistic society, the Quebec government passed Bill 101 in 1977, making French the official language of the province and demanding that it be used in the major industrial, commercial, and financial institutions as well as in public signs and advertisements. While Bill 101 obliges immigrants and all newcomers to Quebec to send their children to francophone schools, the law fully respects the institutional rights of the old-established Anglo community, including their schools, universities, hospitals, and social work agencies.

The Quebec nationalism that had been ethnic and cultural gradually became a territorial nationalism, embracing all citizens of Quebec whatever their origin. This evolving self-understanding was recorded in public statements made by the Catholic bishops. The pastoral letter written by the Canadian Catholic bishops, francophone and anglophone, in the centennial year of 1967 still referred to the French-Canadian nation from sea to sea,[16] with its core and centre in the province of Quebec; while a decade later, two pastoral letters written by the Quebec bishops in 1977 and 1979 respectively defined "the Quebec nation" in pluri-cultural terms,[17] embracing the francophone majority, about eighty percent of the population, the anglophone minority of long standing, and the ethno-cultural communities that have arrived more recently.

I mentioned in chapter 4 that theologians were in disagreement about whether the Quebec nation should remain part of Canada or strive for political sovereignty. Yet federalists and sovereigntists are in perfect agreement that Quebec's cultural identity is fragile, challenged by its location on an English-speaking continent, and therefore in need of institutional protection. That the small francophone society continues to feel threatened is due neither to paranoia nor to aggressive policies adopted by English Canada. The threat is the result of an objective factor: the cultural weight of the English language in North America. The cultural weight of a language is determined by the power of the institutions that mediate it in society. Because in North America industry, commerce, technology, administration, scientific research, and entertainment operate in English, this language puts pressure on the small francophone society and therefore constitutes a threat, especially in Montreal where many of these institutions are located.

There are societies – and Quebec is one of them – that wrestle with the tension between two sets of human rights: the personal rights recognized by the Universal Declaration of Human Rights promulgated by the United Nations in 1948,[18] and the collective rights of political and cultural self-determination recognized in several Covenants of the United Nations in the 1960s.[19] The friction between the rights of a people to protect and promote its national culture and the rights of citizens belonging to minorities can only be resolved by democratically developed intelligent compromises.

There are good reasons then why the Quebec government, supported by all political parties, has rejected the federal policy of multiculturalism. Quebec responds to the new pluralism with the policy of "interculturalism," which fosters interaction between the host culture protected by law and the various cultural communities, all of which deserve respect.[20] While in English Canada the arrival of immigrants does not threaten the English language, in Quebec the French language is in need of legal protection. Bill 22 passed by the Liberal government in 1974 and Bill 101 passed by the Parti Québécois government in 1977 made French the official language of Quebec. Immigrants are obliged to send their children to French schools, and companies of a certain size must carry on their operations in French. People belonging to the various ethno-cultural communities are made to feel that society wants them to integrate as much as possible into the host culture, even as they preserve the memory of their own cultural inheritance. It is safe to say that Quebecers have less spontaneous sympathy for the new arrivals and accept less generously their cultural and religious practices than do the citizens in English-speaking Canada.

What interests me in this chapter is the Christian response to the debate about cultural pluralism in Quebec. Quebec bishops and Christian social justice groups, Catholic and Protestant, call for solidarity with the new arrivals and respect for cultural and religious differences. They are well aware that prejudice in the long run leads to racism. They remind society of the social implications of the love of neighbour. In my opinion, academic theology in Quebec has not reflected extensively on Quebec's cultural pluralism, nor has it been in conversation with the social-scientific and philosophical literature on the topic. Significant exceptions are le Centre de théologie et d'éthique contextuelles québécoises and la Chaire du Canada, Islam, pluralisme et globalization, both in the faculty of theology at the University of Montreal: these centres foster studies that promote the appreciation of Quebec's cultural diversity. The important Christian contributions to the respectful recognition of Quebec's cultural pluralism and the promotion of justice for immigrants and refugees have been made by Christians and Christian centres outside of the academy.

Julien Harvey, the founder of the Jesuit-sponsored Centre justice et foi, gave public lectures and wrote many articles on how to combine, in the light of the Christian message, the defense of Quebec's cultural memory with generous gestures welcoming the new immigrants.[21] The review *Relations*, published by the Centre, continues to pursue this theme. In 1992 Julien Harvey created at the Centre the team Vivre ensemble with the aim of promoting the rights of immigrants and refugees, raising public awareness in regard to their problems, and critically examining the federal and provincial laws that control their lives. Vivre ensemble publishes a substantial bulletin four times a year to educate the public and foster solidarity with citizens of immigrant origin.

Julien Harvey's voice calling for solidarity with immigrants and their families had a certain authority because he was an outspoken nationalist and an advocate of Quebec sovereignty. To combine the affirmation of Quebec's national identity with respect for cultural pluralism, Harvey and his friends recommended the idea of "a common public culture," i.e. a set of values and practices that would enable all Quebecers, whatever their origin, to work together in building a more just society, while leaving them free to follow their cultural customs in regard to family life and community traditions. The common public culture advocated by Julien Harvey supported democratic participation, economic co-operation, the French language, *la laïcité* (the separation of Church and State), the equality of men and women, and the celebration of the national holidays, keeping alive Quebec's cultural memory. Julien Harvey was convinced that Quebecers were a creative people, capable of inviting newcomers to participate in their historical project and, through these exchanges, enrich and expand Quebec's own culture.[22] An appeal for Quebec's openness to pluralism was also made by Fernand Dumont:

> We tend to forget that the creation of nations in modern times represented a surpassing of narrow communities. The tribe assumes the kinship of its members, the filiation from a common origin, symbolized by the great ancestors. The nation is assembled on a basis that is larger and of another kind. It is an historical project that generates new solidarities, fosters a shared cultural heritage, creates institutions of which people are proud and inspires confidence in its historical destiny. That is why the nation is able to accept pluralism, welcoming different types of spirits. Far from cultivating uniformity on the basis of ancestry or race, it sustains its vitality by responding to new influences. Obviously, this openness is not automatic: it requires political vigilance, this other denomination of democracy.[23]

Through its Ministère de l'Immigration et des Communautés culturelles and its Conseil des relations interculturelles, the government of Quebec published over the years many statements on Quebec's openness to pluralism, its respect for cultural differences, and the integration of immigrants and their families into the common public culture. In Quebec the public discourse affirms democratic values and avoids remarks that express prejudice or justify discrimination, while in actual fact Quebecers are still unsettled by the new ethnic and religious pluralism, lacking spontaneous sympathy for the new arrivals. Conservative and right-wing voices, a small minority, criticize the government for admitting ever more immigrants and fostering cultural pluralism in Quebec society. Racism in Quebec tends to be hidden behind a politically correct vocabulary, yet it is real, finding expression – for instance – in the high rate of unemployment among Quebecers of Arab or African origin.

SOCIETY AND RELIGIOUS PLURALISM

Related to the lack of spontaneous sympathy for immigrants is the increasing impatience of many Quebecers with the public presence of religious symbols and practices introduced by certain communities, especially by believing Muslim women. Some Quebecers interpret these religious customs as signs that the immigrants resist integration. The growing prejudice against Muslims after 11 September 2001 has also affected Quebec society. Quebec's Human Rights Commission, constituted to apply Quebec's Human Rights Charter to concrete cases, has dispensed certain individuals from conforming to common practices that interfere with their religious observances, for instance allowing police officers to wear beards or Sikh boys to bring their ceremonial knives to school. Some of these accommodations have annoyed Quebecers. A certain resentment against the oppressive Catholicism of the past makes many Quebecers advocate a strict interpretation of *la laïcité*, excluding religious symbols from the public realm and confining the practice of religion to the private sphere. The growing tension over such accommodations persuaded the government in 2007 to set up a Commission, chaired by the sociologist Gérard Bouchard and the philosopher Charles Taylor, to hold hearings throughout the province, listen to the wishes and aspirations of the people, and come up with a set of public policies that would foster social peace and harmony in Quebec.[24]

Among the briefs submitted to the Bouchard-Taylor Commission were theological statements on religious and cultural pluralism made by several Christian groups, including a brief from the Quebec bishops, a twelve-page document analyzing the debated issues in the light of the Christian message. I wish to quote two paragraphs from this brief, one on the welcome of refugees and immigrants and the other on the future of the nation.[25]

> It seems important to us to start thinking about how we welcome the other. The way we welcome the other sheds light on the moral quality of our society. The wisdom literature of religious traditions provides many maxims insisting on the need to offer hospitality to visitors. Hospitality is also emphasized in the Christian tradition, culminating in the parable of the final judgment where Jesus identifies himself as the stranger: "I was a stranger and you welcomed me." (Matthew 25:35). For this welcome to be authentic, it has to take into account the needs of refugees and immigrants. They need to be respected, both as individuals and as groups. An overly individualistic understanding of human rights risks erasing the presence and the needs of religious and ethnic communities, which actually serve as links to the larger society. Promoting an immigration policy and welcoming newcomers require the ability to recognize their positive contribution and to make personal and collective adaptations that allow them to be included in the host society.

At the same time, the bishops did not overlook the responsibility of their own small nation, linguistically and culturally singular in North America, to defend its historical continuity and make it thrive in the changing circumstances of the future.

> By recognizing the various groups and communities which each have their own "we", it is necessary to move ahead with the construction of a global "we", one of a society required to integrate the richness of its parts, in *fidelity* to its own history and in *openness* to those who come to join it. With its roots in the past it will not deny, this "we" is oriented to the future, ready to be transformed through democratic dialogue and the implementation of a *projet de société*. The adjustments or accommodations adopted to take into consideration particular circumstances will be beneficial since they express a profound respect of persons and facilitate their participation in a common conversation.

The brief submitted to the Bouchard-Taylor Commission by le Centre justice et foi also offers theological reflections on Quebec's cultural pluralism and the fidelity of society to its historical memory.[26] These two briefs offer practical wisdom in the light of the Gospel on how to relate the new pluralism to the affirmation of Quebec's collective identity.

The Bouchard-Taylor Report, published in May 2008, produced a lively debate in Quebec. Jacques Racine, whom we have met several times in these pages, presented a thoughtful evaluation of the Report at the 2011 meeting of la Société canadienne de théologie.[27] He was pleased that the Report called for a generous acceptance of the plurality of cultural practices and advocated an open *laïcité*, i.e. a separation of religion and the State that does not exclude the co-operation between them. At the same time, with many readers of the Report, Jacques Racine regretted the inadequate picture it drew of Quebec's cultural and religious past, without appreciating the efforts of Quebecers to create their society and its social institutions under difficult colonial conditions. Nor did the Report recognize the historical contribution of the Catholic Church to the survival of the French-Canadian nation. It dwelled on the fearfulness of the Quebec people, rather than on their creativity.

In response to the Report, a major debate took place in the pages of the newspaper *Le Devoir* between two groups I shall call "pluralists" and "culturalists."[28] The pluralists agreed with the Report, praised the plural character of Quebec society, and recognized a purely civic understanding of the nation, seemingly without protecting Quebec's historical continuity and its cultural memory. The culturalists, by contrast, criticized the Report for not protecting Quebec's inherited culture and the memory of its history, and for seemingly confining its concern to the defense of Quebec's new cultural pluralism and respect for the human rights of immigrants and their communities. Since the Bouchard-Taylor Report had recommended the adoption of *une Charte de la laïcité* defining the State's neutrality in regard to religion, the ongoing debate between pluralists and culturalists increasingly concentrated on this issue: should *la laïcité* be strict or should it be open? Should people working for the government be prevented from exhibiting religious symbols, for instance wearing the Islamic veil, or should they be free to wear what they wish? The Bouchard-Taylor Report had recommended that only people exercising high functions in government should be prohibited from exhibiting religious signs, while people employed by the government on a lower level, in particular in schools and hospitals, should not see their religious freedom curtailed. The pluralists accepted this recommendation, while the culturalists argued strongly against it: they wanted the government's religious neutrality consistently applied on all levels, high and low, including schools and hospitals. In 2013 the Parti Québécois government announced it would submit a Charter to the National Assembly that consecrated the position of the culturalists, yet as I am writing these lines in October 2013, the public debate continues and no one knows what the outcome will be.

Le Centre justice et foi regrets this heated debate. With the Catholic bishops and a number of prominent intellectuals, the Centre insists that the urgent task of the nation is to combine the pluralist and culturalist concerns, not to choose between them. The dynamic self-making of a people in history includes both openness to change in response to new challenges and fidelity to the memory of its foundational experiences. By welcoming immigrants and refugees, the Centre argues, Quebecers open themselves to social interactions capable of renewing their own culture and making it flourish in as yet unexpected ways. Impressive already at this time is the contribution to Quebec's francophone culture made by novelists, playwrights, painters, musicians, and actors of recent immigrant origin. Since the Centre supports *la laïcité ouverte*, it agrees with the Bouchard-Taylor Report that people working in schools and hospitals should be free to wear the religious symbols they choose. What worries us in particular is that the strict *laïcité* proposed by the government limits the freedom of Muslim women and makes Muslims feel that they cannot become Quebecers in the full sense.

At the same time, we strongly disagree with commentators in the anglophone press and certain angry Quebecers who accuse the culturalists and the present government, demanding the exclusion of religious signs on all levels, of racism or xenophobia. This indictment is unjust. Racism does exist in Quebec as it does in Canada and deserves to be denounced in both societies. Yet, as I mentioned above, the theoretical basis of the position of the culturalists is the collective right of cultural self-determination, recognized by the United Nations. The tension between the human right of a people to promote its national culture and the human rights of individuals and groups to pursue their own cultural and religious ideals, can only be resolved by democratically developed intelligent compromises.

APOLOGIES TO NATIVE PEOPLES

Until fairly recently, awareness of the Native peoples was successfully repressed in Canada. The public paid no attention to the colonial status imposed on them (the Indian Act of 1876). Prejudice and voluntary ignorance became the dominant ideology that made the Native peoples invisible in Canada.

In the 1960s the Amerindians started to organize demonstrations against the unjust conditions inflicted on them; and in the 1980s they brought to light the human damage, previously hidden, produced by the residential schools that Aboriginal children had been forced to attend. In the 1870s the federal government had instituted these schools to integrate the Aboriginal children into the mainstream of Canadian life. Added to this scandal was that the Churches were willing to operate these schools. Now some Amerindians, survivors of these schools, decided to go to court, accusing members of the staff, mainly priests and brothers, of having inflicted on them brutal physical punishment, and even worse, having molested them sexually. These court cases, reported in the mass media, raised the awareness of Canadians in regard to the residential schools and the tragic fate of the Amerindians in their country. What was scandalous was not only the cruel treatment inflicted on some of the pupils, but the very idea of forcibly separating children from their parents, forbidding them to speak their mother tongue and denouncing their cultural inheritance as evil, an educational program approved at that time by the Christian Churches. What these schools intended, in the words of one supporter, was "to kill the Indian in the child."[29] Former prime minister Paul Martin, speaking in April 2013 in support of the Native protest movement IDLE NO MORE, described the Canadian government policy in regard to the Amerindians as "cultural genocide."[30]

Deeply touched by this new knowledge, the Christian Churches made sincere apologies to the Native peoples.[31] In 2008, Prime Minister Stephen Harper himself, speaking in Parliament, offered a formal apology to the Native peoples for the residential school system set up by the Canadian government.[32] Persuaded by these apologies that the Canadian cultural consciousness was changing, the Native peoples intensified their protest movement and multiplied their demonstrations, calling upon the government to dismantle the colonial legislation and negotiate new treaties, nation to nation. While the government was unwilling to do this, it responded to the increasing restlessness of the Native people by setting up, in 2009, the Truth and Reconciliation Commission to bring to light the entire story of the residential schools, raise the consciousness of Canadians, and foster mutual respect and social solidarity between them and the Aboriginal population.

This is the historical context for the decision of la Société canadienne de théologie to hold its meeting of 2011 on the topic of reconciliation, in particular the reconciliation of Quebecers with the Aboriginal nations. Among the speakers were Nicole O'Bomsavin, a Native woman with a doctorate in anthropology, who analyzed without resentment her experience in Quebec society, and Jean-François Roussel, professor of theology at the University of Montreal, who showed that, with a few remarkable exceptions,[33] the substantial literature produced over the years by Quebec theologians has almost totally ignored the existence of the Native peoples.

One significant exception is the work of Achiel Peelman, a Catholic theologian at St Paul University in Ottawa, who chose to live in different Native communities, studied their religious practices, became friends with Native spiritual leaders, and produced two books, *Le Christ est amérindien* (1992) and *L'Esprit est amérindien: Quand la religion amérindienne rencontre le christianisme* (2004).[34]

The collective blindness of intellectuals, including theologians, was further explored at the meeting of 2011. In his lecture on this topic Jean Richard, a theologian already mentioned several times, made an observation that I had never heard before, yet that convinced me immediately. This is what he said. While educated people in the West, in church and society, have integrated the Holocaust into their consciousness, a similar transformation of consciousness has not taken place in regard to another violent happening of giant proportions, the colonial conquest of Western empire. This worldwide conquest has killed millions of people, exploited entire populations, robbed them of their treasures, destroyed their cultural inheritance, and produced drastic structural inequalities in the global society that have been perpetuated up to the present day. Yet we are hardly aware of this history. When observers in the West, however well educated, try to understand what is happening in the world, they do so without attention to this colonial conquest and its consequences. We tend to look at the world as if it never happened. Jean Richard argued that this distorted historical consciousness explains why the Native peoples have been invisible in Quebec and why their tragic fate has not attracted the attention of intellectuals, including theologians. People of good will have remained ignorant of the government's colonial policies.

In his lecture Jean Richard remembered the history of Quebec, the foundation of the colony, and the subjugation of the Native peoples, and then described the humiliation, dispossession, and disintegration inflicted on them by the conquerors. This appalling violence, he argued, is an essential dimension of our society which we refuse to recognize. Can this indifference to the suffering of others, he asked, take place without personal guilt? Quebec theologians are obliged, Richard holds, to wrestle with the difficult question of whether structural sins committed by a society produce personal guilt among its members.

In search of an answer, Jean Richard turned to Karl Jaspers' famous book on the German guilt for the crimes committed by the Nazi regime and the violence unleashed in World War II.[35] To gain a better understanding of the question, Jaspers distinguishes between four different kinds of guilt, distinctions, Richard believes, which are relevant for all societies.

(1) There is the "criminal guilt" of persons who commit evil deeds, break the law, destroy human life, and merit condemnation in a court of law. In Germany after the war, this was dealt with by the international court at Nuremberg.

(2) "Personal guilt" is contracted by persons who participate in various degrees in the unjust or evil deeds done by the State or other institutions to which they belong. This is the guilt on which the German Catholic bishops focused after the war: they laid down that a German is guilty to the extent that he or she has collaborated with the criminal Nazi enterprise. According to this level of analysis, Germans opposed to Hitler who withdrew from public life are free of all reproach.

(3) "Political guilt" is shared by all citizens for the evil done by their nation; it is based on the collective solidarity constitutive of a society and the common fate shared by all the citizens. Based on the principle of solidarity, religious communities pay large amounts of money as compensation for the criminal sexual aggressions committed by one of their members, even though their members as a whole are not personally guilty of any transgression. In post-war Germany the principle of solidarity meant that all citizens, including anti-Nazi resisters, had to accept the reparations imposed upon their country, even if this caused

hardships for the innocent. German Protestant church groups focused on political guilt: they published declarations confessing that "we Germans" started a war that killed millions of people, and accept the reparations imposed as God's punishment.[36] German Protestants created a penitential community, Aktion Sühnezeichen, whose members volunteered to become helpers and servants in Jewish communities in Israel and other parts. Most of the young people who participated in these penitential activities actually came from anti-Nazi families: they assumed their country's political guilt out of social solidarity.

According to Jean Richard, political guilt, thus defined, burdens Canadians and Quebecers. Church leaders and politicians recognized this when they offered public apologies to the Native peoples for the residential school system and the hardship and humiliation inflicted upon them over the centuries. Jean Richard proposed that reconciliation with the Native peoples will be impossible unless Canadians and Quebecers experience a conversion of the heart and willingly acknowledge their political guilt. There are no signs, Richard opines, that Canadians and Quebecers are ready for this.

(4) "Universal guilt" – a controversial idea introduced by Jaspers – is based on the interconnectedness of events in the world and the call to unconditional solidarity with all human beings. The injustice and the suffering inflicted upon others are not totally external to us who are more fortunate. It is generally recognized today that the poverty of countries in the South and the misery inflicted upon their people are connected to the wealth accumulated in the North. Because my cup of coffee in the morning relates me to the coffee picker in the South, I am not totally innocent of the exploitative conditions imposed on him. Jaspers calls this "metaphysical guilt," yet he does not account for it in metaphysical terms. Universal guilt, I suggest, is an ethical imperative. Since we are called – called by God – to universal solidarity, we are deeply troubled by the world we have created, marked as it is by massive inequalities. I am ninety years old and still active, while there are regions where people die at fifty or even younger. I live longer than they because I profit from Canada's wealth acquired by an exploitative economic system. Though I am not personally guilty of this inequality, I refuse to regard myself as totally innocent. This is the human situation: on the one hand we are called to universal solidarity, and on the other we are unable to live up to it.

Discussing the interrelation between personal and social sin in chapter 3, I concluded that none of us are completely innocent, thus recognizing the ambiguity of human existence. While this interpretation of the human condition is widely acknowledged in the Protestant theological tradition, it is rarely found among Catholic theologians. We tended to think that as persons grow in holiness, they distance themselves increasingly from sin. This is the time for Catholics to rethink their theological anthropology.

Reflecting on a possible reconciliation between the people of Quebec and the Aboriginals, Jean Richard concluded that what is need is an awakening to a new consciousness on the part of Quebecers (and Canadians), an awareness of the oppression and violence that are part of our history. We have to be willing to lose our innocence. But guided by the thought of Karl Jaspers, Richard went further: he came to recognize more generally the ambiguity of human existence in an unjust world. In his lecture he acknowledged the influence of Paul Tillich. Humans are torn between sin and grace. The human family has constituted itself in its history through institutions that distribute wealth and power unjustly; at the same time, humans are called by God to the love of neighbour and to solidarity with the poor, the weak, and the excluded, a summons that demands more than they are ever able to do. This universal loss of innocence is a theme rarely developed in Quebec theology. Jean Richard was driven to it by reflecting on the presence of the Native peoples among us.

11

Concluding Reflections

In this concluding chapter I wish to comment on three issues repeatedly referred to in this book: (1) the influence of Vatican Council II on the Quebec theologians; (2) the theological affinity between their ideas and the thought of Fernand Dumont; and (3) the impact of the hope created by the Quiet Revolution on the orientation of their theology. In the final section I shall confess my own theological orientation, which has been shaped by different experiences.

THE INFLUENCE OF VATICAN COUNCIL II

In chapters 1 and 2 we saw the influence of two theological positions adopted by Vatican Council II on the bishops and theologians of Quebec: the relative autonomy of the particular Church and the need for the dialogue of faith and culture. The Council recognized the creativity of the regional or national Church and assigned it the task of proclaiming the Gospel in a discourse that made sense to the people. In order to guide this proclamation, theology had to become contextual, taking into account the situation of society and listening to its culture. Implicit in this demand was the recognition of theological pluralism in the Church. While the papal office protects the unity of the universal Church and the identity of the Christian message, the particular Churches are asked to express the same message in a manner relevant to their cultural context. "Indeed this accommodated preaching of the revealed Word ought to remain the law of all evangelization. For thus the ability to express Christ's message in its own way is developed in each nation."[1] By accommodated preaching the Council did not encourage conformity to the world; it advocated instead a critical dialogue with culture, discerning its destructive potential and recognizing in it truths and values in keeping with God's Word. Proclaiming the Gospel purifies the given culture and enhances its wisdom by integrating it into the Christian message.

In critical dialogue with contemporary Western culture, the Council deplored the dark side of modernity – its individualistic, utilitarian, and materialistic currents; at the same time, it praised its humanizing virtues, such as freedom, equality, justice, and democratic co-responsibility for the common good. "Thus we are witnessing the birth of a new humanism, one in which human beings are defined first of all by their responsibility towards one another and towards history."[2]

The Dumont Report and the Quebec theologians embraced the innovative ecclesiology of Vatican II. In his commentary on the conciliar teaching, Joseph Ratzinger explained in what sense this ecclesiology was new. He recalled that Pius XII had written his encyclical on Christ's mystical body in 1943 to move beyond the purely institutional concept of the Catholic Church, yet the encyclical's "too-pointed idea of the Church's visibility made it all but impossible to give any status to Christians separated from Rome."[3] That is why the Council complemented the image of Christ's body with that of the People of God. According to Joseph Ratzinger, the Council wanted to show that

> the Church is not a rounded-off and finished reality, defined once and for all and thus something beyond time and space. Rather, in its real essence the Church remains a Church on the way and represents in itself the history of God's dealing with humankind: the God who since the days of Adam and Abel has been seeking man out and has been travelling through history with him in the accomplishment of his covenant.[4]

I remember the day when the presidents of the Council, responding to the demand of many bishops, announced the insertion of a new chapter on the People of God in *Lumen Gentium*, the conciliar document on the Church. The purpose of this chapter was to move beyond the institutional and hierarchical concept of the Church: it was to emphasise that the Church is the believing community of the baptized, a family of brothers and sisters, and at the same time the blessed portion of humanity, touched and transformed by divine grace. The people of God is the Church and, in a wider sense, the whole of humanity summoned by God in Jesus Christ. This ecclesiology allowed the Council (1) to recognize non-Catholic Christians and their Churches as part of the ecclesial mystery, (2) to hear an echo of God's Word in the wisdom of the world religions, and (3) to acknowledge God's grace operative in non-believers, summoning them to practice love, justice, and truth. To say that Jesus is greater than the Church – the title of our chapter 5 – not only expresses the frustration of Catholics with the ecclesiastical hierarchy, but on a more profound level proclaims the redemptive presence of God's Word in the whole of human history.

The Quebec theologians discussed in chapter 6 on faith and justice followed the teaching of Vatican II that the Christian life includes the commitment to social justice. The radical version of this commitment, "the option for the poor," was subsequently adopted by the Latin American bishops and, following them, by the Canadian bishops and a wide network of theologians and activists in all parts of the Church. In traditional society, the spiritual life and the ideal of holiness did not include concern for the victims of society. It was only in modern times that Christians recognized that God's Word summoned them to struggle for social justice and assume responsibility for their society. To emphasize this innovative message, John Paul II introduced a new vocabulary into Catholic social teaching: he referred to men and women as "subjects," i.e. agents co-responsible for their society and, more generally, for all institutions to which they belong.[5] John Paul II's praise of the subject character of human beings was an implicit critique of the Poland of his day, a society of the Soviet bloc, that refused to recognize people's freedom and co-responsibility. In his own country decisions were made at the top, and the people, the great majority, had to obey. Even if the decision of the government is wise, it is defective, the pope argued, if it has been arrived at without listening to the people. I do not know whether John Paul II realized that his emphasis on the subject character of men and women produced frustration among thoughtful Catholics, excluded as they are from co-responsibility in the Church.

While Vatican Council II affirmed the autonomy of human beings, the freedom to create their culture and society according to their own ethical aspirations, it also warned them of a false sense of autonomy, the refusal to accept their dependence upon a truth and an order that transcended them. The subject character of human beings is grounded in God's gift freely bestowed. This gift calls people to assume responsibility for their history. Mindful of the sinful dimension operative in man's making of man, the Vatican Council discredited the idea of an inevitable progress in human history. What continues, despite human sin, is the divine summons towards the humanization of culture and society.

The theologians discussed in chapter 9 on faith and the magisterium were influenced by the historical fact – a surprise to many Catholics – that Vatican Council II changed the Church's official teaching on several issues of faith and morals. Moving beyond past ecclesiastical teaching, the Council affirmed the universal destination of divine redemption, the inclusion of non-Catholic Churches in the ecclesial mystery, the theological appreciation of the world religions, and the biblical foundation of human rights and religious liberty.

These changes raise questions in regard to the magisterium, for which Catholics, and theologians in particular, have to find an answer. We considered Cardinal Ratzinger's bold proposal to apply the historical-critical method to the understanding of the magisterium, thus recognizing that it, like theology itself, is contextual.[6] Quebec theologians tend to look upon the magisterium not as a fixed, unchanging authority, but as an agency, sustained by the Holy Spirit, that decides upon Christian truth and practice in dialogue with the believing community and their theologians.

It deserves to be mentioned in this context that Vatican Council II was not a sudden Pentecost, an unexpected gift from heaven; it was in fact prepared by renewal movements in the Church started after World War I by theologians, pastors, and active lay people, movements that became stronger after World War II. A good number of theologians associated with these movements – one thinks of Marie-Dominque Chenu, Yves Congar, Henri de Lubac, and Karl Rahner – had actually been sanctioned by the Roman magisterium. In Quebec, prior to the Council, the progressive Dominican review *Maintenant* attracted a circle of intellectual Catholics, Fernand Dumont among them, who fostered the emergence of a Catholicism appropriate for the new society. The theologians of the renewal left behind the neo-scholasticism of the past, engaged in dialogue with modern thought and modern culture, and tried to communicate the Gospel in a manner understandable to their contemporaries. The reform-oriented theologians were present at Vatican Council II, and the movements they represented had a strong impact on the conciliar teaching. Today the theological and pastoral currents that call for renewal are often frowned upon by the hierarchy, yet remembering what happened at the Council, their proponents are confident that these calls will be heard in due time and rejuvenate the life of the Church.

THE THOUGHT OF FERNAND DUMONT

There was little direct influence of Fernand Dumont on the Quebec theologians discussed in this book. This, at least, is my impression. He joined the theological debate in the 1960s with his articles in *Maintenant* and his book of 1964, *Pour la conversion de la pensée chrétienne*, yet these writings are rarely quoted. His effect was on theologians with whom he worked in common projects. It must be remembered that Dumont was a philosopher and social scientist who, late in his life, became a professional theologian and then published *L'institution de la théologie* in 1987 and *Une foi partagée* in 1996. *L'institution de la théologie* is a brilliant study that makes an original contribution to Catholic theology on the world scale. Since the complexity of Dumont's thought and his elevated literary style have prevented this study from being widely received in Quebec, I wrote a hundred-page essay on his book, soon to be published in French by Novalis, that emphasizes its pastoral and practical significance. I believe that Fernand Dumont, as an accomplished phenomenologist, had a great sensibility for the theological ideas discussed and explored by theologians in Quebec. He developed his own ideas in conversation with theirs. When he produced his theological books late in his life, he felt that he was part of a theological movement in the Quebec Church. For this reason there is a definite affinity between Dumont's thought and the thought of theologians in Quebec. Of the many ideas they shared, I wish to mention three: the experience of faith, the doctrine of God, and the necessary dialogue in the Church.

(1) In Dumont's philosophy, experience is the starting point. In his *L'institution de la théologie*, he shows that Christian faith is experience: it is a believing response to the message and the life of Jesus Christ as recorded in Scripture and celebrated in the Church's liturgy. Christian faith is generated by listening to God's Word. In the days of Dumont's youth, children were introduced to this experience by the first culture to which they belonged. Yet already at that time, faith experienced in the second culture mediated by education was a

rupture, a conversion to a new horizon. In the secular world in particular, faith is a transforming experience. It first creates a distance from culture and society and then embraces them in a new way. Because Christian faith is an experience, it cannot be equated with the calm acceptance of a creed. In a secular culture, faith remains uncertain; it must be sustained by an ongoing encounter with God's Word; it passes through periods of doubt and is rekindled by new insights into the Gospel. Faith as rupture moves the heart from self-love to other-love, even to the possibility of loving God.

Faith, Dumont argues, creates community. It is shared with others and communicated in words. What Christians believe are stories of salvation, historical events, and words that reveal God's truth, especially the marvellous happenings that Jesus talked about in images, symbols, parables, beatitudes, and messianic promises. Doctrines have been important in the life of the Church: they prevent false interpretations of the story of human salvation. But doctrines do not replace the stories told in Scripture and celebrated in the sacramental liturgy. Dumont recognizes that the Church must formulate doctrinal norms to protect the divine truth and preserve Christian unity, yet he thinks that the multiplication of these norms has deleterious pastoral consequences. After the Reformation and, more especially, since the nineteenth century, the magisterium has proliferated the production of norms, a pastoral practice that demands obedience, rather than fostering religious experience. If obedience to doctrine replaces the experience of faith, Catholics will cease to be spiritually nourished by their religion and instead experience it as a heavy burden.

The theologians mentioned in the present study look upon faith as a conversion of the heart and the opening to a new horizon. Since they now live in a secular society and since they have moved beyond the faith of their parents, they experience their faith in the Gospel as a rupture, creating a distance from the dominant culture and from their inherited piety. Challenged by the unresolved problems of their society and their Church, they reread the Scriptures and rethink the tradition to discover new insights and be able to articulate the Good News as God's redemptive message for their time. They share the position of Fernand Dumont that at this time and in the future, Catholics will remain believers only if their faith is kept alive by meditative practices and spiritual experiences. Jacques Grand'Maison's proposal for the new evangelization of Catholics estranged from the Church called for deepening the encounter with Christ and sharing the faith experience in small communities. The exegetes and theologians discussed in chapter 5, "Jesus Greater than the Church," made the personal encounter with the man of Nazareth the heart of the faith experience, a moment of discontinuity, the entry into an alternative way of seeing life and of living it. For the theologians for whom faith and social engagement go hand in hand, discussed in chapter 6, and for theologians committed to women's liberation, discussed in chapter 7, faith is also a rupture, implying a No to the world and conversion to a new horizon. For all of these theologians just as for Dumont, Christian faith produces restlessness. Faith in Jesus is reassuring, yet it continues to raise questions and searches for meaning in times of change. For these theologians, faith has the paradoxical effects of revealing the sin of the world and the coming crisis and, at the same time, producing hope and prompting social engagement.

(2) We saw in chapters 2 and 3 that the dialogue of faith with modern culture, especially the discovery of people's collective responsibility for their society, convinced Maurice Blondel and, after him, many theologians including Fernand Dumont to move beyond traditional theism by turning to panentheism, affirming God's immanence in human history. Dumont sought to demonstrate that an internal dynamics operative in people's lives carries them forward and relates them to a Transcendence, albeit without a name. The name of this Transcendence is revealed to us in the life and preaching of Jesus Christ. Blondel argued that the proclamation of the biblical God is credible because it sheds light on people's experience of the mystery that is operative in their lives.

Involved in Dumont's theological proposals, as I pointed out, are two issues, the dynamic orientation of human life towards Transcendence and the panentheistic theology of God as the gracious Insider. I insisted on this distinction because in my book *Man Becoming* I fully agreed with the turn to panentheism, yet did not share the conviction that implicit in human becoming is a relation to Transcendence. I prefer to think that the openness of humans to the divine reality is mediated by God's grace, an unmerited gift, summoning them to transcend their self-concern by turning to the Other in love.

It is my impression that the Quebec theologians accept explicitly or implicitly the turn to panentheism. They hold that God is a presence in human history, the ground of the world's becoming, the matrix of man's making of man, the horizon of people's efforts to become themselves. Several theologians also share with Dumont the position that human life has a built-in religious orientation: I mentioned in particular Jean Richard, Jacques Grand'Maison, Élisabeth Lacelle, Richard Bergeron, and André Charron. The latter qualifies his position by conceding that people who live superficial lives are not affected by this religious orientation. I mentioned that I fail to be convinced of the religious orientation of human life, or – using Paul Tillich's vocabulary – that all human beings have "an ultimate concern." I am persuaded that there are dedicated secular people, committed to several causes – for instance, scientific research, political reform, and family life – which they are unable to subsume under a single concern. Instead, their fidelity to the different causes, which demands dividing their time and energy, makes them aware of the finitude that marks all human life.

(3) Reflecting on the self-understanding of men and women in modern culture, Dumont concludes that contemporary Catholics want to be co-responsible for society and for the Church. The Dumont Report, summarizing the aspirations of Quebec Catholics, calls for the creation of forums in the Church, at which the believing community and their ordained pastors can engage in dialogue at regular intervals. Vatican Council II has recognized the active share of the baptized people in Christ's priestly and prophetic ministry, yet this share remains an empty promise unless there exist institutional spaces for a creative exchange of ideas. Dumont believes that institutions that give lay people a voice are in keeping with the Church's papal-episcopal structure. Since the Church is of divine origin, he argues, its self-organization is part of its message to the world. Its structure, combining authority, participation, and freedom, should be a model for the world, prompting people to take a critical look at their own society and struggle to make it more humane. With Paul VI's encyclical *Ecclesiam Suam* (1964), Dumont believes that intra-ecclesial dialogue belongs to the essence of the Church.

We have seen that the theologians of Quebec also regard intra-ecclesial dialogue as an essential dimension of the Church. In producing their books and articles, they see themselves in dialogue with their colleagues and their students as well as with the ecclesiastical magisterium. They tend to be on good terms with their bishops, exchange ideas with them, and co-operate with them in the writing of their pastoral letters and theological statements. After the Council, many Quebec bishops organized synods in their dioceses: they wanted to hear what the Gospel meant to the people in the parishes, even though present church law prevented them from responding positively to many of the suggestions made by the people. Eventually Rome ordered the bishops to control the agenda of the synods and remind the people of the Church's official teaching.[7] This instruction was one further sign that Rome was returning to the monarchical understanding of the papacy, an understanding of which Quebec theologians have been consistently critical.

With Fernand Dumont, the theologians discussed in this study acknowledge the newness brought by the Quiet Revolution as well as its rootedness in the history of Quebec and its Church. With Dumont, they look upon both society and the Church as "un héritage et un projet." What is taking place in the Church is "rupture," breaking away from the Catholicism of yesterday, and at the same time, even more strongly, "fidelity" to the Gospel, the Catholic tradition, and the history of Quebec.

We were reminded in several chapters that vast numbers of Quebecers have come to look upon their Catholic past as part of *la grande noirceur*: they lost their faith, removed themselves from the Church, and are ashamed of their history because of the Church's powerful presence in it. Many Quebecers, anguishing over their identity, attribute their uncertainty to the new pluralism produced by recent immigration, rather than acknowledging that their rupture with the Catholic past prevents them from feeling rooted in their history and firm in their identity.

With Dumont, the theologians discussed in this book have a strong sense of being Québécois and Québécoises: they experience no identity crisis, many of them think of themselves – with Dumont – as nationalists. What troubles them is the "deculturation" of their society – the term is Dumont's – i.e. the invasion of individualism and utilitarianism, undermining the inherited social solidarity and discouraging people from becoming engaged in civil society. While the theologians support their society's entry into modernity, they are critical of many of its cultural consequences. They believe that faith in the Gospel, if widely spread, would make an important contribution to society's well-being, acknowledging at the same time that the commitment to secular humanism also helps to make society more just and more humane.

THE HOPE OF THE QUIET REVOLUTION

Like all the Churches of the West, the Church of Quebec has entered modernity, yet it has done this in very particular historical circumstances. The Quiet Revolution released great hope: Quebecers felt that, for the first time in their history, they were able to create a society according to their own aspirations. Joining this social experiment with enthusiasm, engaged Catholics read the Gospel in a new light, a phenomenon well documented in the Dumont Report. Catholics were convinced that a change had taken place in society and in the Church that could not be reversed. With Fernand Dumont, the Quebec theologians demonstrated that the Christian message sustained Quebecers in their project of cultural and political self-determination. They offered theological reasons for approving Quebec's turn to social democracy, the institutions of public welfare, the Charter of Human Rights and Freedoms, the adoption of French as the public language, and the affirmation of Quebec's national identity. With the Dumont Commission, they hoped that the pastoral policies adopted by the bishops would support the emergence of a Catholicism that corresponded to the aspirations of the new Quebec. They believed in the creativity of the Church, capable of developing its own theology, its own catechesis, its own liturgy, and its own spirituality – all within the legal framework of the universal Church presided over by the pope. In the years following the Quiet Revolution, right into the 1970s, a good number of Catholics, theologians among them, trusting the messianic promises of Jesus, joined radical political movements, intent on creating a just and egalitarian society beyond the capitalist system.[8]

The experience of social hope inspired by the Quiet Revolution made Catholic theology action-oriented: it looked upon the Gospel as the initiation into a new way of life. It focused on the innerworldly meaning of divine revelation, the power to illuminate the world so that we can see it rightly and transform it. I quoted Jacques Racine, who remarked that theologians believed that their work contributed to the building of the new Quebec. For them the Gospel was transformative truth.

With Fernand Dumont the theologians felt that abstract truth is not good enough; what counts is relevance, providing answers to people's urgent questions and responding to their spiritual aspirations. Dumont and theologians recognized the cognitive content of divine revelation, yet realizing that conceptual truth leaves us and the world unchanged, they wanted theology to bring out the relevance of dogma, its power to address people in their present predicament.

Looking at their past, Quebecers often accuse themselves of having been excessively passive, submissive to British political and economic power and obedient to their priests and bishops. This memory of past passivity – whether it be historically correct or not – is the reason why contemporary Quebec theologians emphasize people's self-responsibility and their power to become social actors.

The emphasis on self-responsibility remains even when the values of the Quiet Revolution are losing their hold on society and Quebec is become increasingly dominated by the neo-liberal world culture. I have quoted above the sombre judgment of Fernand Dumont and mentioned Jacques Grand'Maison's political anger. Yet the theologians do not give up on their national dream: both federalists and sovereignists believe that Quebecers constitute a nation and that God calls all nations, including Quebec, to become more just, more humane, and more egalitarian. Their radical critique of society is supported by the Quebec bishops in their Labour Day statements of the First of May. As we saw in chapter 6, some Catholic groups and centres, committed to solidarity with the poor, look upon their engagement as resistance to society's mainstream. Even in these changed historical conditions and the fading of the Quiet Revolution's social optimism, theology in Quebec remains on the whole action-oriented, aimed at reforming society or supporting alternative practices. I mentioned that this orientation was questioned in an original way by Anne Fortin's theological approach.

Does the emphasis on action fail to appreciate the Good News as God's unmerited gift? Does it eliminate the mystical dimension of the Christian life? Does it reduce theology to social ethics? Does Quebec theology correspond to what in nineteenth-century Anglicanism was called "muscular Christianity?" I am sensitive to these questions because, belonging to the Augustinian theological tradition, I have no sympathy for Pelagian self-confidence. It is true that the theologians discussed in this book rarely explore the mystical dimension of the Christian life or reflect on the spiritual resources enabling us to think critically and to act. Fernand Dumont and Jacques Grand'Maison, I admit, have a strong sense of the divine gratuity at the heart of human self-making. Quebec theologians as heirs of the Catholic tradition fully recognize that their stance toward the world and, more especially, their option for the poor are grounded on a spirituality, an inner life generated by God's Word, a passionate social concern produced by the Holy Spirit. In their writings, they sometimes suggest that the Gospel is essentially a personal and social ethics. Yet for them ethics is not simply thinking, choosing, and doing the right thing; ethics is a redemptive process, a conversion of the heart, an escape from passivity or self-indulgence, and an entry into the realm of freedom. Quebec theologians recognize the mystical dimension of the Christian life, even if they do not dwell on it.

Creative theological thinking often takes place at centres outside the academy. I mentioned this in chapter 5 on faith and justice and in chapter 10 on the challenge of pluralism: on these issues Catholic centres did important work supplementing what happened at the universities. In the present context, I wish to mention two centres in Quebec City: le Centre Manrése, cultivating Ignatian spirituality, and le Centre d'Études sur Marie-de-l'Incarnation, exploring the spirituality that is part of Quebec's religious history.

SIN AND SALVATION

The theologians of Quebec participated in an exciting historical experiment; they left the past behind, moved into the future, and reconnected with their historical roots in a new way.

My own historical experience has been quite different: it has given me a strong sense of the blindness and sinfulness of the world. It may not be out of place if at the end of this book I write a few pages about my own theological orientation. The memory of the brutality of German fascism, my confusion as a German refugee, and my awareness of having escaped the Holocaust inclined me to accept Saint Augustine's sense of the world's sinfulness and his faith in God's rescuing power. With Augustine I hold that the good in our lives is not wholly of our own making, but a free and ever surprising gift of God. I believe that God's grace offers redemption, rescuing us from internal confusion, self-destructive behaviour, and many external threats to human flourishing. Writing a book on the anti-Jewish rhetoric that was part of Christian preaching almost from the beginning,[9] I came to realize that the sin of the world marks even the life of the Church. Later, during Vatican Council II, I was touched by the social hope expressed in *Gaudium et Spes* and became a liberal, looking with confidence at the future of Western society. This confidence was challenged a few years later by Latin American liberation theology and the 1968 Medellin Conference of the Latin American bishops that revealed the oppressive conditions imposed upon the world by Western empire. With these Latin Americans I made a preferential option for the poor and began to look at society from the perspective of its victims.

Years later, it was the critical theory of the Frankfurt School that made me see the dark side of late modernity: the cultural domination of techno-scientific reason. For Max Horkheimer and Theodor Adorno, the founders of that School, the Holocaust was not a regression to humanity's barbaric past; it was rather the manifestation of the sinister side of late modernity, the use of techno-scientific reason to control people, or even eliminate them, for the benefit of a powerful elite.

If there is hope for Western civilization, according to these thinkers, it will be by the retrieval of ethical reason and the revival of the humanistic tradition. Their cultural analysis opened the eyes of several theologians to the vocation of religion in contemporary society. Christianity and the other world religions are divinely summoned to orient their ethical passion to the promotion of love, justice, and peace and the protection of the *humanum* in co-operation with secular men and women engaged in the same endeavour. In some of his writings, Joseph Ratzinger/Benedict XVI shares the Frankfurt School's radical critique of modernity. In his encyclical *Spe Salvi*, the pope even cites Horkheimer and Adorno, two atheist German Jews, though papal encyclicals normally only cite ecclesiastical texts, mainly previous papal encyclicals.

It is not surprising that my theology has a strong affinity with the Catholic Left in Quebec, with activists and theologians urged by the Gospel to resist economic and cultural empire and support groups and movements engaged in the reconstruction of society from the bottom up. Yet as I stand in the Augustinian tradition, I articulate more clearly than my Quebec colleagues that commitment to social justice is sparked by a divine initiative and that we are not saved by doing good, but conversely that doing good is grounded upon saving grace. As an Augustinian, I insist that the struggle for freedom, justice, and peace is not a Promethean endeavour, but the human response to a divine summons. In a book published in the 1970s, I conclude a chapter on liberating social engagement with a few words expressing its mystical dimension:

> The good we do is God's gift to us. In this Christian perspective, action equals passion. While we see, we are being enlightened; while we act, we are being carried forward; while we love, we are being saved from selfishness; and while we embrace all people in solidarity we are being freed inwardly to cross one boundary after another ... We are alive by a power that transcends us.[10]

Christian believers committed to social solidarity are torn between the gratitude they feel for the divine gifts that have shaped their lives and their unwillingness to forget the suffering inflicted upon the poor and oppressed. In today's world, faith in Jesus Christ is not the entry into peace, but into blessed restlessness.

Quebec theologians may not disagree with these reflections. Yet what characterizes them is that they avoid the word "sin" and hesitate to speak of "redemption." The word "sin" reminds them of the moralistic preaching of the pre-conciliar Church, designed to control the culture of Quebec and, in particular, denigrate people's search for sexual happiness. Quebec theologians find other words to express the malice in society and the human heart. In the parishes, even the penitential confession at the beginning of Mass does not mention the word "sin"; priests find alternative ways of confessing our infidelities. Quebec theologians also tend to avoid the word "redemption." Naming Jesus "redeemer" or "saviour" reminds them of the pre-conciliar preaching that fostered people's self-doubt and their helplessness, limiting the promised divine rescue to the purely spiritual order. Saying that the Gospel "saves" us suggests to Quebecers that the Christian message deals with our souls and leaves history unchanged. Quebec theologians look for a different vocabulary to express the impact of Jesus on their lives and their history.

In chapter 10, I expressed my appreciation of Jean Richard's presentation on the sin of the world. Human beings share in the blindness of their society in regard to its evil practices. Canadians, Richard insists, are unaware of the colonial condition inflicted upon the Native peoples. When we recognize the truth, we experience certain guilt feelings, even though we are personally innocent of the crimes committed in the past. As long as colonial structures oppress people and make them suffer, our conscience remains troubled because we do not do enough to work for their rescue. Jean Richard's troubling reflections confirm my own conviction that sin, forgiveness, and redemption are theological concepts we cannot afford to put on the back burner.

The emphasis on humanity's responsibility for its history also explains why Quebec theologians say very little about resurrection and eternal life. I fully agree with them that the Gospel is a message for this world – Jesus prayed that God's will be done on Earth – and that for this reason Christians should not be preoccupied with the world to come. Since our own future is hidden in God, we need not ask many questions. Yet when I think of the Jews crammed into cattle trains on the way to Auschwitz or the millions of children starving to death in the poor countries of the South, then the resurrection of Jesus acquires central importance. Without life beyond their death, there would be no Good News for them. In the resurrection of the persecuted and crucified Jesus, God has rehabilitated all the victims of history.

I mentioned above that Benedict XVI's encyclical *Spe Salvi* refers with sympathy to the philosophers of the Frankfurt School and engages in dialogue with them about God and evil. Since this text is not well known, I shall quote the following paragraphs.

> The atheism of the nineteenth and twentieth century is – in its origins and aims – a type of moralism: a protest against the injustices of the world and world history. A world marked by so much injustice, innocent suffering and cynicism of power cannot be the work of a good God. A God with responsibility for such a world would not be a just God, much less a good God. It is for the sake of morality that this God has to be contested. Since there is no God to create justice, it seems man himself is now called to establish justice. If in the face of this world's suffering, protest against God is understandable, the claim that humanity can and must do what no God actually does or is able to do is presumptuous and false.
>
> No one and nothing can answer for centuries of suffering. No one and nothing can guarantee that the cynicism of power – whatever beguiling ideological mask it adopts – will cease to dominate the world. This is why the great thinkers of the Frankfurt School, Max Horkheimer and Theodor W. Adorno, were equally critical of atheism and theism. Horkheimer radically excluded the possibility of ever finding a this-worldly substitute for God, while at the same time he rejected the image of a

> good and just God. In an extreme radicalization of the Old Testament prohibition of images, he speaks of a "longing for the totally Other" that remains inaccessible – a cry of yearning directed at world history. Adorno also firmly upheld this total rejection of images, which meant the exclusion of any "image" of a loving God. On the other hand, he constantly emphasized the "negative" dialectic and asserted that justice – true justice – would require a world "where not only present suffering would be wiped out, but also that which is irrevocably past would be undone". This would mean, however – to express it with positive and hence, for him, inadequate symbols – that there can be no justice without a resurrection of the dead.[11]

I mentioned in chapter 3 that according to Fernand Dumont, faith in God generates questions for which there are no easy answers. While the theologians studied in this book say little about the message of eternal life, they courageously confront the problems, conflicts, and failures of their society and seek responses to these questions in the Gospel and the Catholic tradition. In critical dialogue with contemporary thought, they try to show that God's revelation in Jesus Christ is a relevant message for the people of Quebec.

Notes

PREFACE

1 "How Moving to Quebec Has Affected My Theology," *Toronto Journal of Theology* 26/1 (2010): 33–46.
2 Ibid., 44.
3 Stanley French, "Considérations sur l'histoire et l'esprit de la philosophie au Canada français," *Cité libre* no. 68 (June–July 1964): 20–6.
4 A name given to the era during which Maurice Duplessis was Quebec's premier.
5 Fernand Dumont, "Dix années, c'est peu dans la vie d'une Église," *Le Devoir*, 8 April 1982.
6 René-Michel Roberge, "Un théologien à découvrir: Fernand Dumont," *Laval théologique et philosophique*, 55 / 1 (1999): 31–47.
7 Rémi Parent, *L'Église, c'est vous* (Montreal: Paulines, 1982).

INTRODUCTION

1 The 4th decree of the 32nd General Congregation of the Society of Jesus, held in 1975 in Rome.
2 Gregory Baum, *The Church in Quebec* (Toronto: Novalis, 1991).
3 David Seljak, "The Catholic Church and Public Politics in Quebec," in *Rethinking Church, State and Modernity*, edited by David Lyon et al. (Toronto: University of Toronto Press, 2000), 131–48.
4 Carolyn Sharp, "Critical Theologies in Quebec," and Monique Dumais, "Critical Feminist Theologies in Quebec," in *Intersecting Voices*, edited by Don Schweitzer et al. (Toronto: Novalis, 2004), 67–82 and 83–95.

5 See Gregory Baum, "How Moving to Montreal Has Affected My Theology," *Toronto Journal of Theology* 26/1 (2010): 33–46.
6 Benedict XVI, encyclical *Spe Salvi* (2008), no. 22.

CHAPTER ONE

1 This phrase is an adaptation of the second sentence in Jean-Philippe Warren's book *L'art vivant* (Montreal: Boréal, 2011).
2 The section on the Quiet Revolution is an edited version of pages from my article "Catholicism and Secularization in Quebec," in *Rethinking Church, State and Modernity*, edited by David Lyon et al. (Toronto: University of Toronto Press, 2000), 149–52.
3 Debated among historians and social scientists is the question of whether the Quiet Revolution was a significant turning point or simply a social evolution of the kind that took place in all Western societies. See chapter 2.
4 Pierre Elliot Trudeau, ed., *La grève de l'amiante* (Montreal: Cité Libre, 1956).
5 Yvan Lamonde, ed., *Cité Libre. Une Anthologie* (Montreal: Alain Stanké, 1991).
6 Gérard Dion and Louis O'Neill published the manifesto *Immoralité politique dans la Province du Québec* in 1956 and the book *Le chrétien et les élections* (Montreal: Éditions de l'homme) in 1960.
7 É.-Martin Meunier and Jean-Philippe Warren, *Sortir de la 'Grande Noirceur'* (Sillery, QC: Septentrion, 2002).
8 C. Shilling and P. Mellar, "Durkheim. Morality and Modernity: Collective Effervescence," *British Journal of Sociology* 49 (June 1998): 193–209.
9 Quebec's confessional school system was abolished in 2005.
10 Martin Roy, *Une réforme dans la fidélité: La revue Maintenant [1962–1974]* (Quebec: PUL, 2012).
11 Yves Beaulieu et al., *Le renouveau communautaire chrétien au Québec* (Montreal: Fides, 1974).
12 *Lumen Gentium*, no. 13.
13 The conciliar document on the bishops, *Christus Dominus*, no. 12. In his book *The Catholic Origins of Quebec's Quiet Revolution* (Montreal & Kingston: McGill-Queen's University Press, 2005), Michael Gauvreau deals with the Church in the 1960s without acknowledging the impact of Vatican Council II, an omission that makes his analysis unreliable.
14 Fernand Dumont, *Récit d'une émigration* (Montreal: Boréal, 1997), 176–80.
15 The following three pages are an edited version of pages from the chapter "The Dumont Commisssion: Democratizing the Catholic Church," in my *The Church in Quebec* (Ottawa: Novalis, 1991), 52–60.

16 The Dumont Commission, *L'Église du Québec: un héritage, un projet* (Montreal: Fides, 1971).
17 Ibid., 95.
18 Ibid., 114.
19 Ibid., 115.
20 Ibid., 259.
21 Ibid., 103.
22 Ibid., 135.
23 Ibid., 112.
24 Fernand Dumont, personal communication.
25 Serge Cantin, dir., *Fernand Dumont: Un témoin de l'homme – Entretiens* (Montreal: Hexagone, 2000), 135–48.
26 Gérard Marier, "Le renouveau charismatique," in *Encyclopédie de l'Agora*, http://agora.qc.ca/documents/spiritualite--le_renouveau_charismatique_par_gerard_marier (accessed 20 May 2013).
27 Nicole Laurin, "L'énigme de la sociologie québécoise," in *Sociologie et société québécoise*, edited by Céline Saint-Pierre et al. (Montreal: Presses de l'Université de Montréal, 2006), 161.
28 Fernand Dumont, *Pour la conversion de la pensée chrétienne* (Montreal: Éditions HMH, 1964).
29 Ibid., 116.
30 Robert Schwartzwald, "The 'Civic Presence' of Father Marie-Alain Couturier, O.P., in Quebec," *Quebec Studies* 10 (Spring/Summer 1990): 149.
31 This quotation is taken from John Dear's article "Abraham's Heschel's Prophetic Judaism," *National Catholic Reporter*, 16 June 2011.
32 Gregory Baum, "Commentaires," in *30 ans de révolution tranquille*, edited by Marc Lesage et al. (Montreal: Bellarmin, 1989), 67–73.
33 Robert Bellah, "Civil Religion in America," in his *Beyond Belief* (New York: Harper & Row, 1974), 168–89.
34 David Martin, *A General Theory of Secularization* (Oxford, UK: Blackwell, 1978).
35 Gregory Baum, "Catholicism and Secularization in Quebec," in my *The Church in Quebec* (Ottawa: Novalis, 1991), 15–48.
36 Claude Corbo, *L'éducation pour tous: Une anthologie du Rapport Parent* (Montreal: Presses de l'Université de Montréal, 2002).
37 Gregory Baum, "*Le Devoir*, Forum for the Exchange of Ideas," in *The Public Intellectual in Canada*, edited by Nelson Wiseman (Toronto: University of Toronto Press, 2013), 83–95.
38 J.G. Mallory, "The MacDonald Commission," *Canadian Journal of Political Science* 19 (September 1986): 597–613.

39 Fernand Dumont, *Raisons communes* (Montreal: Boréal, 1995), 12.
40 Carolyn Sharp, "Critical Theologies in Quebec," in *Intersecting Voices*, edited by Don Schweitzer et al. (Toronto: Novalis, 2004), 67–82.
41 Guy Rocher, "Un bilan du Rapport Parent: vers la démocratisation," *Bulletin d'Histoire politique* 12 (Winter 2004): 117–28.
42 Gilles Routhier, "Les évolutions de l'enseignement théologique au Canada," in *La théologie à l'Université. Statut, programmes et évolutions*, edited by M. Deneken and F. Messner (Geneva: Labor et Fides, 2009), 111–34; Gilles Routhier, "Le Canada francophone," in *Le devenir de la théologie catholique mondiale depuis Vatican II 1965–1999*, edited by G. Doré (Paris: Beauchesne, 2000), 259–317.
43 Gilles Routhier, "Conclusion," in *Les Évaluations de l'enseignement théologique au Canada*, http://theo.kuleuven.be/insect/assets/file/worldwide_canada-routhier.pdf (accessed 20 May 2013).
44 Gregory Baum, "Politisés chrétiens," in *The Church in Quebec*, 67–90.
45 http://gtcq.blogspot.com/2010/05/groupe-de-theologie-contextuelle.html (accessed 20 May 2013).

CHAPTER TWO

1 André Naud, "La théologie au Québec: héritage ou projet?" *L'Église canadienne* (Oct. 1972): 230–5.
2 Joseph Ratzinger, *Theological Highlights of Vatican II* (New York: Paulist Press, 1966), 111–12.
3 Gilles Routhier, "Vatican II comme modernisation de l'Église catholique du Québec," in *Modernité et religion au Québec* (Quebec: Presses de l'Université Laval, 2010), 42.
4 *Christus Dominus*, no. 12.
5 *Gaudium et Spes*, no. 44.
6 Ibid., no. 62.
7 *Lumen Gentium*, no. 62.
8 John Paul II, the encyclical *Redemptoris Missio* (1990), no. 52.
9 Gregory Baum, "The Labour Pope in Canada," *The Ecumenist* 23 (Jan.–Feb. 1985): 17–23; and "Faith and Culture," *The Ecumenist* 24 (Nov.–Dec. 1985): 9–13.
10 Baum, "The Labour Pope in Canada," 19.
11 *Dei Verbum*, no. 24.
12 Baum, "The Labour Pope in Canada," 18.
13 Jacques Racine, "Comme des dieux ou la lutte aux idoles," in *Des théologies en mutation* (Montreal: Fides, 2002), 178.

14 Gregory Baum, "Political Theology in Canada," in *Intersecting Voices: Critical Theologies in a Land of Diversity*, edited by Don Schweitzer et al. (Ottawa: Novalis, 2004), 49–66.

15 Paul Avis, "Apologetics," in *The Oxford Companion to Christian Thought* (Oxford, UK: Oxford University Press, 2000), 32.

16 Gregory Baum, *The Pastoral Constitution on the Church in the Modern World* (New York: Paulist Press, 1967), 182–208.

17 Christian Duquoc, "Théologie," *Catholicisme*, vol. 14, column 1080.

18 http://eglisecatholiquedequebec.org/babillard/documents/MemoireCardinalMarcOuellet.pdf (accessed 20 May 2013).

19 http://www.eveques.qc.ca/Listes/Documents/2007-12-12a.pdf (accessed 20 May 2013).

20 See Yves Lamonde and Esther Trépanier, eds., *L'avènement de la modernité culturelle au Québec* (Quebec: Presses de l'Université Laval, 1986); Gilles Bourque et al., *La société libérale duplessiste* (Montreal: Presses de l'Université de Montréal, 1994); Jacques Rouillard, "La révolution tranquille: rupture ou tournant?" *Journal of Canadian Studies / Revue d'études canadiennes* 32, no. 4 (Winter 1998): 23–51.

21 Benedict XVI, the encyclical *Spe Salvi* (2008), no. 22.

22 *Gaudium et Spes*, no. 55.

23 Transcendental Thomists, influenced by Kant, focus on the categories in the mind that, sustained by the divine presence, enable humans to recognize the world and know the truth.

24 Gregory Baum, *Man Becoming* (New York: Herder & Herder, 1970 / Seabury Press, 1979).

25 *Gaudium et Spes*, no. 22.

26 Benedict XVI, encyclical *Caritas in Veritate* (2009), no. 56. See also the sentence in the same encyclical "A humanism which excludes God is an inhuman humanism," no. 78.

CHAPTER THREE

1 Julien Massicotte, *Culture et herméneutique: L'interprétation dans l'œuvre de Fernand Dumont* (Quebec: Nota Bene, 2006), 16l.

2 Fernand Dumont, *Récit d'une émigration* (Montreal: Boréal, 1997).

3 For a substantial introduction, see René-Michel Roberge, "Un théologien à découvrir: Fernand Dumont," *Laval Théologique et Philosophique* 55 (February 1999): 31–47.

4 Fernand Dumont, *Une foi partagée* (Montreal: Bellarmin, 1996), 11.

5 Dumont, *Récit d'une émigration*, 244.

6 Dumont, *Une foi partagée,* 18.
7 Ibid., 19.
8 Fernand Dumont, *Raisons communes* (Montreal: Boréal, 1995), 212.
9 Cited in Maurice Zundel, *Dans le silence de Dieu*, tome 2 (Quebec: Anne Sigier, 2002), 160.
10 Cited in André Charron, "Catholicisme culturel et identité chrétienne," in *Religion, sécularisation, modernité*, edited by Brigitte Caulier (Quebec: Presses de l'Université Laval, 1996), 183.
11 Jean-Claude Breton, "Pourquoi prier alors? À l'écoute de Marcel Légaut," in *Dieu agit-il dans l'histoire?* edited by Roger Mager (Montreal: Fides, 2006), 137–50.
12 Charron, "Catholicisme culturelle et identité chrétienne," in *Religion, sécularisation, modernité*, 183.
13 Brigitte Haentjens, "Rencontres essentielles," *Relations* 750 (August 2011): 10.
14 Dumont, *Une foi partagée*, 82–3.
15 Joseph Ratzinger, *Introduction to Christianity* (New York: Herder & Herder, 1969), 64.
16 Ibid., 153–54.
17 Pierre Lucier, *La foi comme héritage et projet dans l'œuvre de Fernand Dumont* (Quebec: Presses de l'Université Laval, 1999).
18 Gaston Bachelard, *L'eau et les rêves* (Paris: José Corti, 1942), 25, cited in Julien Massicotte, *Culture et herméneutique* (Quebec: Nota Bene, 2006), 15–16.
19 Riccardo Petrella, *Désir d'humanité: Le droit de rêver* (Montreal: Écosociété, 2004).
20 Robert Hurley, *Hermeneutics and Catechesis: Biblical Interpretation in the* Come to the Father *Catechetical Series* (Lanham, MD: University Press of America, 1997).
21 Dumont, *Une foi partagée*, 151.
22 Fernand Dumont, *L'institution de la théologie* (1987), in *Œuvres complètes* (Quebec: Presses de l'Université Laval, 2008), vol. IV, 327–8.
23 Dumont, *Une foi partagée*, 145–6.
24 Joseph Ratzinger, *Introduction to Christianity* (New York: Herder and Herder, 196), 193.
25 *Gaudium et Spes*, no. 44.

CHAPTER FOUR

1 We have as yet no biography of Jacques Grand'Maison. His pastoral engagements have been studied in two long articles by É.-Martin Meunier, "Intellectuel-militant catholique et théologie de l'engagement:

la consécration d'un prophète en Saint-Jérôme," in *Société: Le chainon manquant* 20/21 (Summer 1999): 255–311, and "Jacques Grand'Maison et la Révolution tranquille," in *Mens, Revue d'histoire intellectuelle de l'Amérique française* 3 (Spring 2003): 149–91.

2 Jacques Grand'Maison, *Une foi ensouchée dans ce pays* (Montreal: Leméac, 1979), 15–16.

3 Jacques Grand'Maison, *Mitan de la vie* (Montreal: Léméac, 1976), 21–2.

4 Ibid., 84.

5 Jacques Grand'Maison, *La second évangélisation*, vol. I (Montreal: Fides, 1973), 76.

6 Rabbi Michael Lerner, *Tikkun*, 5 August 2011.

7 Jacques Grand'Maison, *Crise de prophétisme* (Montreal: Action Catholique canadienne, 1965).

8 Jacques Grand'Maison, *La seconde évangélisation*, vol. II, tome 1 (Montreal: Fides, 1973), 151.

9 Grand'Maison, *Crise de prophétisme*, 297.

10 *Gaudium et Spes*, no. 44.

11 "The baptized are in their own way sharers in the priestly, prophetic and kingly functions of Christ." *Lumen Gentium*, no. 31.

12 See chapter 1, p. 14.

13 Gregory Baum, "Le prophète fuit l'idéologie," translated by Jean-Claude Breton, in *Crise de prophétisme hier et aujourd'hui*, edited by Guy Lapointe (Montreal: Fides, 1990), 33–48. The English original was published in Gregory Baum, *The Church in Quebec* (Ottawa: Novalis, 1991), 91–107.

14 Jacques Grand'Maison, *La seconde évangélisation* (Montreal: Fides, 1973).

15 Ibid., vol. I, 69–176.

16 The French translation: Johann Adam Möhler, *L'Unité dans l'Église ou le principe du Catholicisme* (Paris: Cerf, 1938).

17 Grand'Maison refers especially to Victor Turner, *The Ritual Process: Structure and Anti-Structure* (Chicago: Aldine, 1969).

18 Karl Rahner, *The Shape of the Church to Come* (New York: Seabury Press, 1974).

19 "Le Rome postconciliaire a gardé les contrôles majeurs: elle est retournée à sa quotidienneté tridentine." Grand'Maison, *La seconde évangélisation*, vol. 2, tome 1, 92.

20 "On relativise les erreurs passées du Magistère par l'histoire et on absolutise l'infaillibilité du Magistère présent en se reliant exclusivement à l'Esprit et au Royaume." Grand'Maison, *La seconde évangélisation*, vol. 2, tome 1, 103.

21 United Nations International Covenants on Civil and Political Rights in Walter Laqueur, ed., *The Human Rights Reader* (New York: New American Library, 1990), 215–24.
22 Gregory Baum, *Nationalism, Religion, and Ethics* (Montreal & Kingston: McGill-Queen's University Press, 2001).
23 Jacques Grand'Maison, *Nationalisme et religion* (Montreal: Beauchemin, 1970).
24 Gregory Baum, *Nationalism, Religion and Ethics*, 155–6.
25 Jacques Grand'Maison, *Une foi ensouchée dans ce pays*, 26.
26 Jacques Grand'Maison, *La nouvelle classe et l'avenir du Québec* (Montreal: Alain Stanké, 1979).
27 *La justice sociale comme bonne nouvelle: Messages sociaux, économiques et politiques des évêques du Québec* (Montreal: Bellarmin, 1984), 137–44.
28 Jean Richard, "Les projets de société québécoise: essai de lecture théologique," in *Projet de société et lecture chrétienne*, edited by Camil Menard and Florent Villeneuve (Montreal: Fides, 1997), 339–68.
29 George Grant, *Lament for a Nation: The Defeat of Canadian Nationalism* (Toronto: McClelland & Stewart, 1965).
30 Louis Vaillancourt, "La crise du Canada à la lumière de Douglas J. Hall," *Laval théologique et philosophique* 51, no. 3 (Oct. 1995): 584–604.
31 Jacques Grand'Maison, *Au seuil critique d'un nouvel âge* (Montreal: Leméac, 1979).
32 Jacques Grand'Maison, *Une foi ensouchée dans ce pays*, 39–40.
33 Gregory Baum, "Le prophète fuit l'idéologie," in *Crise de prophétisme hier et aujourd'hui*, edited by Guy Lapointe (Montréal: Fides, 1990), 33–48.
34 Jacques Grand'Maison, "L'univers culturel de Vignault, de Félix Leclerc, de Miron tient davantage du cocon à habiter, à protéger des autres. Tendance semblable aussi dans un syndicalisme de plus en plus corporatiste ... Et que dire du 'cocooning' religieux de bien des communautés chrétiennes, de mouvements spiritualistes et d'expériences pastorales des dernières décennies?" in *Crise de prophétisme hier et aujourd'hui*, edited by Guy Lapointe, 337.
35 Henning Mankell, *Les chaussures italiennes* (Paris: le Seuil, 2009), 125.
36 Jacques Grand'Maison, *Nouveaux modèles sociaux et développement* (Montreal: Hurtubise, 1972).
37 Jacques Grand'Maison, *Les tiers* (Montreal: Fides, 1986).
38 "Il y a eu de l'enfer là-dedans, puis il y eu des expériences de fraternité," quoted in É-Martin Meunier, "Jacques Grand'Maison et la Révolution tranquille," *Mens* 3 (Spring 2003): 149–91.
39 The apostolic exhortation *Reconciliatio et Paenitentia* (1984), no. 16.

CHAPTER FIVE

1 Albert Nolan, *Jesus before Christianity* (London: Darton, Longman and Todd, 1976).
2 Jacques Grand'Maison, *La seconde évangélisation* (Montreal: Fides, 1973), vol. 2, tome 1, 167–74.
3 Jean-Paul Audet, *La Didaché: Instructions des Apôtres* (Paris: Gabalda, 1958).
4 Jean-Paul Audet, *Le projet évangélique de Jésus* [1969] (Orford, QC: Éditions des sources, 1998).
5 Ibid., 140.
6 André Charron, dir. *Jésus? De l'histoire à la foi* (Montreal: Fides, 1974).
7 André Charron, dir. *Après Jésus: Autorité et liberté dans le peuple de Dieu* (Montreal: Fides, 1977).
8 Leonard Audet, "Le Royaume, le centre de la prédication de Jésus," in *Jésus?* 25–37.
9 André Myre, "Les titres christologiques: évolution," in *Jésus?* 159–74.
10 Léonard Audet, "Le pluralisme dans l'Église primitive," in *Après Jésus*, 181–98.
11 Roland Proulx, "Le changement dans l'Ancien Testament," in *Après Jésus*, 99–114; André Myre, "Le changement dans le Nouveau Testament: l'ouverture au païens," in *Après Jésus*, 115–63.
12 Jean-Louis d'Aragon, "L'autorité dans l'Église," in *Après Jésus*, 31–49.
13 Jean-Claude Petit et al., eds., *Jésus: Christ universel?* (Montreal: Fides, 1990).
14 Normand Provencher, "La singularité de Jésus et l'universalité du Christ," in *Jésus: Christ universel?* 9–24.
15 Normand Provencher, "Bilan d'un congrès," in *Jésus: Christ universel?* 263–8.
16 Alain Gignac et al., eds., *Le Christ est mort pour nous: Études sémiotiques, féministes et sotériologiques en l'honneur à Olivette Genest* (Montreal: Médiapaul, 2005), 13.
17 Denise Couture, "À propos du corps féministe d'Olivette Genest," in *Le Christ est mort pour nous*, 235–42.
18 Olivette Genest, *Le discours du Nouveau Testament sur la mort de Jésus: Épîtres et Apocalypse* (Quebec: Presses de l'Université Laval, 1995), 245.
19 Anne Fortin, *L'annonce de la bonne nouvelle aux pauvres* (Montreal: Médiapaul, 2005).
20 Carolyn Sharp, "Critical theologies in Quebec," in *Intersecting Voices*, edited by Don Schweitzer et al. (Ottawa: Novalis, 2004) 67–82.

21 Anne Fortin, "Lire: le geste de théologie de l'Écriture," in Michel Beaudin et al., eds., *Des théologies en mutations* (Montreal: Fides, 2002), 293–308; also "L'an zéro de la Christologie," in *La théologie: pour quoi, pour qui … et comment?* edited by Jean-Guy Nadeau et al. (Montreal: Fides, 2000), 147–60.

22 In English translation, see Pius Parsch, *The Liturgy of the Mass* (St Louis, MO: Herder, 1942) and *Know and Live the Mass* (New York: Catholic Book Pub. Co., 1952).

23 Quoted in Jacques Grand'Maison, *La seconde évangélisation*, vol. II, tome 1 (Montreal: Fides, 1973), 151.

24 http://www.culture-et-foi.com/coupsdecoeur/livres/denis.htm (accessed 20 May 2013).

25 Rémi Parent, *l'Église c'est vous* (Montreal: Éditions Pauline, 1982).

26 Ibid., 7.

27 Charles Valois, *Le courage de changer* (Montreal: Novalis, 2009), 142–7.

28 Rémi Parent, *Une Église de baptizés: pour surmonter l'opposition clerc/laïcs* (Montreal: Paulines, 1987); the English translation is *A Church of the Baptized: Overcoming the Tension Between the Clergy and the Laity* (New York: Paulist Press, 1989).

29 Joseph Ratzinger, *Die christliche Brüderlichkeit* (Munich: Kösel Verlag, 1960).

30 Ibid., 60.

31 Rémi Parent, *La vie, un corps à corps avec la mort* (Montreal: Paulines, 1996).

32 Michel Beaudin, *Obéissance et solidarité* (Montreal: Fides, 1989).

33 Richard Bergeron, *Obéissance de Jésus et vérité de l'homme* (Montreal: Fides, 1988).

34 Richard Bergeron, "Mon parcours théologique 1950–2000," in *Des théologies en mutation*, edited by Michel Beaudin et al. (Montreal: Fides, 2002), 63–80.

35 Richard Bergeron, "Pour une spiritualité du troisième millénaire," *Religiologiques* 20 (Autumn 1999): 231–46.

36 Richard Bergeron, *Renaître à la spiritualité* (Montreal: Fides, 2002).

37 Pierre Pelletier, "Richard Bergeron sort de ses gongs," *Présence* (21 October 2003): 33–4.

38 See chapter 3, p. 64.

39 Richard Bergeron, *Et pourquoi pas Jésus?* (Montreal: Novalis, 2009).

40 Robert Hurley, "Postcolonial Biblical Studies," *The Ecumenist* 47 (Summer 2010): 11–14.

41 Richard Horsley, *Jesus and Empire* (Minneapolis: Fortress Press, 2003); *Jesus in Context: Power, People and Performance* (Minneapolis: Fortress

Press, 2008); *Jesus and the Powers: Conflict, Covenant, and the Hope of the Poor* (Minneapolis: Fortress Press, 2010).

42 Assemblée des évêques du Québec, *Jésus Christ, chemin d'humanisation* (Montreal: Médiapaul, 2004).

43 *Gaudium et Spes*, no. 22.

44 Ibid., no. 3.

45 John Paul II, encyclical *Redemptor Hominis* (1979), no. 14.

CHAPTER SIX

1 "From Words to Action," in *Do Justice: The Social Teaching of the Canadian Bishops*, edited by E.F. Sheridan (Montreal: Paulines, 1987), 315.

2 Ibid., 316.

3 "Ethical Reflections on the Economic Crisis," in *Do Justice*, 399–410.

4 "From Words to Action," 400.

5 The expression "the option for the poor" was not yet used in the Medellin Documents; it was used and defined by the Latin American Bishops Conference at Puebla in 1979 in the Final Document, no. 1134. See John Eagleson et al., eds., *Puebla and Beyond* (Maryknoll, NY: Orbis, 1979), 260–1. The option for the poor is called "preferential" because it extends solidarity to the oppressed; only after oppression has been overcome will solidarity become universal.

6 "The Medellin Documents," in *The Gospel of Peace and Justice*, edited by Joseph Gremillio (Maryknoll, NY: Orbis, 1976), 445–76.

7 World Synod of Bishops 1971, "Justice in the World," in *The Gospel of Peace and Justice*, 513–29.

8 John Paul II, the encyclical *Laborem Exercens*, no. 8 (last paragraph).

9 Gregory Baum, *Compassion and Solidarity* [1987] (Toronto: Anansi, 1992).

10 With Thomas Merton (1915–1968) the Catholic mystical tradition has become politically aware.

11 Yvonne Bergeron, "Les messages du 1e mai," in *Intervenir à contre-courant*, edited by Michel Beaudin et al. (Montreal: Fides, 1998), 63–88.

12 "A Society to be Transformed," no. 18, in *Do Justice*, 326–34.

13 Louis O'Neill and Gérard Dion, *L'immoralité politique dans la Province de Québec* http://faculty.marianopolis.edu/c.belanger/QuebecHistory/docs/morality/1.htm (accessed 20 May 2013).

14 Gregory Baum, *The Church in Quebec* (Ottawa: Novalis, 1991), 67–89.

15 Ibid., 86–7.

16 Jean Richard and Louis O'Neill, eds., *La question sociale hier et aujourd'hui: Colloque du centenaire de Rerum novarum* (Quebec: Presses de l'Université Laval, 1993).
17 Claude Ryan, *Mon testament spirituel* (Montreal: Novalis, 2004).
18 Ibid., 178.
19 "Ethical Reflections on Canada's Socio-economic Order," in *Do Justice*, 412.
20 Ibid., 427
21 The following paragraphs are edited versions of texts from my book, *Sign of the Times* (Toronto: Novalis, 2007), 210.
22 Marguerite Mendel, "The Social Economy in Quebec," in *2003 Conference of Latin American Centre for Development and Public Administration*, http://www.envision.ca/pdf/SocialEconomy/SocialEconomyinQuebecMendell.pdf (accessed 20 May 2013).
23 Nancy Neamtan, "The Social Economy," in *Tamarack, Institute for Community Engagement*, 2006, http://tamarackcommunity.ca/g3s10_M4C2.html (accessed 20 May 2013).
24 In her article "La théologie de la rue," in *La theologie: pourquoi? pour qui?* edited by Jean-Guy Nadeau (Montreal: Fides, 1997), 25–30, Vivian Labrie shows that faith helps us to discern the good and evil in society and provides an ethics for a peaceful *vivre ensemble*.
25 Michel Beaudin, "Sotériologie capitaliste et salut chrétien," in *Seul ou avec les autres? Le salut chrétien à l'épreuve de la solidarité*, edited by Jean-Claude Petit et al. (Montreal: Fides, 1992), 237–81; "Une théologie à propos de l'économie? Réflexion sur un itinéraire et sur la mise en chantier d'une pratique théologique," in *La théologie: pour quoi? pour qui?* edited by Jean-Guy Nadeau (Montreal: Fides, 2000), 31–63; "De l'entrée de la théologie en économie à l'entrée de l'économie en théologie," in *Des théologies en mutation*, edited by Michel Beaudin et al. (Montreal: Fides, 2002), 121–71; "La tradition biblique du Jubilé comme expression de la singularité du messianisme judéo-chrétien," in *Figures de messies aujourd'hui*, edited by Michel Beaudin et al. (Montreal: Fides, 2002), 21–58; "Le Dieu du président Bush et le Dieu des théologies contextuelles sauvent-ils?" in *Dieu agit-il dans l'histoire?* edited by Robert Mager (Montreal: Fides, 2006), 115–36; "La violence illimitée s'immisçant par l'alibi de la justice immuable ou infinie, vengeresse de l'attentat contre le World Trade Center," in *Mondialisation, violence et religion*, edited by Pierre Noël (Montreal: Fides, 2009), 53–77.
26 Gilles Dostaler et al., *Capitalisme et pulsion de mort* (Mantilly, France: Pluriel, 2010).

27 Pierre Dansereau, "Le défi du XXIème consiste à transformer l'essor technologique en progrès social," *Le Devoir*, 1 Oct. 2011.

28 I have heard him use the word "stupid" in his lectures in Montreal.

29 Michel Beaudin, "Un projet occupe déjà le terrain: la société comme marché. Fascination du credo néolibéral et solidarité sociale velléitaire chez les gens d'affaires francophones de Montréal," in *Projet de société et lectures chrétiennes*, edited by Camil Ménard et al. (Montreal: Fides, 1997), 57–103.

30 *Sans emploi peut-on vivre?* (1994), *L'économie et son arrière-pays* (1996), *Le pouvoir de l'argent* (1997), *Intervenir à contre-courant* (1998), and *À nous le politique* (2001), all published by Fides, Montreal.

31 Guy Paiement, ed., *Témoins d'une naissance, Vingt textes portant sur une autre manière de voir l'Eucharistie* (Montreal: les Presses de la CSN, 2008).

32 André Beauchamp, *Repères pour demain: Avenir et environnement au Québec* (Montreal: Bellarmin, 1987); *Pour une sagesse de l'environnement* (Montreal: Novalis, 1992); *Électricité est-elle à risque?* (Montreal: Bellarmin, 1996); *Gérer le risque, vaincre la peur* (Montreal: Bellarmin, 1996).

33 André Beauchamp, *Introduction à l'éthique de l'environnement* (Montreal: Paulines, 1993); *Fêtes et saisons: Écologie et création* (Paris: Cerf, 1993); *Environnement et l'Église* (Montreal: Fides, 2008), 993.

34 André Beauchamp, "La paix avec la terre," in *Pacem in terris: Paix sur la terre*, edited by Gregory Baum (Montreal: Novalis, 2013), 81–6.

35 *The Brundtland Report*, no. 11.

36 For André Beauchamp's text, see http://www.diocesevalleyfield.org/?q=node/479 (accessed 20 May 2013).

37 *Imaging God: Dominion as Stewardship* (Grand Rapids, MI: Eerdmans, 1986), by the Montreal-based Protestant theologian Douglas Hall, has been translated into French by the Quebec theologian Louis Vaillancourt as *Être image de Dieu: Le stewardship de l'humain dans la création* (Paris: Cerf, 1998).

38 Lise Baroni et al., *L'utopie de la solidarité au Québec* (Montreal: Paulines, 2011).

39 Ibid., 243–80.

40 Gregory Baum, *Compassion and Solidarity*, 77.

CHAPTER SEVEN

1 Élisabeth Lacelle, *L'incontournable échange* (Montreal: Bellarmin, 1994), 36–40; see also her personal testimony, "1971. J'y était jeune," on the website of Femmes et ministères (http://www.femmes-ministeres.org),

Venez fêter avec nous: 40 ans de ténacité des femmes en Église (accessed 20 May 2013).

2 For the particular Quebec bishops who called for reform, see Marie-Andrée Roy, *Les ouvrières de l'Église* (Montreal: Médiapaul, 1996), 163–71.

3 Lacelle, *L'incontournable échange*, 15–45.

4 Gregory Baum, *Religion and Alienation* (Ottawa: Novalis, 2006), 150–4.

5 Elisabeth Lacelle, *L'incontournable échange*, 278; Francesco Alberino, *Genesis. Mouvement et institution* (Paris: Ramsay, 1991), 57.

6 Lise Baroni et al., eds., *L'utopie de la solidarité au Québec* (Montreal: Pauline, 2011), 137.

7 Lacelle, *L'incontournable échange*, 241–61.

8 The proceedings of the Conference were published in Élisabeth Lacelle, ed., *La femme et la religion au Canada français* (Montreal: Bellarmin, 1979).

9 http://www.lautreparole.org (accessed 20 May 2013).

10 *L'autre Parole, 1976–2011, 35 ans d'écriture et de réécriture* (Gatineau, QC: Éditions À3Brin, 2011), 17–24.

11 http://www.femmes-ministeres.org (accessed 20 May 2013).

12 Sarah Bélanger, *Les soutanes roses* (Montreal: Bellarmin, 1988); Lise Baroni et al., eds., *Voix de femmes, voies de passage* (Montreal:Paulines, 1995); Céline Girardet al., eds., *Voies d'espérence* (Montreal: Paulines, 1996); Jacinthe Fortin, *La 25e heure pour l'Église* (Montreal: Paulines, 2002).

13 Marie-Andrée Roy, "Les femmes, le féminisme et la religion," in *L'étude de la religion au Québec*, edited by Jean-Marc Larouche et al. (Quebec: Presses universitaires de Laval, 2001), 342–59.

14 Marie-Andrée Roy, "Sexe, genre et théologie," in *Franchir le miroir patriarcal*, edited by Monique Dumais (Montreal: Fides, 2007), 13–58.

15 Monique Dumais, "La théologie peut-elle être du genre féminin au Québec?" in *La femme et la religion au Canada français*, 111–26.

16 Louise Melançon, "La prise de parole des femmes dans l'Église," in *Souffles des femmes: Lectures féministes de la religion*, edited by Monique Dumais et al. (Montreal: Paulines, 1989), 15–27.

17 Monique Dumais, "La théologie peut-elle être du genre féminin au Québec?" 124.

18 Monique Dumais, "Sortir Dieu du ghetto masculin," in *Souffles des femmes*, 135–46.

19 Lacelle, *L'incontournable échange*, 26.

20 *L'autre Parole, 1976–2011, 35 ans d'écriture et de réécriture*, 13.

21 Ibid., 39.

22 Louise Melançon, "Quelle figure du Christ pour une théologie non-sexiste," in *Jésus: Christ universel?* edited by Jean-Claude Petit et al. (Montreal: Fides, 1990), 197–208.
23 Élisabeth Lacelle, "Un projet d'Église selon l'humanité nouvelle," in *L'incontournable échange*, 107–17.
24 Lise Baroni and Yvonne Bergeron, *L'utopie de la solidarité au Québec*, 257–66.
25 Yvonne Bergeron, "Jésus de Nazareth et le politique," in *A nous la politique*, edited by Michel Beaudin et al. (Montreal: Fides, 2001), 165–80.
26 *Les femmes aussi faisaient route avec lui* (Montreal: Médiapaul, 1995); the English translation, *Women also Journeyed with Him* (Collegeville, MN: Liturgical Press, 2000).
27 Lacelle, *L'incontournable échange*, 38.
28 The decree on the Church's mission, *Apostolicam Actuositatem*, no. 2.
29 *Gaudium et Spes*, no. 92.
30 Fernande Saint-Martin, *La femme et la société cléricale* (Montreal: Mouvement laïc de langue française, 1976), 15–16, cited in Monique Dumais, "La théologie peut-elle être de genre féminin au Québec?" in *La femme et la religion au Canada français*, 121.
31 http://www.womenpriests.org/classic/appendix.asp (accessed 20 May 2013).
32 http://www.lautreparole.org/articles/406 (accessed May 20 2013)
33 Élisabeth Lacelle, ed., *La femme et la religion au Québec*, 33–42.
34 Ibid., 148.
35 Anita Caron, ed., *Femmes et pouvoir dans l'Église* (Montreal: VLB éditeur, 1991); Anita Caron et al., eds., *Les rapports homme-femme dans l'Église catholique: perceptions, constats, alternatives, Les Cahiers de l'Iref*, no. 4, 1999.
36 Marie-Andrée Roy, *Les ouvrières de l'Église* (Montreal: Médiapaul, 1996).
37 Lise Baroni et al., eds., *Voix de femmes, voies de passages* (Montreal: Paulines, 1995).
38 http://www.vatican.va/roman_curia/pontifical_councils/laity/documents/rc_con_interdic_doc_15081997_en.html (accessed 20 May 2013).
39 Béatrice Gothscheck, "Marie dans l'imaginaire québécois," in *Souffles des femmes*, 75–134.
40 Lacelle, *L'incontournable échange*, 23–4.
41 Moniques Dumais, "D'une morale imposée à une éthique autodéterminée," in *Souffles des femmes*, 109–34.
42 Ibid., 114.
43 Ibid., 114–15.

44 Ibid., 112. From Pius XII, "Speech to Italian Women," 21 October 1945.
45 Ibid., 118.
46 http://www.marievictoirelouis.net/document.php?id=678 (accessed 20 May 2013).

CHAPTER EIGHT

1 Robert Mager et al., eds., *Modernité et religion au Québec* (Quebec: Presses de l'Université Laval, 2010).
2 Maxime Allard, "Maintenant, symptôme pour comprendre le Québec de 1962," in *Modernité et religion au Québec*, 27–40.
3 Gilles Routhier, "Vatican II comme modernisation de l'Église catholique du Québec," in *Modernité et religion au Québec*, 41–54.
4 Jean-Guy Bissonnette et al., eds., *Milieux et témoignages* (Ottawa: Leméac, 1982); Fernand Dumont et al., eds., *Entre le temple et l'exile* (Ottawa: Leméac, 1982).
5 Dumont et al., eds., *Entre le temple et l'exile*, 223–31.
6 Raymond Lemieux, "Le catholicisme québécois: une question de culture," *Sociologie et société* 22 (October 1990): 145–64. See also Raymond Lemieux, "Croyances et incroyances: une économie du sens commun," in *Croyances et incroyances au Québec*, edited by André Charron et al. (Quebec: Presses de l'Université Laval, 1992), 11–86; and "Les croyances: nébuleuse ou univers organisé?" in *Les croyances des Québécois. Esquisses pour une approche sociologique*, edited by Raymond Lemieux et al. (Quebec: Presses de l'Université Laval, 1992), 23–89.
7 E. Martin Meunier, Jean-François Laniel, and Jean-Christophe Demers, "Permanence et recomposition de la 'religion culturelle': Aperçu socio-historique du catholicisme québécois (1970-2006)," in *Modernité et religion au Québec*, 79–128. See also "La religion au Québec: Regards croisés sur une intrigue moderne," *Globe, Revue internationale d'études québécoises*, vol. 10, no. 2 (2007)/vol. 11, no. 1 (2008).
8 This section is an edited version of a text taken from my article "Catholicism and Secularization in Quebec," in *Rethinking Church, State, and Modernity*, edited by David Lyon et al. (Toronto: University of Toronto Press, 2000), 149–65.
9 *Risquer l'avenir: Bilan d'enquête et prospectives* (Montreal: Fides, 1992). See also *Voies d'avenir: Résumé de la recherche* (Montreal: Fides, 1992).
10 *Risquer l'avenir*, 7–23.
11 See Peter Berger, *The Sacred Canopy* [1967] (New York: Anchor Books, 1990).

12 *Risquer l'avenir*, 76.
13 Micheline Milot, *Une religion à transmettre?* (Quebec: Presses de l'Université Laval, 1991), 63.
14 Gregory Baum, *Religion and Alienation*, 2nd ed. (Ottawa: Novalis, 2006), 148–54.
15 *L'avenir des communautés chrétiennes: Rapport du congrès provincial tenu à Montréal en octobre 1992* (Montreal: Fides, 1993).
16 Ibid., 95–111.
17 Peter L. Berger et al., eds., *The Desecularization of the World: Resurgent Religion and World Politics* (Grand Rapids, MI: Eerdmans, 1999).
18 See Cardinal Ratzinger's sermon of 18 April 2005 given at the Mass prior to the election of a new pope: http://www.vatican.va/gpII/documents/homily-pro-eligendo-pontifice_20050418_en.html (accessed 20 May 2013).
19 Socrates, "The unexamined life is not worth living," quoted in Plato's Dialogues in *The Apology* dealing with Socrates' death.
20 Encyclical *Caritas in Veritate*, 2009, no. 78.
21 Benedict XVI, 27 October 2011, "Address at the Meeting for Peace at Assisi."
22 Gregory Baum, "The Response of a Theologian to Charles Taylor's *A Secular Age*," *Modern Theology* 26 (July 2010): 363–81.
23 See Bernard Émond, *Il y a trop d'images* (Montreal: Lux Éditeur, 2011), 10–13.
24 Nancy Huston, "Éthique et religion," *Le Devoir*, 16 November 2011.

CHAPTER NINE

1 *Apostolicam Actuositatem*, no. 2.
2 *Lumen Gentium*, no. 4.
3 Paul VI, the encyclical *Ecclesiam Suam*, 1964, no. 113.
4 H. Denzinger, ed., *Enchiridion Symbolorum*, no. 1351.
5 Pius XII, the encyclical *Mystici Corporis* (1943), no. 22.
6 *Gaudium et Spes*, no. 22.
7 See the website for the Vatican, Roman Curia, Pontifical Commissions, International Theological Commission, "The Hope of Salvation for Infants Who Die without Being Baptized" (2007), http://www.vatican.va/roman_curia/congregations/cfaith/cti_documents/rc_con_cfaith_doc_20070419_un-baptised-infants_en.html (accessed 3 October 2013).
8 "The Interpretation of Dogma" II, 4, in *Irish Theological Quarterly* (December 1990): 251–77.
9 A French translation of the *nota* was published in *La Documentation Catholique*, 5 and 19 August 2001.

10 "Catholics in America," *National Catholic Reporter*, 28 October–10 November 2011.
11 Louise Melançon, "Magistère et théologie: Parcours et témoignage d'une théologienne," in *Des théologies en mutations*, edited by Michel Beaudin et al. (Montreal: Fides 2003), 111–17.
12 Sophie Tremblay, "Du murmure au cri: l'émergence d'une parole croyante dans le Réseau 'Culture et Foi,'" in *Des théologies en mutations*, 331–41.
13 André Naud, *Les dogmes et le respect de l'intelligence: Plaidoyer inspiré par Simone Weil* (Montreal: Fides, 2002).
14 Armand Veilleux, "Qu'arrive-t-il à l'Église aujourd'hui?" 8 February 2010, http://www.scourmont.be/Armand/writings/louvain-2010.htm (accessed 20 May 2013).
15 Peter Berger, ed., *The Desecularization of the World* (Grand Rapids, MI: Eerdmans, 1999).
16 Charles Taylor, *The Secular Age* (Cambridge, MA: Harvard University Press, 2007).
17 The role of the magisterium and the place of doctrinal norms in the Church are treated in an entire chapter of Fernand Dumont's *L'institut de la théologie*, 221–60.
18 Karl Rahner, *Faith in a Wintery Season* (New York: Herder & Herder, 1989), 161–2.
19 Gregory Baum, "The Church's Tomorrow," *The Ecumenist* 47 (Summer 2010): 6–10.

CHAPTER TEN

1 Charles Taylor, *A Secular Age* (Cambridge, MA: Harvard University Press, 2007), 114–28.
2 Bernard Lambert, *Le problème oecuménique* (Paris: Centurion, 1962); Bernard Lambert, *De Rome à Jérusalem: Itinéraire de Vatican II* (Paris: Centurion, 1965).
3 Jean-Marie Tillard, *Eucharistie, pâque de l'Église* (Paris: Cerf, 1964); Jean-Marie Tillard, *Église d'églises, Ecclésiologie de communion* (Paris: Cerf, 1987).
4 The instruction *Dominus Jesus*, Congregation of the Doctrine of the Faith, 2000, http://www.vatican.va/roman_curia/congregations/cfaith/documents/rc_con_cfaith_doc_20000806_dominus-iesus_en.html (accessed 2 May 2013).
5 http://www.vatican.va/holy_father/benedict_xvi/speeches/2011/november/documents/hf_ben-xvi_spe_20111119_corpo-diplom_en.html (accessed 20 May 2013).

6 Assemblée des évêques catholiques du Québec, "Est-ce que toutes les religions se valent?" (2005), http://www.eveques.qc.ca/documents/2005/20050616f.html (accessed 20 May 2013).
7 John Paul II, the encyclical *Redemptoris Missio* (1900), no. 56.
8 Assemblée des évêques catholiques du Québec, *Le dialogue interreligieux dans un Québec pluraliste* (Montreal: Médiapaul, 2007).
9 *Redemptoris Missio*, no. 55.
10 *Le dialogue interreligieux dans un Québec pluraliste*, 48.
11 Islam in Europe Committee, *Final Report*, http://islamineurope.blogspot.ca/2010/11/belgium-final-report-of-intercultural.html (accessed 20 May 2013).
12 Église catholique de Montréal, *Proposer aujourd'hui Jésus Christ, Projet diocésain d'éducation à la foi* (2003), 10.
13 http://www.eveques.qc.ca/Listes/Documents/2012-02-17.pdf (accessed 20 May 2013).
14 Gregory Baum, *Amazing Church* (Toronto: Novalis, 2005), 125–34.
15 The subsequent paragraphs are edited versions of texts taken from my article "The Church and Pluralism in Quebec," in *Doing Ethics in a Pluralistic World*, edited by Phyllis Airhart et al. (Waterloo, ON: Wilfred Laurier University Press, 2002), 39–56.
16 Canadian Catholic Bishops Conference, "On the Occasion of the Hundredth Year of Confederation," in *Do Justice!* edited by E.F. Sheridan (Montreal: Paulines, 1987), 122–34.
17 Assemblée des évêques du Québec, "La charte de la langue française au Québec" (1977), in *La justice sociale comme Bonne Nouvelle*, edited by Gérard Rocher (Montreal: Bellarmin, 1984), 111–18; "Le peuple québécois et son avenir politique," (1979), in *La justice sociale comme Bonne Nouvelle*, 137–44.
18 Walter Laqueur, ed., *The Human Rights Reader* (New York: New American Library, 1990), 197.
19 Ibid., 216.
20 Gérard Bouchard, *L'interculturel* (Montreal: Boréal, 2012).
21 Élisabeth Garant, ed., *Justice sociale, ouverture et nationalisme au Québec: Regards de Julien Hervé* (Montreal: Novalis, 2004).
22 Gregory Baum, "Julien Harvey: homme de foi, homme du pays," in *Justice sociale, ouverture et nationalisme au Québec*, 9–24.
23 Fernand Dumont, *Raisons communes* (Montreal: Boréal, 1995), 89.
24 "Le Rapport Bouchard-Taylor." http://www.scribd.com/doc/3053017/rapport-de-la-commission-BouchardTaylor-version-integrale (accessed 20 May 2013).

25 Assemblée des évêques du Québec, *Mémoire présenté à la Commission Bouchard-Taylor*, 12 December 2007, http://www.eveques.qc.ca/Listes/Documents/2007-12-12a.pdf, 4 (accessed 20 May 2013).
26 Le Centre justice et foi, *Mémoire présenté à la Commission Bouchard-Taylor*, December 2007, http://cjf.qc.ca/upload/cjf_memoires/2_Memoire_CJF_Bouchard-Taylor_Dec2007.pdf (accessed 20 May 2013).
27 Jacques Racine, "Le Rapport de la Commission Bouchard-Taylor: Identité, mémoire et religion," a lecture delivered at the 2011 meeting of la Société canadienne de théologie.
28 I have analyzed this debate in "Le Devoir: Forum for the Exchange of Ideas," in *The Public Intellectual in Canada*, edited by Nelson Wiseman (Toronto: University of Toronto Press, 2013), 83–97.
29 Cited in the apology pronounced by Prime Minster Stephen Harper in Parliament on 11 June 2008, http://www.cbc.ca/news/canada/story/2008/06/11/pm-statement.html (accessed 20 May 2013).
30 See Paul Martin's speech of 26 April 2013, http://www.cbc.ca/news/canada/montreal/story/2013/04/26/truth-and-reconciliation-saganash-paul-martin.html (accessed 20 May 2013).
31 Gregory Baum, "Canadian Churches Repent of Their Identification with Colonialism," Proceedings of the Conference of the international review *Concilium*, held in Montreal in April 2013, to be published in 2014.
32 http://www.cbc.ca/news/canada/story/2008/06/11/pm-statement.html (accessed 20 May 2013).
33 See Denise Couture and Jean-François Roussel, "Préparer une théologie contextuelle en solidarité entre Autochtones et Allochtones au Québec," *Théoforum* 39/3 (2008): 259–86.
34 Achiel Peelman, *Le Christ est amérindien* (Montreal: Novalis, 1992), English translation *Christ is a Native American* (Maryknoll, NY: Orbis Books, 1995), and *L'Esprit est amérindien: Quand la religion indienne rencontre le christianisme* (Montreal: Médiapaul, 2004).
35 Karl Jaspers, *The Question of German Guilt* [1946] (New York: Fordham University Press, 2000).
36 Gregory Baum, *The Church for Others* (Grand Rapids, MI: Eerdmans, 1996), 45–58.

CHAPTER ELEVEN

1 *Gaudium et Spes*.
2 Ibid., no. 55.

3 Joseph Ratzinger, *Theological Highlights of Vatican II* [1966], (New York: Paulist Press, 2009), 74.

4 Ibid., 75.

5 In his encyclical *Laborem Exercens* (1981), no. 6, John Paul II argues that workers are not objects of production; instead they are subjects of production, co-responsible for the industrial process. In the encyclical *Sollicitudo Rei Socialis* (1987), no. 15, the pope recognizes "the creative subjectivity of the citizens," i.e. their co-responsibility for society as a whole.

6 See pages 170–1.

7 Instruction on Diocesan Synods (1997) jointly published by the Congregation for Bishops and the Congregation for the Evangelizing of People.

8 Gregory Baum, "The Catholic Left in Quebec," in *Culture and Social Change: Social Movements in Quebec and Ontario*, edited by Colin Leys and Marguerite Mendel (Montreal: Black Rose, 1992), 140–54.

9 Gregory Baum, *The Jews and the Gospel* (New York: Newman Press, 1961).

10 Gregory Baum, *Religion and Alienation* [1975] (Toronto: Novalis, 2006), 211.

11 Benedict XVI, encyclical *Spe Salvi* (2007), no. 42.

Index